No peace without war.
No love without sorrow.

HONOR *and* CIRCUMSTANCE

— THE HIGHLAND LEGACY SERIES BOOK 4 —

RENÉE GALLANT

Also By Renée Gallant

The Highland Legacy Series
Whispers of Deception (Book 1)
Betrayal's Legacy (Book 2)
Sassenach (Book 3)

Short Stories
A Finger for Each Cigarette
With Words We Weave – A Celebration of the Past
With Words We Weave: Texas High Plains Writers 2020 Anthology

Chapter One

January 1746, Scotland

ACCORDING TO THE FIRST LETTER received in October 1745, the Highlanders had risen out of the mist like the grim reaper with an army of demons wielding broadswords, Lochaber axes, and rudimentary weapons constructed of scythes banded to the end of long poles, one swipe of which would take the legs clean off a horse or remove a man's head from his shoulders. Calum's father, the Laird Beinnmaree, sounded almost gleeful in his horrific descriptions of the battle and General John Cope's cowardly retreat. Only ten days before this triumphant attack at Prestonpans, Prince Charles Edward Stuart and his ragtag army had strolled through the gates of Edinburgh and taken the town without firing a single shot. The uprising had seemed a roaring success with the Highlanders and their prince, sending the king's army running.

The small portion of the MacKinnon clan left behind at Gleann Eader received the next letter just after Christmas, and within three days' time, Elaina and Calum were prepared to leave the safety and sanctuary of Calum's childhood home on a mission to save his mother's life. If they weren't too late already.

Elaina thought the fight between the siblings might become worse than the war itself when Isobel wanted to load up her tot of a boy, Jamie, and travel with Elaina and Calum to her mother's side. The four remaining MacKinnons stood in the drawing room of Isobel Tulley's home, where Isobel had removed the stitches that held closed the wounds of Elaina's battle with the Campbells. Elaina's fingers traveled absently to the scar across her throat. If only a heart could be healed by stitching it up. Her wee nephew Jamie sidled closer to his mother, drawing Elaina's attention back to Isobel and Calum, who stood toe to toe in the failing light of a frigid January afternoon floating through the large window. Though she was cozy standing in the warmth from the blazing fire in the hearth, Elaina shivered as if a mouse had scurried across her grave.

The look on Calum's face told everyone what he thought about his sister's proposal even before he said, "Absolutely not. Ye cannae drag a babe straight into a war, Isobel."

"I'm no baby!" Jamie yelled at his uncle, kicking him in the shin.

Elaina stifled a laugh behind her hand as her husband lunged at the little imp, missing him by a hair's breadth.

Jamie dove behind a chair far enough away from his uncle that Calum couldn't make a sudden grab for him.

Calum rubbed his leg while glaring at his sister.

Watching the war of words from a safe distance as well, Elaina could understand Isobel's plight but also Calum's reasoning. Besides the trip being so dangerous, the lad would slow them down and, according to the letter, time was of the essence.

Isobel stood a good two heads shorter than her younger brother, but that didn't stop her from standing toe to toe with him, her fists smashed into her hips and the vein in the side of her neck bulging. "Ye are no' my keeper, Calum MacKinnon. I am a grown woman, and I will do as I please."

"Nay, this time ye willna. 'Tis too dangerous. We will gather Mam and bring her back. Ye need to be here gettin' things ready. Ye need to send for the healer and gather the women. We will return as quickly as God allows."

Isobel narrowed her eyes. "And if she is too sick to bring her home? What then?"

Jamie cowered lower behind the chair, peeking out at his mother as her voice rose louder.

"Why do ye no leave yer wife behind if it is too dangerous, brother?" Isobel waved a hand in Elaina's direction.

Elaina arched an eyebrow at her. "Don't bring me into this."

"Do ye think she be stronger than I? Do ye no' think I be as skilled with a sword or an herb?"

"Nay, Isobel," Calum sighed, rolling his eyes toward the ceiling.

Elaina thought him awfully brave to take his eyes off his sister at the moment.

"I cannae leave her again. No' after… Well, Freya is still out there, and I cannae leave her."

Isobel had no response to that. The last time Calum had left his wife to travel with his father and brother to escort Prince Charles Edward Stuart into the Highlands, an old foe led to the MacKinnons by Calum's ex-betrothed Freya MacKenzie had brutally attacked Elaina. She had lost the child she was carrying and come close to losing her own life too.

Isobel's eyes flitted to Elaina's and held them for a moment before she spun in a swish of skirts and stormed from the room. Jamie cast a baleful glare at his uncle before he followed on her heels.

Calum pinched the bridge of his nose before turning to look at Elaina. "Do *ye* understand?" His voice was a near whisper that echoed the furrow in his brow and the sorrow in his gaze.

"I do." Elaina moved to his side. "We must hurry, but have some sympathy for your sister, Calum. She will be here alone. I would be just as angry."

"Nay," Calum said, pulling her close. "I would fear for my life if I were to attempt to leave ye behind."

Elaina laughed as she tried to staunch the tears she felt inching toward the surface. She didn't want to leave Isobel. She didn't want to leave Gleann Eader. They were safe here. Well…safer than out there where war raged and men ran about with scythes bound to poles.

Calum kissed the top of her head. "Go. Ye must rest. We've a long hard journey on the morrow. I've a few more matters to settle and then I will come to you." With a tight squeeze, he left her standing in the middle of the parlor with a chill scurrying across her skin and through her heart.

Elaina glanced around the now empty parlor and heaved a sigh. Who could rest when such uncertainty tainted the very air she breathed? Trailing a hand along each piece of furniture, down the door frame as she left the parlor, and along the winding banister to the second floor that held their bedroom, she tried to brand into her memory all the textures and smells of Isobel Tulley's home. Calum's sister had been kind enough to allow them to stay with her over the past year. So much had happened in this cozy home. Her fingertips swept the wall underneath the family portraits lining the hallway as she thought of all the laughter and tears that had filled this home. Once again, she was leaving a place that she loved. A place she might never return to, just as she had over a year ago when she'd left Duart Manor and her life as an English lady.

She spent the next hour trying to decide what to take and what to leave. In the end, she decided to leave the things that were most important to her. The pendant her mother had presented her with before they sailed from the colonies to England, not so long ago, but it now felt like a lifetime. Her pitiful attempt at sewing a gown for her and Calum's babe who was now not of this world. If she left them here, surely she would return.

Elaina wiped away her tears and readied herself for bed. Not long after she had climbed under the heavy blanket, Calum joined her, smelling of the bright air of winter with a touch of hay from the stables. Wrapping his arms around her, he kissed the top of her head. She snuggled into him and closed her eyes.

But sleep evaded Elaina. She felt it did Calum as well. Though neither spoke through the night, the rhythm of his breathing told Elaina that he too lay thinking about what their journey might bring. Dawn had not yet broken when Elaina made her way to the little graveyard that lay behind Isobel's home. She stood in the pale gray light with her hand on her son's gravestone, but her gaze rested beyond the dormant garden of remembrance toward the flat plain that a scant few months ago had seen the prince and his small entourage setting out for war. Rhona, the Lady Beinnmaree, had been none too happy about her husband's surprise of having delivered Prince Charles to their Highland home, nor thrilled about joining him on his jaunt to take over the throne of England, but she had followed her husband and now paid the price with a broken leg and an infection that would not heal. Elaina prayed they would not be too late.

"Are ye scared?" Isobel whispered from behind her.

"Christ almighty." Elaina whipped about so fast she nearly fell, catching herself on the stone cherub.

Isobel giggled and grasped Elaina's hand, righting her from the stone. "I'm sorry. I didna mean to frighten ye."

Elaina clamped her other hand to her chest, waiting for her heart to slow so she could find her words. "Jesus, Mary, and Joseph. Don't sneak up on a person," she admonished, but squeezed Isobel's hand.

They stood for a moment, no words spoken, and the whistle of the wind through the trees the only sound.

"Aye, I'm scared," Elaina finally answered. "Part of me wishes to stay behind with you and Jamie. But the rest of me…the heart of me needs to be with my husband."

"That I understand." Isobel cast a longing glance at her husband's grave.

"I'm sorry. I didn't mea—"

Isobel waved away Elaina's apology, stepping closer to her sister-in-law until their hands lay hidden between the warm wool of their skirts. Winter had come to the Highlands and with it bitterly cold and unpredictable winter storms and the threat of death not only from a stray fever or illness but now from a redcoat's rifle or bayonet…or in Rhona's case, a wayward horse.

Elaina squeezed Isobel's hand. "I don't want to leave you behind."

"And I dinna wish to be left." Isobel turned to Elaina and took both of her hands, clasping them together and covering them with her own. "Death comes for us all, sister," she whispered. "Only God kens the time or the place. I pray it doesna come for ye nor the rest of my kin for a verra long time."

"Those are my prayers as well."

"Bring her home to me, Elaina," Isobel whispered.

"I will do my very best."

The two women made their way back to the house as the morning lightened from gray to pink. Elaina only looked back once after their tearful goodbyes. There, on the hilltop behind the main house, silhouetted against the rising sun, Isobel stood with her skirts blowing in the early morning breeze, her son by her side, the only two of Calum's family left in Gleann Eader. All others had gone with the fledgling army to roust King George, the Hanoverian usurper, from the throne.

Elaina's heart broke for Isobel, but who knew what they were riding into? The latest letter had held no news of the Jacobite uprising, only the terrible word of Rhona's accident and subsequent illness. No information of where the prince's troops were, nor what had happened since Prestonpans many months ago. Had General Cope's men regrouped? Did he have the rebels on the run? What was the status of the war? The best place for Isobel and Jamie was at Gleann Eader. It would kill them all if anything happened to wee Jamie, even if he sometimes had a temper like a…well, like a Highlander.

Chapter Two

ELAINA AND CALUM SKIRTED THE town of Falkirk, leading their mounts off the winding road and down a trail, into the thickets of brush and trees. They were careful to follow the advice of Father Duncan, whom they'd had the pleasure of staying with the previous eve after three nights of sleeping on the frozen ground. They headed in the opposite direction from where a battle had raged less than a week earlier, avoiding the boggy marsh. Elaina hoped they'd at least had the decency to bury the dead men. The dead horses were another issue entirely. The stench of the burned animals sporadically assaulted her when the wind would shift directions during its ever-swirling dance. She shivered, thinking about screaming Highlanders removing the legs of the British dragoons' horses with their crude weaponry. It must have been like Satan's spawns themselves had emerged on that misty morning. Elaina had heard a Highland war cry more than once, and she thanked heaven that they had been coming to save her and she did not have to fight against them. The sound would scare you half to death if you'd never heard it before and finish the task if you had.

As the sound of hoofbeats approached from the east, Elaina and Calum both pulled their pistols and pointed them in that direction. When a rider rounded a curve, Elaina cried out, "Ainsley," as she and the young man slid from their horses simultaneously and embraced.

Ainsley lifted her from the ground.

"Look at you! You become more of a man every time you leave my presence." Elaina wrinkled her nose at him. "Lord, you smell like one too."

"Well, I've only one other set of clothes, and I didna wish to soil them with the blood of the English. I was waitin' for ye to get here so ye could wash these for me." The sixteen-year-old grinned down at her.

"Dinna let him guilt ye into washin' his things. The lad is quite capable of scrubbin' his own stench out of his own clothes," a stern female voice said from over Elaina's shoulder.

Startled by the woman she had not seen, she twirled around. "Caitir!" Elaina felt her world almost complete as she ran to her friend and held her in a tight embrace.

"Ye look well, Elaina. Much better than when I left ye. Ye have recovered then?" Caitir whispered.

"Aye," Elaina whispered into her hair as she squeezed her friend tighter. The vision of her infant son's grave flitted through her mind, and she pushed it aside at the sound of her husband's voice.

"Cousin," Calum said, and Elaina transferred Caitir into his arms. "Is she close by?" he asked.

"About an hour's ride," Caitir said when Calum finally released his stranglehold. "We came for the surgeon or for herbs if one cannae be found. Neither is easy to come by at the moment."

"She is no' improved then?" Calum asked.

Caitir merely shook her head.

"Well," Elaina said, "she is still alive. We will thank God for that. Now, where are you to obtain herbs or a physician from?"

"Come." Ainsley turned to mount his horse. "Steel yerselves. 'Tis no' a pretty sight."

Elaina's stomach swirled in a knot at the thought of what they were about to encounter. Ainsley and Caitir led the way through the dormant, ice-covered foliage and shrubs until they came to a wider trail. She would still not call it a road. A few minutes later, they came upon a small village and filed one by one down a lane, toward a big fine house in a clearing.

"Slaton House," Caitir said as they slid from their horses. "Belongs...belonged to a colonel who fought for the English. He died in the battle defending his King George to the end. 'Tis where they have taken the injured. If Rhona had broken her leg here, it wadna be so hard to have her treated. But as it is, this is the lot we received."

Ainsley, who had not yet moved from beside his horse, glanced over his shoulder at Elaina and Calum. "There is another thing, and if ye would be more taken to stayin' put wi' the horses, we'd no think less of ye," Ainsley said.

Calum raised his brow in question.

"In exchange for the herbs, we may be required to be of some assistance to the wounded and the people caring for them. It is the least that we could do."

"If it is the least that we can do for my mother, then let us do it," Calum said.

Elaina laid a hand on his arm and gave it a squeeze.

He placed his on hers. His muscles were taut, and lines furrowed between his brows. It was the only outward sign of the concern that she knew raged within his heart.

She, too, felt time slipping away from them, but perhaps God would grant his mother mercy if they bestowed that mercy on others.

They lashed the horses to a dormant laurel tree whose branches, thick and twisted, nearly grazed the frozen ground. As they approached the house, Elaina saw Ainsley shrug as if adjusting his coat…or his nerves. Just what were they about to walk into?

Ainsley opened the door to the fine house without knocking. Elaina and Calum followed their guides inside to a horrific scene. The good colonel's home reeked of blood and excrement. His beautiful rugs and once high-polished floors had been soaked with the sacrifices of men who had fought for their lives, for their king, whichever side they remained loyal to.

Elaina pulled her cloak up over her nose and mouth, but even the thick wool couldn't suffuse the odors assaulting her senses. The moans and wails of injured men attacked her ears as the air about her took her breath, and she wanted to flee from the carnage. She wanted to return to Gleann Eader and pretend none of these horrors existed. Auld Ruadh's crinkled face worried its way through her mind, and the thought of her friend and uncle possibly lying dead or shattered almost took her to her knees. But if he had perished or were badly wounded, certainly Caitir would have mentioned it in the letter they had received. She closed her eyes as if that would help expel the thought from her head.

"Mayhap ye should take her outside," a graveled voice traveled through the din of the surrounding noise.

She opened her eyes and found herself staring into a bloodied apron. Her gaze followed the long torso up to the grim face of a gray-haired man before her. He held a saw in one hand and a crimson-stained towel in the other.

"I will be fine in a moment." Elaina lowered her cloak and attempted to pull herself together.

"If ye say." The man looked doubtful. "The lasses could use another set of hands in the blue salon three doors down the hallway there." He cocked his head toward what had once probably been a lovely hallway. Now the damask walls were dulled brown from unknown fluids of various kinds, the covering torn in places and portraits knocked askew.

"Doctor Conley, this is my cousin Calum," Caitir addressed the man who resembled the grim reaper. "He and Ainsley need a moment of yer time. Elaina and I will see if we can make use of ourselves." She took Elaina's arm and led her down the darkened hallway. "Just breathe in and out."

"I remember fine how to breathe." Elaina cast a sideways glance at her friend.

"Well, then why are ye pantin' like yer givin' birth?" Caitir snickered at the glare Elaina pinned her with. "I dinna wish to say that ye will grow accustomed to it, because who would want to see these poor men in this state and not be sorely affected by the pitiful nature of the situation? Unfortunately, it gets easier. Yer senses dull, and the whole of it 'tis not so overwhelming."

A young lass who could have been no older than twelve years in age nearly trampled the pair as she barreled from the room they were about to enter. She carried a large pot in each hand.

"Can ye lend a hand to Mrs. Gibbons?" she yelled over her shoulder as she scurried down the hallway. "I'm to fetch more water." And she was gone.

Elaina followed Caitir through the doorway to find row upon row of men laid out on the floor and only one woman scurrying between them. The kerchief in the woman's hair had lost its hold on strings of gray that now curled about, sticking to her neck and forehead. Her face glowed a mottled red from her exertions.

"Thank God." The woman straightened and wiped the sweat from her brow. "You." She snapped her fingers at Elaina. "Can ye take the twelve men at that end of the room? There is drinkin' water in the bucket by the window and a chamber pot in the corner there."

Elaina glanced to the end of the room the woman had motioned to. Removing her cloak and gloves, she placed them on the back of a chair that seemed to be the cleanest place in the room. She then rolled up her sleeves and approached the man closest to her. She stared at him in surprise, then glanced back at the woman who was most definitely a Scot and back to the man who, no mistaking, was a member of the British army. Her gaze scanned the room. Injured soldiers from both sides lay side by side, each being tended to as if they were equals, as if their clothing did not put them at warring odds with one another. In this room…in this house, they were merely injured men rather than members of opposing armies.

Elaina hurried to the bucket of water and lugged it back to the injured British soldier. She tried to give him water, but he tossed about in a fevered state, jerking his head away from her touch and the tin cup she had scooped water into. "Shh," she attempted to soothe. "Drink." She held his head with one hand and touched the cup to his lips with the other. Blood-soaked rags encircled his head and dipped down to cover one eye. His skin burned into her hand as she cupped his head, urging him to swallow.

The Scottish woman in charge scurried by her and dropped a handful of rags at her feet. "They're clean," she said over her shoulder. "I just cannae scrub all the blood out."

Elaina picked up a rag and dipped it in the water bucket, then drew it across the man's skin, sending him into a fit of shivers. "I know," she whispered. "'Tis cruel of me." She slid the rag down his throat and across the part of his chest that she could reach. "But we must cool you off."

"Abigail?" The young man forced the word from his throat, tossing his head.

"Quiet now." She squeezed his hand. "You are safe."

The man's youth had come through with that one word. He could be no more than eighteen, perhaps, as his life hung in a delicate balance between this world and the next. She hated to leave his side, but she also needed to attend to the other eleven men now in her care. "I will return. You rest."

The soldier clutched at her. "Don't leave me, Abigail. Stay."

The pleading gaze from his one icy blue eye impaled her heart. Elaina could feel tears building in her throat, but she choked them down. Tears would be of no use. "Rest, my dear. I'm not going far. I will be back before you know it." With great reluctance, she pried her hand from his and picked up the water bucket, moving on to the next man.

A Scot, now missing his left arm from the elbow down, was in jovial spirits in spite of receiving so great a wound in battle. "Eh, I dinna ken what I'll do now, what with only one arm. Ply an ol' widow woman wi' me charms, I suppose. What say ye? Do ye think this bonnie mug could do the trick?" He winked at Elaina.

"I dare say you are quite the charmer." She handed him the cup of water. "I'm certain you could sweep a widow off her feet with nary a problem."

The first soldier she had tended cried out for Abigail, drawing the attention of them both.

"Yon lad is in a bad way, is he no'?" The now solemn Scot pointed his empty cup at the young man. "'Tis a pity. Such a young 'un. Me, well, I've had me turn about the earth. God has been good to me. Look at me now. Fit as a fiddle. Why they willnae let me loose, I dinna ken. I can still wield a sword wi' me right hand."

Elaina tore her gaze from the young British soldier. "True, you might could swing a sword, and you've only lost your arm to the elbow, so it shouldn't disturb your balance overmuch, but how do you propose to protect yourself? You cannot wield a targe."

"Aye. I would have to puzzle that one out, lass. Move along and let me think. These other men need tendin' too, more than I." He gave a nod to the men on past him, some members of the British army and some not. "'Tis a fine thing, them tendin' to the enemies injured as such they are. For underneath their blood red coats, they are mere men, and off the battlefield, I call several friend."

The melancholy that had taken over the jovial man drew Elaina's attention back to him.

"Go on, lass. I'll be fine. But next time ye come 'round, see if ye can sneak me something stronger than water. It's bloody cold sittin' on this floor."

"I will see what I can find, sir." Elaina ducked her head at the man.

"Ollie's the name. Ye are welcome to use it. There'll be no 'sirs' aimed at me, thank ye kindly."

Elaina couldn't help but laugh as she grabbed up the bucket to move on. "All right then, Ollie it 'tis. I am Elaina. You may call me that as well. If you've need of anything…"

"So ye are no Abigail, then?" Ollie glanced over at the soldier, who now whispered the mystery woman's name.

"No. I am not Abigail." Elaina sighed, thinking how terribly sad this entire situation was.

"Dinna fash about the lad. Ye move along, and I'll sit wi' him until ye can return." Ollie pushed himself to his knees and crawled one-armed over to the young man.

Elaina didn't know if her heart could take much more, and this was only the beginning. She wondered if Calum and Ainsley were finding what they needed or if they too had turned their attention to the casualties of the battle. She watched Caitir move among her throng of men with gentle ease, giving a sweet smile to each of them.

With a deep breath, Elaina took up her bucket and made her way through her assigned men, administering water and adjusting bandages. She glanced up as a man straggled through the door with a jug on his shoulder, nearly tripping over a body and coming close to losing his vessel. His gaze darted around the room in an almost panicked dance until it landed on Mrs. Gibbons.

"I was told ye've need of this." The Scotsman plunked the jug upon the seat of the chair that held Elaina's cloak. "There's nay laudanum to be had anywhere. This'll have to do."

Mrs. Gibbons exhaled a breath that caused her shoulders to droop. The weariness in her bones was evident but for a moment, just long enough for Elaina to wonder about the toll that this war was taking on everyone. The older woman wiped the sweat from her brow with the sleeve of her dress. "Thank ye kindly, Walter," she said while her gaze traveled about the room full of men—some groaning, others thrashing about, gnashing their teeth. "This'll have to do, won't it? God have mercy on these men." She then straightened her spine, crossed the room, and took the jug of whisky from the chair.

"I'll bring ye more soon," he said. His gaze roamed over the bodies of the injured and dying, pity and sorrow clearly etched upon his face, before he turned and disappeared out of the door.

Mrs. Gibbons waved the women over and divided the jug of spirits into three pitchers. They all set about treating the men in the most pain.

When it was his turn, Ollie took a small swig but refused more when Elaina tried to push it at him. "Give it to the lad, miss. Lord kens he needs it worse than this tough ol' codger."

Elaina crouched beside the young man and dribbled the mind-numbing whisky into his mouth a little at a time.

"Stay wi' him, lass. That's the calmest he's been in hours. I'll tend the rest of the men." Ollie pushed himself to his feet and took up the pitcher with his remaining hand.

"You shouldn't—" Elaina started to say.

Ollie snorted. "I'm a tough auld goat. It'll take more than a missing arm to keep me down."

Elaina watched him amble over to one of the injured and shook her head in amazement. Such a strong and good heart. If only there were more like him. She settled herself beside the young soldier and took up his hand.

He mumbled incoherently about Abigail and springtime.

She brushed a soothing stroke across his cheek with her knuckles.

His eyes fluttered open, and he stared at her, his icy blue eye clouded with the effects of the whisky. "You returned to me," he whispered.

"Aye. I told you I would." Elaina squeezed his hand.

He raised their hands to his cheek and laid his head against them.

A torrent of helplessness washed over Elaina. With her free hand, she brushed a wayward strand of hair from his forehead. With a lack of any way to help the dying young man, she whispered the words of a lullaby to him, a song her mother had sung many times when Elaina had been a young girl and was sick with fever. She closed her eyes, leaving their joined hands against his cheek and gently stroking his forehead with the other.

A hand on her shoulder jolted her from the world she had retreated to in her mind. A world filled with the hills of the colony of North Carolina. A place where her mother still lived, and the ravages of war did not surround her.

"Is this him?" Mrs. Gibbons asked.

Elaina blinked into the dimmed light of the room. She didn't know how long she had sat with her hand linked to the young soldier, but the sun hung low and candles and oil lamps had been lit about the place.

A pair of black boots appeared on the other side of the young lad's prone body, and a soldier squatted down beside them. "Yes, it is him," the man whispered. "How long have you sat here, miss?"

Elaina glanced up at the man asking the question—a British soldier taking in the horrible wounds of one of his fallen comrades with a pained look etched upon his face. "I-I have no idea," she mumbled, dropping her gaze to his boots.

"He is gone, miss. He is dead. I thank you for sitting with my brother and comforting him in his time of passing."

"Dead? No, he…" She looked at the young man with their hands still clasped to his cheek and his face turned toward her own, but his half-lidded gaze saw nothing any longer. She was no longer the mysterious Abigail. She moved to unfold her legs and groaned with the stiffness that had overtaken them.

The dead man's brother rose up as well, offering his hand to help her to her feet. "Is there any way I can repay you?"

Elaina waved away the offered hand. A gallant gesture, but she couldn't bring herself to touch him. It was an irrational fear that if he physically made contact, he would recognize her and immediately arrest her for treason. She shook her head, keeping her face turned toward the floor, wringing her hands and trying to keep tears at bay. "There is no need," she said.

"Have we met somewhere? Are you a relation of the colonel?"

Her hands froze. "No. No relation," she mumbled. "I am sorry for your loss, Officer. I-I must go." Her heart seized in her throat. Surprised by the choked sound of her voice, Elaina dashed at the tears running down her cheeks and fled the room.

"Wait!" the officer yelled after her.

Elaina did not slow her escape. As she turned the corner and stumbled down the hallway toward the front of the house, a familiar voice called out.

"Mistress!"

She glanced up.

Ainsley waved a ball of muslin tied with a piece of hemp at her.

Calum appeared at his side, looking ragged and worn. Blood stained the cuffs of his shirt and many of his curls had escaped the leather binding that held the rest together at his neck. "What's amiss?" he asked as he fell into step with her.

"I just…I just need some air." She barreled out of the door and into the frigid evening air and didn't stop moving until she reached the tree that held their horses. She leaned her head against a frozen branch, a sob escaping from her throat. She stifled a scream when a large hand clamped down on her shoulder.

"There, there." Calum scooped her into his embrace.

Elaina collapsed into his arms. "Why am I crying? I feel like I am always crying anymore." She sniffled into his chest.

"'Tis never easy to see men in such a state, *mo chridhe*. Ye are human, Elaina, and it doesnae mean that ye are weak to cry." He placed a soft kiss against the top of her head.

"Well, I don't like it," she whispered. She froze in her husband's arms and then whipped her head around toward the sound of running footsteps. She nearly collapsed at the sight of Caitir running toward them.

"Here, ye'll catch yer death and then where would be," she scolded as she slipped Elaina's cloak about her shoulders. "Gloves too. Now, let's be on our way before anythin' else happens. We've been gone long enough. Rhona needs these herbs."

"Well, let us be on then." Calum helped Elaina onto her horse before mounting his. "Ye can fill us in on what happened to Mam and what is going on with the war as we ride. The letter spoke of none of it."

Ainsley and Calum rode side by side. Elaina cast a glance over her shoulder to see a soldier standing in the doorway, watching them as they rode away.

Elaina clicked at her steed, speeding it up, until she was close enough to the two men to feel the safety of Calum's presence and to hear Ainsley's explanation of Rhona's accident.

"It was a surprise attack, a bit before dawn. Complete chaos reigned for a bit. Most men were exuberant with our win, while others were draggin' their fallen comrades in to be treated. Yer mam stepped out the doorway of a sick house just as a frightened, riderless mare bolted through the camp. 'Twas a terrible break. The healers cleaned and set her leg as best they could and sewed her up." Ainsley's voice dropped to a whisper. "But she is no' well."

"And my father?"

"She insisted he continue on with the prince. He didna want to leave her, but at the time she wasna as sick as she is now. The prince and the rebels moved south and eventually into England."

"England?" was the only word that would come out of Elaina's mouth. She nearly drew her horse to a stop to keep from falling out of the saddle at the shock. "England?" she said again, her voice squeaking like a mouse. She turned and stared at Caitir who rode beside her.

She nodded her affirmation. "Aye. Made it to Derby."

She stopped her horse then, and everyone else followed suit. "That…that's just a few days' march from London."

"Aye, 'tis, Elaina. I've nay heard anythin' since. The Jacobites could have taken the throne by now," Ainsley said, his face beaming with pride.

Elaina was unsure what to feel. Relief? Fear? Pride? Shame? After sitting in that room with injured men from both sides, her thoughts went straight to the number of lives that must have been lost…from both sides. Grief seized her throat, and she swallowed a lump. She would not cry again. Not today.

"Rhona," she said, as if reminding herself of their current mission. "Take us to Rhona."

Ainsley nodded and turned his horse back to the trail, leading them through their bleak surroundings. It seemed as if nothing could survive winter in Scotland. She prayed that was not the case for Rhona.

Near to dark, the four approached an elongated stone cottage with a thatched roof sitting barren in front of a ridge of rolling hills. In the spring it was probably quite lovely and picturesque, but in the dead of winter that is exactly what it looked like…dead. A swirl of gray smoke rising from the chimney was the only sign of life. Ainsley slid to the frozen ground first, with the others following suit. After securing their horses, Elaina, Caitir, and Calum followed Ainsley as he stepped through the doorway of the cotter's house after a gentle tap on the door. Elaina could smell the infection as she entered the small dwelling. The woman of the home stood by a small wooden table wringing her plump hands. Her hair was woven into a severe braid, her face pink from the heat of the home. It was stifling. And in the dead of winter, no less. A pair of twin boys aged close to thirteen or so stood solemn-faced behind what had to be their mother as she spoke in hushed tones to Ainsley.

Caitir stepped around Elaina with a gentle hand to her shoulder. She pulled a bowl down from one of the wooden shelves lining the stone wall of the house with all the ease of having lived with this woman and her children for nigh on a week or more. She set about grinding and mixing different herbs together, forming them into a paste with hot water from an iron kettle suspended over the blazing fire.

A long sheet of muslin hung in a haphazard half circle in the far corner of the room. Elaina, drawn to the makeshift screen and the elongated shadow that danced beyond it in the light of a hidden candle, crossed the room and with a deep breath stepped behind it.

"*Mo nighean.* My daughter." Rhona's voice shook with the shivering that racked her delicate frame. She was withering just like a flower in winter, shrinking into herself.

Elaina took Rhona's frail hand in her own, her mother-in-law's fever burning Elaina's hands that were still cold from the hours-long ride to this place. She brushed Rhona's hair back from her face and kissed her forehead. Her once glorious fiery curls lay matted and dull. "May I?" she whispered, searching Rhona's glassy hazel eyes as she nodded toward the blanket covering the woman's injury.

Her mother-in-law gave a weak smile and a small nod before turning her face to the wall.

Elaina gently lifted the blanket and then heard Calum's sharp intake of breath behind her. The leg was gray. Not the color that living flesh should have. The leg was dying and taking Rhona with it. Elaina stepped to the side so Calum could be with his mother. Caitir joined them, lifting the putrid muslin from her aunt's leg. Rhona winced and clenched her teeth as Caitir washed the angry wound and spread her brewed concoction across it.

"We must get her to Edinburgh," Elaina said, startling everyone.

Calum turned and stared at his wife. "We cannae go to Edinburgh."

"We can. Your father said in his letter that the Jacobites occupied it. Besides, it's closer than Gleann Eader, and time is of the essence."

"Ye are an outlaw. Ye are wanted for murder. It is dangerous enough being this far south," Calum hissed, keeping his voice low as he gave a nervous look over his shoulder at the milky shadows beyond the curtain surrounding them.

"She needs a physician. Your mother is going to die if she stays here. We can sneak in after dark and take her to my ho—to Duart Manor." Elaina caught herself as she spoke of her brother's estate. The brother whom her parents had raised to believe was her blood, but he was not. He was the son of a British earl, and she the daughter of a rebel Highlander. Now, she and William stood on the opposing sides of a war.

"And if William is there?" Caitir asked, still bent over Rhona's injury.

"Why would William be there? Certainly, he would be with the British regiment, wherever they are." Elaina stepped from behind the curtain, back into the main room of the small cottage and away from the protests to the most sensible answer. "Have ye paper and ink, madam?" she asked the woman.

The woman spun in a swirl of brown skirts, her gray braid also swinging with the momentum of her swift turn of direction. She was probably eager to get them out of her home. Elaina couldn't blame her. She returned with the requested items, spreading them on the table.

"Have you a wagon, also?"

The woman shook her head.

"Ainsley, I need you to find us a wagon and a team to pull it." Elaina sat at the table, the quill scratching with urgency at the paper. "Have ye horses?"

Elaina whispered to the twins, again clinging to their mother's skirt and now watching her with growing interest.

"Nay," the woman spoke. "My husband took them when he left with Prince Charles." She made the sign of the cross in front of her.

Elaina bent her head over her papers, trying to think as she scratched out the urgent letter. She tapped the feathers of the quill against the crooked bridge of her nose, then turned and whispered to the woman, "Might I ask a favor of you and your sons? Will you allow them to take our horses and deliver this letter?" Elaina looked over her shoulder to make certain that Calum and Caitir were still out of earshot. "I ask on behalf of Micheil MacKinnon, the Laird Beinnmaree of Gleann Eader. A very special acquaintance of the prince himself. You may keep the two horses as payment," she added at the woman's hesitation.

Elaina realized she'd have a time explaining to Calum about their missing horses. She couldn't very well tell him she had sent the two boys off on a private mission, so she decided to tell him she promised the horses to the woman in payment for caring for Rhona and allowing her to rest in her home, which wasn't a complete falsehood.

The woman stared at her before giving a slight nod of her head. She then turned and whispered to her two sons.

Elaina could see the excitement on their faces as they scurried about donning the warmest clothes they owned. Elaina followed them outside. "I need you to deliver this letter. Do you know your way around these parts?"

"Aye," one boy answered. "We travel with our da all the time. I have been close to there." He tapped his finger on the letter Elaina handed him.

"Good. God's speed and thank you, truly. By all means, be careful. I couldn't live with myself if anything happened to either of you."

"Dinna worry about us, madam," the other boy said as he swung up into the saddle of Caitir's horse. "We willna let ye down."

His brother mounted Ainsley's steed, and the two boys sped off, both lying low over the horses' necks.

Chapter Three

Two days later, under cover of darkness, Ainsley steered the team of horses down the lane leading to Duart Manor. The gravel of the lane crunching under the wheels of the wagon sounded much louder to Elaina than it probably was. She gazed up at the two-story manse she had once feared she would never see again. It looked sad and abandoned. No candles flickered in the windows. The torches were lit outside of the stables, however, and Elaina wondered if William had hired a new coachman or if he had been too busy mounting a defense against the Jacobites.

Rhona moaned under the pile of furs they had her wrapped in.

"Shhh, *mo mhàthair*," Calum whispered from the back of the wagon.

Elaina tapped Ainsley's arm for him to stop the wagon and then she slid down and took a few tentative steps toward the back entrance of the manor.

"Who goes there?" a voice called out from the darkness of the path leading to the house.

Elaina already held a pistol in her hand and now pointed it into the black hole between the rose bushes, whose limbs were bare from the bitter bite of winter but remained thick enough that they hid the man well. "Is the master of the house at home?" she asked.

"I am the master of the house, madam."

The man's odd half-strangled voice and his answer gave Elaina pause. "I ask again. Is the master of the house at home? Do not make me shoot you."

A large bumbling form shot around from the side of the rose bushes, tackling Elaina onto the rough surface of the path and sending her pistol flying.

She and her attacker rolled around, struggling and grunting for several moments before Elaina could catch enough wind to speak. "Mrs. Davies," she groaned, still struggling with the soft yet incredibly strong form. "Dammit, woman! It is me, Elaina."

All movement stopped. "My lady?" a chubby hand found Elaina's face, feeling of it as if the blasted cook were blind and trying to identify her.

"Please, get off of me," Elaina croaked, being suffocated while Mrs. Davies patted her face like bannock dough.

"Oh, my heavens, my lady. I am so sorry. We didna ken who was sneakin' 'round in the dead of night. One canna be too careful." The woman finally rolled off Elaina.

A pair of hands grabbed her, lifting her to her feet.

Hearing snorts and giggles coming from the vicinity of her companions, Elaina leveled a glare through the inky darkness that no one could see. "I see how it is. Just let me get attacked and sit back and laugh about it. Some friends—"

Someone much taller than Elaina wrapped her in a bear hug, crushing her face to his chest.

"Eads?" she whispered into the dressing coat that smelled faintly of pipe smoke and lemon oil.

"I can't believe you were going to shoot me, my lady." Her former butler squeezed her harder, if that were possible, before holding her at arm's reach. "You have been with the savages for way too long. I am glad you have returned to civilization."

"I didn't recognize your voice," Elaina said, grasping the man's arms.

"I was trying to sound like Lord Spencer."

Elaina snorted. "Well, you need practice. You sounded more like a strangled goat."

Eads laughed, and Elaina realized she didn't think she had ever heard the man laugh. It was a pleasant sound.

"Well, let's get ye inside and out of this blasted cold," Mrs. Davies said.

"I have a sick woman with me. She needs a physician in the most serious of ways. I assume that Lord Spencer is not here since you are acting in his stead?" Elaina asked Eads.

"Yes, madam. He is not home at present."

"Good. We need a bed, food, and a doctor."

"I might say ye need a bath as well," Mrs. Davies mumbled.

Elaina, who had been tapping around in the darkness with her foot, offered a snort while she collected her wayward pistol. "Yes, we all might need one of those as well, but first things first. Is there anyone we can send for the physician?"

"I am afraid they have all gone with one side or the other," Eads said.

Elaina stared at the outline of him. "All of them?"

"I believe so, my lady." Eads sounded reluctant to have to deliver the news.

What in the bloody hell were they going to do now? The weight of the man's statement bore down on her. She stomped her foot like a child. She wanted to jump up and down and scream. *You damn fool,* she chastised herself. *If she dies, it is your fault for not attempting the trip to Gleann Eader.*

"Come." Mrs. Davies's voice had taken on the authoritative tone she used with her kitchen help. "Let's get her inside. I am as good as any healer in these parts. Let me look at her."

"Might we get a warm welcome as well?" Ainsley said from behind the trio.

"Well, ye might if I kent who ye was," Mrs. Davies turned toward the sound of his voice.

"It's Ainsley," Elaina whispered in the woman's ear.

"Ainsley? 'Tis not. Ainsley is but a lad. This is a grown man standin' before me with his deep voice and towerin' over me like a giant."

Elaina studied Ainsley's shadowy form. His changes had been subtle while being around him daily, but, now on the grounds of their former home, she realized just how much the boy had grown. He had been through a lot in the past year or so. Hell, they all had. They were not the same people who had ridden away from Duart Manor that frozen morning with Ainsley's dead brother, Angus, behind them. The act of taking the murdered boy home to his parents had changed everyone's lives forever. Some for the better, some for the worse.

Ainsley wrapped the cook up in a bear hug until she started thumping him on the arms with her fists, her protests muffled by his coat. "Ye'll smother me to death if ye dinna let me loose."

"I would like one of those too." Caitir stepped forward, embracing the cook and the butler in turn.

"Well, I'll be." The cook sniffled. "Enough. Inside. I'll set Missie to work feedin' the lot of ye, and I will see about yer companion. Come along." Mrs. Davies clapped her hands at them in between sniffles, and the group set about unloading Rhona from the wagon.

Chapter Four

Elaina insisted everyone traveling with her, including herself, stay downstairs in the servants' quarters. She gave Eads and Mrs. Davies each permission to move to rooms upstairs. "I will explain it all later," she said when they questioned her as to why. That alone told her that William must not have informed the help about the happenings of the past year. "Let us get Rhona tended to, and then I will tell you everything."

It was funny how scents lingered in the recesses of your mind, only to drown you in a flood of memories when you least expected it. Walking through the kitchen area, the smell of the fires being stirred and bannocks already being prepared at first brought a warm feeling of sentimentality, but the pad of her boots on the stone kitchen floor and the smell of snow in the air threw her into a whirlwind of memories of sitting by the fire with a young Angus brushing her hair and then the feeling of the cold stones under her body as she lay crumpled in a heap weeping over the loss of him days later. She bit the insides of her cheeks to keep the tears at bay. There was no time to relive the past. She had mourned her friend for a long time. Now she needed to concentrate on the joy he'd brought to this house with his short life. More important matters lay ahead. Another life hung in the small gap between living and dying, and Elaina felt it her duty to do all she could to save her mother-in-law.

Calum eased his mother down onto Mrs. Davies's bed, grimacing as she moaned in her fevered state at the movement. Ainsley set about stoking the fire while Caitir and Mrs. Davies scurried from the room to gather supplies. Calum knelt by the head of the bed and, with a gentle touch, moved Rhona's limp curls away from her face.

The lines etching his furrowed brow as his mother tossed with fever matched the bands squeezing Elaina's heart. The situation did not bode well. She wanted to kiss the lines smooth. She wanted to ease the pain and uncertainty so clearly written upon his face, but Elaina had never witnessed someone so ill recover from their wounds. Nothing but time would tell, but how much time did they have?

Caitir and Mrs. Davies returned, and the plump cook and household healer shooed Elaina and Calum from the room. "Ainsley, stay." Mrs. Davies laid a hand on the lad's arm as he turned to go as well. "I need ye to hold her," Elaina heard Mrs. Davies whisper to him as she and Calum exited the room.

Calum's grip tightened on her hand. He'd heard her as well.

Elaina pulled him into the kitchen and away from whatever Mrs. Davies had planned. She plopped down on the bench that spanned the length of the table in the kitchen.

Calum followed suit.

Exhaustion pulled heavily on her bones as Missie, the young cook's assistant, poured them both a dram of whisky and set a plate of cold sliced chicken before them. "The bannocks will be ready shortly," she said in a whisper that no one spoke above. The somberness of the situation seemed to warrant it.

Elaina hated to tell the lass she was too tired to chew. After a burning gulp of whisky, she crossed her arms on the tabletop and laid her head on them.

Calum did the same, and they sat staring at each other, the light of the fire in the hearth dancing on Calum's skin and flickering in his hazel eyes.

The corner of her mouth turned up in what she hoped resembled an encouraging smile. His did the same. It was the saddest smile she thought she had ever seen, and she wondered if hers looked that hopeless. She inched her hand across the table worn smooth with years of food preparations, and spanning the short distance between them, she locked index fingers with him, giving his a squeeze. He returned in kind, and she closed her eyes, that slightest touch of skin on skin exuding an intimacy she had not felt in near a week.

Rhona's muffled cries startled her from a light slumber she hadn't even known that she had fallen into.

Calum gave a start as well, squeezing his eyes shut as the tortured sounds continued to carry down the hallway. "I need air," he mumbled, staggering up from his seat, and then he disappeared out of the kitchen door and into the night.

Elaina thought if he had wanted company, he would have dragged her with him. Instead, she stayed in her seat, giving him time to clear his head and harness his emotions.

Missie's slight form pulled the hot bannocks from the fire, depositing the iron skillet with a clunk upon the trivet waiting on the table.

What was daily life like here at Duart Manor without the Spencer family present, Elaina wondered, picking at the steaming disk of oat bread. "How long has Lord Spencer been gone?" she asked Missie. "Sit, please." She waved the girl to sit and visit with her, pushing the whisky toward her and the pan of bannocks.

Missie refilled Elaina's glass before pouring herself a small one. "He came back only once after ye…well, after ye took Angus home." Her blonde head bowed over the cup she held with both hands. "It has been a sight lonely here without ye, my lady. Without all of ye."

"What did he tell you of the situation? Did he tell you why I have not returned?"

"No, my lady. He moved from his bedchambers to his office and back. He took his meals in one or the other. I believe Eads asked him one time, and that one time was all it took to realize that we mustn't speak of ye. We thought ye dead until…"

"Until I surprised you in the middle of the night?" Elaina smiled.

"No." The young girl's eyes remained upon her cup. "Until I saw the broadsheet with yer likeness, my lady, and realized ye were wanted for the murder of a British officer. That certainly explained Lord Spencer's foul mood."

Elaina's smile faded from her lips. "Yes, I suppose it would." She picked at a small nick in the tabletop, feeling small and almost ashamed over having caused her brother such angst. In her defense, the English had planned to hang her anyway for the accidental murder of a member of the Black Watch, and the English bastard she actually killed in cold blood had murdered Ainsley's brother, Angus.

"Did ye do it?" Missie asked, almost as if she didn't want to hear the answer.

A sigh escaped Elaina as Mrs. Davies, Caitir, and a pale Ainsley entered the kitchen, followed by Eads. Ainsley headed straight for the spirits, throwing back a cup before he too left out the back door, into the night.

"Poor lad," Mrs. Davies said, her gaze following the retreating figure. "I'm no' sure it didn't hurt him as much as it hurt Lady Beinnmaree."

"I need you all to sit for a moment." Elaina nodded to the benches around the table. "We have much to discuss, and I don't know how much time we have. Fetch you each a mug first. You will need to fortify yourselves."

A few minutes later, after Elaina had related the happenings of her imprisonment, learning the truth of who she was, her marriage to Calum, and all the other terrible things that had happened to her along the way, Mrs. Davies, Eads, and Missie sat staring at her as if not believing what they had heard.

"I never liked that man, Rabbie," Eads said, referring to the coachman who had killed Elaina's parents and tried to kill her more than once.

"I cannae believe ye are truly Scottish." Missie studied Elaina as if she had discovered a new species of life.

"'Tis true," Caitir said. "She is a Scot through and through."

"Well, it certainly explains her temper," Mrs. Davies mumbled before gulping down her drink and refilling her cup.

Elaina rolled her eyes. "Why is that the first thing anyone ever says?"

"Well," Eads started, his voice cracking on the short word. He cleared his throat and began again. "Well, you have never attempted to kill one of us. Even when half of the staff disrupted the mourning of your parents with quite the *brouhaha*."

Elaina snickered, thinking back to the day she had laid her parents to rest and the scene she had come upon in the kitchen. Flour everywhere…Mrs. Davies spitting mad, and little Angus holding his own with the substantial-sized cook. "Who had the temper that day?" Elaina raised a brow at the cook.

Mrs. Davies's face turned as red as the burning coals in the hearth fire. "Never ye mind. That's in the past. We are in the here and now. What on earth is Lord Spencer going to say if he comes home to find a gaggle of rebels in his kitchen?" The cook kneaded her plump hands.

Elaina thought she might rub the skin right off.

"He needn't find out," the almost always silent Missie said, drawing the attention of the entire group. She held their gaze instead of looking away as she normally did. "They can stay hidden in the lower quarters with us. Lady Elaina has always been kind to us, not to mention that she has been to hell and back over the last year. Besides, the odds of his returning are slim to none, as long as the war continues. I for one will keep your presence secret."

"As will I," Eads said.

"And I." Mrs. Davies reached across the table and squeezed Elaina's hand in an unusual show of affection.

Elaina squeezed hers in return. The loyalty of the group warmed her heart and comforted her soul.

Chapter Five

S HE FOUND CALUM DOWN BEHIND the gardens, in the little clearing where she and Angus and Ainsley had spent much of their time together before Angus's murder. He sat on the splitting stump, his face buried in his hands. Elaina dropped to the frozen ground beside him, laying her head on his knee, and he placed a warm hand upon it, his thumb making little circles against her hair. Elaina stared out into the moonless night.

The clouds had moved in, bringing the threat of snow with them. Eads had gifted Elaina with the stunning and horrific news that the English had retaken control of Edinburgh just as soon as the Jacobite army left. She had brought Rhona right into enemy territory. She debated about informing Calum, but decided it could wait. The Jacobites had added few men to their army, many fewer than expected, having yet to see the French reinforcements promised by the prince. Rumors flew around like midges during the summer months—abundant and annoying. At times, the Cause seemed worthwhile. After all, the Jacobite army had walked straight into Edinburgh without a fight, although the castle had always remained under government control. Then Prince Charles and his legion of Highland warriors had made it as far as Derby. Elaina felt it to be more a matter of luck than brilliant strategy, and just how long could their luck hold out?

"Do ye think she will live?" Calum's voice startled her back into the present and the black stillness that surrounded them.

Elaina hesitated, considering carefully before answering. Rhona's leg certainly did not look good, and if the infection had spread as far as she was afraid it had, Rhona's prospects were slim. "I don't know," was as truthful an answer as she could give.

"It looks frightful," Calum whispered.

"That it does."

They sat in silence a bit longer, Calum's thumb still rubbing her head and her arms wrapped around his leg. "How long do ye think we can safely stay here?" he asked.

"As long as we need to. No one knows we are here. If we stay hidden, I think we will be fine."

"For the moment," Calum replied ruefully.

"Do you feel the same as I do? That this is all just blind luck?"

"Aye," he answered. After a moment, he whispered, "*Mo chridhe?* My heart?"

"Yes?" she whispered, squeezing his leg.

"I am bone weary. Let's go to bed, aye? We can plan our next move tomorrow when we see if Mrs. Davies's ministrations have done anythin' to help my mam."

"Wonderful idea. I think I could sleep right here if I weren't afraid I would freeze to death during the night."

"Well, we will have none of that. Come." Calum pulled her to her feet.

Elaina groaned as her half-frozen legs unfolded out from under her. "I'm not sure I ever want to be on the back of a horse again," she moaned as they made their way toward the house, arms wrapped around each other's waists.

"Aye, 'twas a long hard ride. My bum is feelin' it as well." Calum rubbed his backside, then reached down and patted Elaina's. "Tell ye what, I will rub yers if ye rub mine."

Elaina laughed, pulling him closer. "What an obscene offer."

"Obscene? 'Tis only common courtesy for a husband to ease his wife's sufferin'. Ye dinna think it obscene when I rub yer feet."

"I consider that obscene as well."

"How so?"

"When you rub my feet, your hands tend to head north."

"They've a mind of their own. I cannae help it."

"I suppose other things have a mind of their own also?"

Calum chuckled as they reached the door to the house. "Aye. Other things control the world, I believe. They overrule the brain more often than not."

"Greed and lust. Two of the most motivating factors in a man's life."

"Not all men, *mo chridhe,* but yes…most."

The kitchen had been abandoned by the time they returned to the house.

The fire had been smoored for the evening and all the occupants, she assumed, bedded down for the night. They made their way through the dim room, lit only by the bit of glow from the hearth. Calum snatched a bannock as they passed the table. He broke it, handing Elaina half. She nibbled on it, the oats gritting between her teeth. Something about the smell of the kitchen, the coolness of the night, and the earthy taste of the bannock reminded her of her own mother, who had secretly supported the Cause for all of her life and been beaten to death for it. Greed had killed her mother and her father. A madman's obsession with money and his twisted thoughts on how to get his hands on it. Now, lust might take the life of Calum's mother. His father's lust for fame and fortune had brought Rhona into this fight against her will. Where her husband went, she followed. Elaina would have done the same. But now Rhona fought for her life while her husband fought for suppression of the English and was hell bent on making certain the prince knew of his loyalty and sacrifice so that in the end, if victorious, Micheil MacKinnon—the Laird Beinnmaree of Gleann Eader—would rise to power alongside the heir to the throne of England and be rewarded justly.

Greed and lust, two of the seven deadly sins, and Elaina believed them to be what would eventually upend the Jacobite upheaval. They might be victorious at the moment, but she had met the Duke of Cumberland, King George's younger son, and knew that if the king called for him to return from the fight in Flanders, he would return, and there would be hell to pay. Prince Charles Edward Stuart seemed a godly yet prideful man. Add pride to greed and lust, and you had a volatile mix that could only end in disaster.

Chapter Six

Several days later, Mrs. Davies shook her head at Elaina before she left Rhona's room after having changed the bandages on her wound. After three days of Mrs. Davies's doctoring, there were no improvements to be seen.

Elaina sat on the stool next to the invalid's bed, the seat of it still warmed by the cook's substantial form, and tried to ignore the almost sweet smell of infection that hung in the room. She plunged a rag into the bowl of cold water on the table by the bedside, squeezing the water from the cloth and watching the ripples in the water expand to the edges of the bowl, held captive in their small vessel. Elaina had the feeling that the waves caused by this war would not be contained in a tidy little circle. The repercussions would be felt for thousands of miles and hundreds of generations. How could they not be? It was war, after all. Look at the deaths that had already occurred. These men had families—both sides, English and Scottish. The Glorious Revolution had taken place in the 1600s, and here they sat in the middle of the eighteenth century fighting the same fight. How long could it continue?

Rhona moaned, bringing Elaina out of her troublesome thoughts. She had more urgent matters to worry about, like trying to save her husband's mother from the death that knocked at her door. Drawing the wet rag across Rhona's forehead and down her neck, Elaina could only whisper soothing words to the woman who jerked her head, trying to escape the coolness of the water.

"It's all right," Elaina whispered. "Rest. Be still."

"My la—ahem…mistress," Eads stuttered from the doorway.

"Yes, what is it?" Elaina looked over shoulder.

Eads, whose face was a lovely shade of pink, stared at her, his chest heaving as his breath came quick and shallow. He opened his mouth but shut it again with a snap.

"What is it?" Elaina repeated, standing to face him, dread creeping down her spine.

"A messenger came…"

"Go on."

"Lord Spencer is to arrive within the hour with a group of British officers. We are to prepare a meal for them and ready the rooms. They will stay at the house." The words tumbled out in a rush.

The rag hit the floor. "Jesus Christ almighty," Elaina whispered, making the sign of the cross. "Are you certain? How can it be?"

Eads ignored her questions and asked his own. "Calum and Ainsley are moving the horses and the wagon to the woods. Mrs. MacKinnon is too weak to move, yes?"

"Yes. There is nothing to be done except for us to stay hidden. There should be no reason for them to come down to the servants' quarters. You and Mrs. Davies shall have to board with us. I hope you don't mind sharing a room with a bunch of Jacobite rebels." A terrifying thought crossed Elaina's mind. *What if one of the stable hands does take exception to housing rebels? It will be the perfect opportunity to turn us all in.* She wrung her hands as she asked, "Do you think that any of the other servants mind? What I mean is, are we safe here?"

"I can only speak for the three of us. We will not reveal your presence. But, in truth, I don't think the stable hands will either. I don't think you have any-thing to fear."

"Thank you, Eads," she said. His words gave her a small bit of comfort.

William had let most of the household staff go when he'd returned the last time. Missie had informed her that Lord Spencer had announced there was no need to keep them on if no one would be living at Duart Manor the majority of the time. He had offered no other explanation. That was when the remainder of the staff believed Elaina to be dead. Well, nothing could be done. What would be would be. They had to stay out of William's way and pray that he and the officers would not tarry long.

"Prepare the house," Elaina said needlessly. The butler had already turned for the door. "Don't worry, Eads. It will all be fine."

"I pray as much, my lady." He bowed his head to her.

"Eads—"

The stately butler held up a hand. "I know you do not wish for us to call you by that title, but the late Lord and Lady Spencer raised you from only a few months old. Your entire life you lived as their daughter. They loved you as their own. In their eyes, you belonged to them. They gave you a home, an education, and, I dare say, a wonderful life. Blood is not the only thing that makes a family, my lady. I will not sully their memory by shunning their daughter. You *are* a lady, whether or not you believe it of yourself. It is your title, and that is how I will refer to you. Now, I have duties to perform. I bid you good morning." Eads bowed and left Elaina staring at the empty doorway, her mouth gaping open.

In the wilds of the Highlands, it was easier to push thoughts of her childhood back and believe her life to be something other than what it had been. But, here in her grandmother's home with servants who had known the parents who'd raised her, it grew increasingly difficult to push her family from her mind.

Retrieving the rag from the floor, Elaina rinsed it off in the bowl and returned to attending her mother-in-law.

"Mary, mother of God, what are we to do?" A breathless Caitir tumbled into the room, dropping to the floor next to the bed.

"Nothing," Elaina said. "We are to do nothing except stay quiet and out of sight."

"They will hang us."

"They will *not* hang us. They will not know we are here, and what have we done, anyway? Not one of us has raised a hand in the rebellion… Well, except Ainsley, but how are they to know that? Don't fret."

It would have been easier if Elaina had believed her own words. What else would the officers or her brother think if they found a group of Scots hiding in the servants' quarters, one of them dying from a large, inflamed wound to the leg and another wanted for murder? The answer was obvious, and Elaina feared there would be no argument that could save them.

Elaina and Caitir pitched in with the meal preparations for the approaching officers. No one wanted Lord Spencer wandering down to the kitchen to check on the progress of upcoming nourishment. Soon the kitchen overflowed with the scent of roasting meat and toasting bread. Elaina carved cheeses, trying not to panic over the thought of being trapped in the same house as those who hunted her. If she could have taken Rhona anywhere else, she would have, but there had been nowhere else to go, and Elaina had felt they would be safe at her family home in a city occupied with Jacobites. She could not have anticipated that Prince Charles would have invaded England, that Edinburgh would have already returned to English rule, or that her brother would return accompanied by a gaggle of officers.

After returning from hiding the horses, Calum sat by his mother's side, mopping her brow while everyone else ran around in a tizzy, trying not to panic at the approaching British military.

Ainsley burst through the kitchen door. "They are coming down the lane."

"How many?" Mrs. Davies asked, wiping sweat from her brow with the edge of her apron.

"At least ten."

Mrs. Davies nodded, studying the food before her. "Good. I think we'll have plenty. Missie, clean yerself up. You'll help serve."

The poor child looked like she wanted to throw up on her shoes, and Elaina felt much the same.

As the first round of food made its way upstairs, Elaina, Ainsley, and Caitir joined Calum and Rhona in Mrs. Davies's room and closed the door behind them. The heat coming off the fire in the hearth baked the small room and the nervous, sweating bodies that hid within. Elaina sat by the wall, her knees drawn up to her chest and her face buried in her skirts. Her ears rang with the silence of the room. Rhona's labored breathing and quiet moans were the only sounds. Drawing breath had become difficult, heat or no heat. Elaina feared that if she were to suck in a deep lungful, her brother would surely hear her through the floor separating them. Laughable, but her comrades seemed to stifle their own breaths as well.

Elaina listened to the faint sound of footsteps on the stairs to the main floor as Eads and Missie, she assumed, carried nourishment to her brother and his guests. She wished she had thought to grab a hunk of cheese herself, or a scone. Her stomach grumbled at the thought of the men upstairs, feasting. She glanced up to see if anyone else had heard it, and all eyes were on her. She snorted, burying her face into the folds of her skirts, trying to muffle the nervous laughter that threatened to erupt. The sniffles and snorts around her made matters worse; tears ran from her eyes, and her neck ached from holding back.

A light rap sounded on the door, instantly sobering the room as all heads swiveled toward it.

Mrs. Davies slipped through with a small tray as if she had heard Elaina's stomach as well. "Eads says they plan to stay but a couple of days at most," she whispered, handing the small platter to Caitir.

Surely to goodness they could survive two days without being found out. Elaina had popped a piece of dried fruit into her mouth when Missie barreled through the door and into Mrs. Davies. If the latter hadn't been of such substantial size, Elaina believed the two would have tumbled head over heels.

"What on earth—"

Missie slapped a hand over the cook's mouth. "There is trouble," she hissed over the rest of Mrs. Davies's muffled exclamation.

"What kind of trouble?" Calum asked, the entire group getting to their feet.

"A stable hand brought in a peasant woman and her child. He found them hiding in the stables. Claims the woman had stolen some food. The woman refuses to speak at all. The boy, however, is howling in Gaelic for his *seanmhair.*"

His grandmother. Elaina's heart dropped to her feet. She snatched Missie by her arms, whirling her around to face her. "What does the child look like?"

"Like a heathen, and he acts as one too. He kicked Lord Spencer in the shin when he tried to speak to him."

"Mother of God." Elaina stifled a giggle. "Give me your apron. Now!" she barked at Missie's wide-eyed stare. "I need a kerchief for my hair." She turned to Caitir, who scrambled into action.

"Ye cannae be meanin' to go up there." Calum looked appalled. "Let them handle it."

"One of the officers is threatenin' to arrest her and toss her into the Tolbooth Prison. He accuses her of treason because the lad speaks only Gaelic," Missie offered.

"I have to go." Elaina took the kerchief from Caitir.

Calum moved to stand in front of Elaina, his voice rising as he protested. "Ye are out of yer mind. Ye cannae go walkin' into a room full of redcoats over a strange woman and her child."

Elaina pinned the kerchief to her head, tucking any stray hairs underneath it while studying her husband's face. "It is my fault," she offered pensively.

"How can it be yer fault?" Calum raised his brow.

"I'll fix it." Elaina ran from the room and up the stairs before Calum could stop her.

She smoothed her apron before opening the door to the formal dining hall and glanced over her shoulder. Calum, silent as a cat and looking just as fierce with fury blazing in his eyes, took the stairs two at a time. Giving a small squeal, she squeezed through the door, slamming it behind her as he reached the landing. She tried to dislodge her heart from her throat as she leaned panting against the door.

Glancing up, Elaina found all eyes on her. William stared slack-jawed in open disbelief.

She cleared her throat and curtsied before the men. "My lord, forgive me." She gave them the best version of a proper British accent that she could muster.

"Annie Lanie!" Wee Jamie broke loose from his mother's grasp and wrapped himself around Elaina's leg.

"You know these people?" William growled through clenched teeth.

"Aye, my lord. 'Tis my sister and my nephew. I am truly sorry for any misunderstanding."

Jamie stuck his tongue out at William as Elaina hoisted him up to her hip.

"May I, my lord?" Elaina's voice came strangled as she fought to keep a smile from her face.

William gave the briefest of nods, and Elaina snatched a scone from a nearby platter and shoved it into Jamie's hands, hoping to keep the toddler's mouth full and therefore silent. She edged her way over to stand beside Isobel. "If you would, my lord. You can take any missin' food from my pay. I asked them to wait for me in the stables until you and your visitors retired for the eve. She is a recent widow, and I bid her come to me, hopin' I could find her work in the city."

"Well, she could have said as much." An officer eyed Isobel with disdain. "Or does she only speak that dreadful language her brat has been spouting?"

Isobel made to take a step toward him.

Elaina grabbed her hand, squeezing it tight. "Begging her pardon, she has a distrust of men, especially—"

William waved a hand through the air. "Who am I to deprive a widow woman and her child food? Now, if you will kindly take your family to the servants' quarters, I shall settle matters after we finish dinner." He glared at Elaina with a fire she had not seen in some time.

"Aye, my lord." She curtsied again and dragged Isobel and Jamie through the door, nearly knocking Calum from the landing he remained planted on.

Chapter Seven

"WHAT IN THE ALMIGHTY HELL do ye think ye're doin'?" Calum growled through his teeth after the group had retreated to Rhona's room. "Ye just waltz into the room like ye are no' a wanted woman, like ye've no cares in the world. I swear to God ye are goin' to be the death of me!" He paced the floor as he ranted, running his fingers through his curls. He circled back on Elaina. "What would ye have done if they had recognized ye?"

"I suppose they would have taken me with Isobel to the Tolbooth." Elaina should have known better than to use sarcasm as a defense, but the statement left her mouth before it could register in her brain.

"Do ye think it's funny? Do ye ken what they do to women in there? 'Tis one of the worst places on earth ye would want to be jailed in. If ye thought the gaol at Balquhidder to be a terrible place, ye would think ye had gone straight to hell in the Tolbooth."

Elaina swallowed hard. Even the mention of her time in the gaol at Balquhidder made her stomach turn.

Isobel laid a hand on Calum's arm. "Ease up, brother. She meant well. Nothin' happened. She saved Jamie and me from arrest. We are all safe." Her gaze turned to her mother.

Calum closed his eyes and sighed. His shoulders dropped, and his fists unclenched. Then his eyes flew open, and he turned on Isobel. "What are ye doin' here in the first place? Did I no' tell ye it was too dangerous?"

Isobel stood toe to toe with her brother, glaring up at him with her fists on her hips. Both of the siblings' hair curled in wild swirls about their heads, only Isobel's had the fiery color their mother's had once held, which matched her temper. "Och, aye, ye told me, but ye also told me ye were bringin' my mam home to me, and here ye are in Edinburgh and no' Gleann Eader. I suppose ye would just come stragglin' on home after ye buried her and tell me I had lost my mam."

Calum's voice dropped to a whisper. "She will not die."

Isobel's eyes lost their fire, and her expression changed from the hard-set jaw of fierce anger to tears in her eyes as she turned toward Rhona. "She does no' look like she will live."

"We are doin' the best we can do. All the physicians went with Prince Charles and the rebellion. How did ye come to be here?" Calum asked again.

"I sent for her." Elaina laid her hand on his arm.

Calum stared down at her. "Why? It is too dangerous."

"Dinna chew on her, brother. We had already left Gleann Eader when I met up with the messenger. I would have found ye anyway. I could no' sit at home worryin' about my family."

Rhona moaned, drawing everyone's attention. Jamie stood beside the bed, pulling the rag across his grandmother's forehead and whispering to her in Gaelic. He had taken the cloth from Caitir, who stood behind the child, one hand on his shoulder and the other wiping at a tear rolling down her cheek. Ainsley leaned against the wall beside the hearth, his eyes on the boy.

It had taken a child's love of his grandmother to draw the adults in the room back to what mattered the most. Not the rebellion, the Jacobites, nor Elaina and Isobel going against Calum's orders. Rhona, the headstrong woman who held the family together, was losing her battle.

Isobel dropped to her knees beside Jamie and took up her mother's hand. "*Mo mhàthair*," she whispered, raising her mother's hand to her lips. "We are here."

The door to the room opened behind Elaina, and she turned as William stuck his head in, his mouth open to yell at her, she supposed. As his gaze scanned the room, he closed his mouth, then he stepped inside and closed the door behind him.

"She is their mother," Elaina whispered to him, taking his hand. "I had to bring her here, William, to attempt to save her life. She is his *seanmhair*, his grandmother." She nodded her head at wee Jamie.

William stood staring at the invalid who lay covered in sweat, her face a pasty shade of gray. "What is wrong with her?"

"She has broken her leg. Infection has set in. Mrs. Davies has been working for days, but she is not improving."

"Why have you not sent for the physician?"

"There is no physician to be had. They all went with the prince."

William crossed the room to the bed. "May I?" he asked Isobel, who scooted back, giving him space to examine her mother. He pushed back the blanket and lifted the dressing on the wound.

Isobel gasped and clapped a hand over her mouth at the sight of her mother's leg.

"Her leg must be removed if she is to have a chance at living," William stated, placing the dressing once more over the wound.

"Ye cannae take her leg," Calum said.

William turned to him, his blue eyes studying Calum's face. "I am sorry. But it is the only way."

"There are no physicians in the city to perform such duties, in any matter," Calum said.

"I can send for one of ours. How did this happen?" William raised a brow at Elaina.

Elaina stared at him, not wanting to tell him that her mother-in-law had been present at one of the early scuffles in the rebellion. "A farming accident," she muttered, looking beyond him at a spot on the wall.

"A farming accident? In the middle of winter? In Edinburgh?"

"A *farming* accident," Elaina repeated with more emphasis.

William closed his eyes against what Elaina could only believe was his frustration with her. Shaking his head, he opened his eyes and turned to Calum. "I will send for a surgeon. If you wish to save your mother's life, you must abide by what he determines."

Calum gave the slightest nod of his head.

"Now, Elaina. May I speak to you in private?" William growled at his sister.

"Aye," she whispered, following him out of the room with her head down like a scolded child.

Chapter Eight

M rs. Davies, Missie, and Eads huddled together like a tumble of frightened kittens, their eyes on the floor as Elaina and William entered the kitchen. William glanced around the room, and Elaina wondered if this was the first time he had ever been in the servant's area.

"The butler's pantry?" Eads offered, reading his master's mind well.

Missie pointed the way when William raised his brow in question.

Elaina heaved a sigh. Grabbing a lantern, she took charge and led the way, her head held high. If she were going to her own execution, she would do so with honor. Floor to ceiling mahogany cabinets graced the walls of the pantry. Light from the lantern danced off her mother's prized crystal, made by her family's glassworks company. The company had once belonged to Elaina after their mother's death, but with the truth of Elaina's birth and the minor fact that she had killed two British soldiers, she didn't have the heart to ask William about the business. She had forfeited any right she had to it with her deadly acts. There was also the fact that she was the daughter of a dead Scottish Highlander and his wife and not William's true sister at all, though they'd spent their entire lives together. Elaina turned her gaze to William, who stood leaning against the cabinets, studying her.

Though the butler's pantry was a large room, it seemed to crush the air out of Elaina's lungs, and she fidgeted under his scrutiny. "Well, say it, William. We do not have all evening."

"I want to throttle you and hug you at the same time. I am considering which I may do first." He lunged at her, and Elaina squealed and cowered under his height. He took the lantern from her and placed it on a nearby shelf before wrapping her up in his arms.

After a moment, when she had determined he would not strangle her to death, she relaxed and let her arms slide around her brother. "I have missed you, William," she whispered into his chest.

"And I, you, Elaina. Now," he said, holding her at arm's length, "what in the devil do you mean coming to Edinburgh? I thought Calum's family resided in the Highlands?"

"They do. Rhona was visiting a relative near here when the accident happened. We came as fast as we could when we received word."

William crossed his arms in front of him. "So, then, the man named Micheil MacKinnon, who is at the prince's side, is no relation to your husband or the woman lying ill in the next room?"

Elaina stopped breathing.

"It is as I thought, then. What news do you have for me on the rebellion? I assume that to bring the enemy under my roof and put my reputation in harm's way, it must come with a reward of some kind?"

"Why, you cad. I have nothing to do with the Jacobite Cause. I have been at my husband's home in Gleann Eader. As I said, when word came of Rhona's injury, we came as fast as we could."

"And your husband? Am I to believe he remained in the Highlands with you while his clan raised swords against their king?"

Elaina crossed her arms and narrowed her eyes at him. "Are you going to arrest us? What about Ainsley and Caitir? What about poor Isobel and wee Jamie?"

"Wee Jamie I shall just turn over my knee and beat his arse, the heath—"

"You will not touch him." Elaina took a step toward her brother.

"He needs more than that."

"Aye, he probably does, but he has enough distrust of the British without you adding fuel to the fire. I swear to you that we remained at the family home." Elaina left out the part about their plans to join the fight at a future date.

"What do you know of Prince Charles's plans?" William leaned once more against the cabinet and folded his arms.

"Less than you, I'm sure. We thought Edinburgh still under his authority, which is why we thought it might be safe to bring her here."

"So, you admit you are Jacobite loyalists?"

Elaina sighed and threw her head back in frustration. "For Christ's sake, William," she grumbled at the ceiling before turning a burning glare on her brother. "At this point in time, I do not give a rat's arse who sits on the throne of England. I would just like to save my mother-in-law's life while there is still a chance."

"You have softened to her, then?" William whispered.

"Aye." Elaina nodded, tears coming to her eyes. "We have softened to each other."

William stared down at his shoes for a moment. "That is good. I would like to believe you are happy with your new life." He turned his gaze back to her. "You are happy, are you not?"

"That is a difficult question to answer at present," Elaina whispered, a tear sliding down her cheek.

"What is it?" William's gaze seemed to take in her appearance for the first time.

The compassion she saw there was more than she could bear, and she buried her face in her hands and wept.

In two steps, William had reached her and wrapped his arms about her. "With whom did you leave your babe, Elaina?" he whispered.

She couldn't catch her breath enough to speak and merely shook her head against his chest.

"When last I saw you, you stood over me with a broadsword pointed at my neck. Before you left, you told me you were with child. Where is your baby, Elaina?"

The sobs broke forth in uncontrolled waves, and William sank to the floor with her in his arms. He rocked her and smoothed her hair as their father would do when they were children.

He pressed his handkerchief into her hand. "I am sorry, Elaina. God, I am so very sorry."

After several minutes, she gained control of her emotions and told her brother all that had happened in their time apart. She told him about Freya's curse and Rabbie's return. She assured him of the man's death. This time, there was no mistaking. She herself had severed his head from his body. She even told William of her dream of their parents and how they'd held little Thamas Edward in their eternal grasp.

"Thamas Edward. A fine name," William whispered into his sister's hair.

"I thought so." Elaina blew her nose.

"You are such a brave soul," William whispered, clutching her to him.

"I feel like a failure. I have lost my child. I have dragged my family into the heart of a war—"

"Your father-in-law did that, Elaina. Not you. You are merely trying to save a life."

Elaina stared at her hands while she rested the side of her head against her brother's chest. "I did not think that the rebellion would have ever gone this far, William."

"But it has."

"Do you know where the rebels are? Are they any closer to London?" Elaina cringed at the question, but she also needed to know.

"No. They are no closer. In fact, they are retreating." His tone spoke more relief than pride. "We are to have a gathering of captains and generals in several days. We must roust the traitors, Elaina, and I fear Micheil MacKinnon's name is amongst those at the top. If they find them, there will not be much I can do to save him. I need you and your family to know that I will not give your presence away, but nor can I condone any untoward action against the king. My loyalty is to my country, as I am sure you understand?"

Elaina nodded, her mind already running through plans to get word to the Laird Beinnmaree and the prince, although it should be common sense that anyone working that closely with a member of royalty attempting to depose a sitting king would have their name on any number of lists.

"I will send for a physician that I know to be discreet and honorable in his actions. I will have him here on the morrow, Elaina. But for now, you all must remain hidden if you value your lives. Understood?"

Elaina nodded, resting against her brother's shoulder. It was like being in her father's arms once again. Though somewhat distant, he had comforted her tears on many occasions, and William patted her head much the same way as the man he resembled in not only looks and build, but mannerisms and undying loyalty to his king as well.

Chapter Nine

TRUE TO WILLIAM'S WORD, A physician arrived the following morning. The anxious group of Highlanders huddled in the kitchen, hidden from the British officers still at Duart Manor. Calum paced the floor from the east wall to the ovens and back. Unable to be still either, Elaina was on her hands and knees scrubbing soot from the hearth against Mrs. Davies's objections.

Elaina concentrated on the *ssht, ssht, ssht* of the brush against the stones, letting it lull her mind into a place of emptiness. Sweat trickled between her breasts and down the small of her back—the heat from the ovens was quite intense. She didn't know how the substantial Mrs. Davies didn't keep from passing out when performing her duties. She tried not to think about wee Angus and the time he'd brushed her hair with fascination or how she had collapsed on this floor after his death. *There is a plan for all things.* If not for Angus's death, she might have never found out the truth of her identity, nor the fact that Rabbie MacLeod, their coachman, was actually Robert Campbell, the man who had murdered her adoptive parents.

Jamie appeared beside her with a brush of his own, dipped it in the water, and, with a grim fierceness, attacked the stones, matching Elaina's pace. The lad was maturing at a rate that was both admirable and startling. He had the size and mental capacity of children near twice his age. Elaina wasn't certain if that was a good thing or not.

She began to softly sing a tune in rhythm to their scrubbing.

Jamie cast a sideways scowl at her.

"What? You don't like my singing?" Elaina nudged him with her elbow.

"Nay. Ye sound like a goose a'honkin'."

"Jamie!" Isobel scolded, but laughter erupted from Elaina's throat, and she hugged the boy tightly even as he struggled to remove himself from her grasp.

"You are the funniest wee lad, James Micheil Tully." Elaina released her captive, and he grunted in that guttural, throaty way that the Scots had perfected as he scooted out of her reach and returned to his task of scrubbing.

A throat cleared behind her, and Elaina turned to find the physician had finished his examination. She jumped to her feet, and the entire room crowded around the small man.

He pushed his spectacles up his hook of a nose before clearing his throat again. "She is bad off. I mean, ye ken that already. I have something that I would like to try before we take her leg. If we do not see improvement in two days' time, I will have to remove the leg, at least from the knee down."

Calum bowed his head. Closing his eyes, he ran a hand through his undone curls hanging past his shoulders. "Well, it must work. We cannae take her leg. What kind of life would she have?"

"There are many people with a missing limb," the doctor replied. "She could have a peg and do fine."

"And do fine?" Calum growled at the man, who took a step backward.

Elaina lay her hand on Calum's arm.

"We cannae do it. She wadna want it," he whispered.

"We will take this one step at a time, Calum. Do not get ahead of yourself. We will worry about the future when it gets here." Elaina turned her attention to the doctor. "What do we need to do?"

He took a deep breath. "First thing, I need to remove some dead tissue. It will be quite painful, and she may have a limp for the rest of her life if she does not die on us."

Isobel cringed and clapped a hand over her mouth.

The doctor turned to her. "I am sorry to be so blunt. But now is not the time for dancing around the truth of it. The surgery needs to be performed immediately, and I do not want to risk moving her across town. I will perform it here."

"What about the officers upstairs?" Caitir voiced Elaina's thoughts for her.

"I will speak with William." Elaina glanced at the physician, not knowing how much he knew about the situation he was standing in the middle of. He could be arrested for aiding the Jacobites.

"Well, whatever you need to do, you need to do it now," the buzzard of a man said. "It needs to be done straight away. I must fetch some of my things. I shall return within the hour," he said before scurrying out of the kitchen door leading to the gardens. William must have informed him of the importance of discretion.

Eads arrived moments later to deliver the fortuitous news that William and the other military men in residence at Duart Manor were to ride into Edinburgh in but an hour for a gathering of a war council. Although it could not have been a better time, the thought twisted Elaina's wame in a knot. She hadn't time to dwell on the news, however. The surgeon's words had the household, including her, scurrying to ready the small room for his coming duties.

Relief washed over her when word came down from upstairs that the men had left. There were a few finishing touches to see to for Rhona's procedure, but Elaina left them in the capable hands of Mrs. Davies. She had another mission in mind. She knew there to be some laudanum in a cupboard in William's study, at least there used to be, and she climbed the stairs to the main floor to retrieve it.

When she climbed the stairs to the main part of the house, the realization of her situation washed over her, and she braced herself against the baluster. Running her hand along its smooth surface, she realized how certain she'd been that she would never see this house again. What an odd feeling to be home at last but banished to the servants' quarters! But it wasn't home anymore, was it? Not now that she knew the truth of her birth and how she'd come to be with the Spencer family. She thought back to the letters her grandmother had hidden in her desk. The letters from her daughter, Diana Spencer. Letters that her grandmother had never responded to. Elaina now knew the truth of the "great matter" was her and her appearance on the Spencers' doorsteps in the arms of a Highland lass. The portrait of Elaina's adopted mother looked down at her from the wall beside her, and she trailed her fingers lightly over the golden hair in the portrait.

"Thank you," she whispered.

"Now, that's quite odd."

Elaina whirled around in surprise to find a lieutenant in full dress staring at her. "Officer." The squeaky pitch of her voice made her cringe as she managed an awkward curtsy.

"I've never witnessed a servant thanking a portrait before. Frankly, I've never witnessed *anyone* thanking a portrait."

"Well…you see…I was thanking her for hiring me on." How Elaina had the wherewithal to attempt an English accent was beyond her because she hardly had the capacity to breathe.

"How quaint. Now. I have left my pocket watch in my room. If you will fetch it for me, I'll be on my way."

She bobbed again. "Aye, sir." She scurried up the stairs, only to stop at the top of them and look back down. "I forgot... I mean...which room is yours, Lieutenant?"

He stared, his head cocked to the side. "The green room."

Elaina found herself disconcerted by the look he was giving her. "Aye, sir." She scurried away and found herself in her favorite room in the house, though it was now very much different from when she had left more than a year ago. William had furnished the room with a large bed where none had stood before. When she had left to take Angus's body to his family, the room was empty save for a few stray crates and her grandmother's writing desk. The desk remained, and upon it lay the lieutenant's pocket watch. Elaina picked it up, pausing to run her hand along the soft leather writing surface, not sure why she was being sentimental about a piece of furniture. After all, she had never known her grandmother, and from everything she had gathered, she herself was the reason that her grandmother and her mother had stopped talking to each other. Yet, here she was feeling sentimental about a piece of furniture.

You fool, Elaina scolded herself and hurried from the room. She almost toppled down the stairs at the sight of the lieutenant, who had progressed halfway up them.

"I thought perhaps you had gotten lost."

"No, sir. I-I didn't spot it at first, is all."

"Really? I thought 'twas in plain sight on the writing desk. You weren't rummaging through my things, were you, miss?" he asked with a slight quirk in the corner of his mouth. "That could be grounds for dismissal." The slight movement of his lips did not look like the beginnings of a smile. It looked like a cat ready to pounce.

"I would never. How dare you?"

"Tsk, tsk. Is that any way for the help to talk to an officer and a guest?" The lieutenant held out his hand.

Elaina stared at it until he snapped his fingers, and she realized she still held his pocket watch. "Sorry, sir. My mind..." She placed it in his outstretched hand.

His fingers wrapped around her hand, holding her in place, searing through her skin. "Don't miss me while I'm gone. I shall return, and we will see what kind of mischief we can find to get into."

She yanked her hand from his grasp, and he chuckled. He gave her a wink and turned, making his way back down the staircase and out the door without a look back.

Elaina collapsed down onto the step and buried her face in her trembling hands. Acid roiled in her wame, and she fought to keep the eggs she had eaten for breakfast where they belonged and not on her brother's staircase. She would not see the lieutenant again. She planned on never coming up to the living quarters as long as the military guests remained in the home. *Living quarters…merde.*

Suddenly remembering the laudanum, she jumped to her feet and raced to William's study, her original destination before the lieutenant had rudely interrupted her.

"Is something the matter?" Caitir whispered to her when she returned, bottle in hand.

"N-no. Why do you ask?"

"You are white as the snow, that is why."

"I am just concerned for Rhona is all. I couldn't find the laudanum, and I panicked. All is well now." Elaina squeezed past her friend and into the room where the good doctor had laid out all his instruments. She needed to collect herself before she came face to face with her husband.

The doctor gave her an encouraging smile as he took the laudanum from her. "She will thank you for this. It is quite scarce during these times, as I am sure you know."

"Unfortunately, yes. I wish all this bloody fighting would just stop. Beg your pardon," she said at her foul language.

If the doctor took offense, it didn't show. "I wish it as well," he said with a sigh.

Elaina didn't have to wonder at what horrors the man had faced on the battlefield. She had witnessed them well enough at the rudimentary hospital weeks ago. The Scots had treated their English prisoners with compassion. Treating their wounded alongside their own. Now this good doctor was aiding the enemy. Perhaps the entire world had not turned so cold and filled with hate, after all.

"Now, if you will leave me to it." The doctor interrupted Elaina's thoughts.

"Of course."

Elaina passed Calum on her way out of the room. He cast her a curious glance, but before he could open his mouth to question her emotional state, the doctor called him to his mother's bedside.

Chapter Ten

ELAINA, AINSLEY, AND JAMIE STROLLED through the woods behind the manor, leaving Calum, Isobel, and Caitir behind to help the physician if need be. The adults had all agreed that Jamie needed a good romp around the countryside rather than be subjected to what was to come.

"Dis is where ye grew up, Annie Lanie?" Jamie picked up a stone and sent it whizzing, pegging a tree a good distance away. The lad had a wicked arm.

"Nay, I grew up far away in the colonies, in the Royal Province of North Carolina."

"Is it far?"

"It is *quite* far. Across a vast ocean. The trip takes many weeks, sometimes several months, depending on the winds and the weather."

"What's it like? Is it a desert?"

Ainsley snorted a laugh, earning him a scowl from the boy. "'Tis no desert. 'Tis much like yer home, with mountains and trees." He ruffled the boy's curls.

"How do ye ken?" Jamie asked with considerable doubt while chunking another stone. "Have ye been there?"

"I havena been there in person," Ainsley said, his voicing dropping. "I hope to someday. Yer auntie used to tell my brother and me tales when we were younger."

The melancholy in Ainsley's voice constricted Elaina's throat. The memories of Angus brought up by being here at the manor had to be hard for Ainsley too, she realized.

"Ye have a *bràthair*?" The cover of the trees overhead cast shadows upon Jamie's face as he looked at Ainsley, his brow furrowed.

"Aye, I have many brothers and sisters, but this brother I speak of is no longer with us. He is with the spirits, but no worries," Ainsley added, glancing at Elaina, who had tried to keep the grief from her expression. "I will be with him again someday."

"No' soon!" Jamie exclaimed, grabbing Ainsley's hand.

Ainsley barked out a laugh. "Nay, no' soon. Someone has to rescue yer Auntie Elaina when she finds trouble. Come, laddie, and I will show ye where Angus and I would hide when we wanted to scare yer Auntie Elaina." He swooped Jamie onto his shoulders and broke into a jog through the woods.

Jamie leaned over Ainsley's head, dodging low-hanging branches and emitting squeals of laughter as the pair disappeared into the trees.

Elaina followed at a slower pace, her thoughts dwelling on her encounter with the lieutenant earlier. She prayed Ainsley wouldn't have to rescue her anytime soon. Her worries soon turned to fond remembrances of her home in North Carolina. She must ask William if the property remained in the family or if their father had sold it when they came across the ocean. A fair number of people had come and gone from her life in the two and twenty years she had been on this earth. She let their faces drift in and out of her memory. Some brought a smile, others—

Jamie gave an exuberant whoop that brought her out of her melancholy. She wiped her tears and broke into a jog to catch up with her companions.

"Look, Annie Lanie!" Jamie grinned up at her as he pointed at what was at one time a small fall of water into a gentle burn.

Elaina looked around at the area, no longer quite as she remembered. The fall and burn were now much larger than last she had seen them, and a rivulet cut down the hillside where heavy spring rains had likely caused the rocks and mud to loosen. She followed the trail down the hill, standing on her toes to eye the pile of debris that rested against a copse of trees at the bottom.

"Look." Jamie pulled her sleeve, dragging her attention back to a stone that sat wedged into the mud at the water's edge.

Ainsley squatted beside it and used a handful of dead leaves to scrub the mud from the surface.

Elaina kneeled beside Jamie and watched his chubby fingers follow the dips and swirls carved into the rock. "What do you make of it, Ainsley?" she asked, trying not to let her voice give away her unease. She did not have a good history with carvings on rocks.

"I'm nay certain. 'Tis a fair bit worn. I take it to be quite old. Maybe it is a good sign." Ainsley smiled across the rock at Elaina. "Maybe 'tis a sign that all will end well, that the spirits are with us."

Until recently, Elaina had given superstitions little weight, but Calum's ex-betrothed, Freya, and her hex and the eventual loss of Elaina and Calum's child had changed her views. A woman scorned was not to be taken lightly in the Highlands of Scotland. The thought of Freya sent chills down Elaina's spine. Word had spread that the woman had made her escape to the colonies, but what if the sources were wrong? What if she were here, now…in the woods…leaving mysterious stones for her to find? The thought made heat crawl up the back of her neck as she scanned the surrounding tree line.

"Maybe it is time to return to the house. Perhaps the physician has finished." Her voice squeaked at the end of her statement, and she cleared her throat.

"Dinna be afeard, Annie Lanie," Jamie said.

Observant little thing, Elaina thought.

He grabbed her hand, giving it a tug. "'Tis no eye."

Elaina stared at him, not believing he remembered that day in the woods at Gleann Eader and the stone they had found. "No, 'tis no eye, James Micheil, and thank goodness for it, but the sun is inching low, and it will soon turn frigid. Let us go see how your *seanmhair* fared with the doctor and if Mrs. Davies has something warm to fill our bellies with."

"I'll race you," Ainsley said, scrambling to his feet, and the two boys were off.

Elaina grabbed up her skirts and chased after them, letting their exuberant whoops of excitement wash over her and soothe all the melancholy places her mind had gone. She lost herself in the thrill of the chase. It had been some time since she had had a good run, and by the time they reached the house, she was in better spirits. The three of them tumbled to the ground as they reached the gardens behind the manor, and Elaina gasped for air. She watched the clouds scurrying above them as if hastening to get from one place to another.

She heard the approaching footsteps moments before Calum's curly head edged its way into view. His hazel eyes sparkled at her as his curls fell in a halo around his face. "Ye look like a fish lying on the banks of the loch, *mo chridhe.* Ye keep gasping like that, and ye may suck the clouds down from the sky."

Elaina swatted his leg, unable to speak. He looked much more at peace than last she had seen him, which bode well for the physician's efforts. She offered a silent prayer of thanks as she let Calum haul her up from the ground. She leaned into him, taking in the smell of wood smoke and something else. Standing on her toes, she stole a kiss.

"Whisky," she whispered after gleaning the taste of it from his lips.

"Aye, I needed some fortification," he said with a chuckle. "And then some numbing."

"I'm certain you did." After a glance over her shoulder to be certain that Jamie was not within hearing, she lowered her voice. "It was a success, then?" she asked, squeezing his hand.

"We cannae ken yet. Only time will tell."

The sadness in his voice caused Elaina to cup his face in her hands, bringing him to her for another, longer kiss.

"I do love ye so, Elaina," he croaked; then, clearing choked emotions from his throat, he added, "Come, *mo chridhe*." Taking her hand, he steered her toward the house. "Do ye need fortifying or numbing?"

"I need warming."

"Well, whisky will have to do the job for the moment. I'm quite certain they would miss us at the supper table, and then we would have to explain to the lot o' them how we couldnae keep our hands from each other."

Near the entrance to the kitchen, Ainsley snorted.

Elaina elbowed Calum, who didn't bother to hide his laughter. Thank heavens Jamie had run ahead into the house in his usual rambunctious way.

Calum leaned close. "But later," he whispered, letting his teeth graze her ear.

Elaina shivered at his breath on her neck and in anticipation of "later."

Chapter Eleven

T HE HORSE LAID HIS EARS flat against his head, causing Elaina to take a step back to avoid getting bit. She tripped and fell backward into a pair of arms. Her blood ran cold as she stared down at the crimson fabric covering the arms and at hands that were not her husband's.

The horse was an excellent judge of character, for it nipped at the arm holding her up. The soldier scrambled away with the horse's bared teeth just catching his coat sleeve.

"Thank you, sir," Elaina said in her best English accent as she tried to extricate herself without success from the man's grasp.

He chuckled in her ear, sending shivers down her spine. Not the kind of shivers Calum sent, but the kind Rabbie had caused when he was alive. "No worries, madam. You are just the wench I was looking for."

Elaina gritted her teeth to keep from biting the man herself. "What can I help you with?" She glanced up over her shoulder at the man's placid face. "Lieutenant."

The officer offered an amiable smile in return and sat her on a barrel, placing himself between her and the doors to the stables.

Damn Calum for going hunting with Ainsley. She should have gone with them. She glanced beyond her captor's shoulder, out of the door, hoping her husband might have forgotten something and come back to retrieve it.

"No worries, madam," the lieutenant said easily. "We shan't be disturbed."

The hair stood up on Elaina's arms, and she wrapped them around herself to suppress the trembling she could feel starting in her legs.

"Don't worry about that either, madam. This is a business meeting. You needn't worry about your blessed virtue."

"What can I help you with? I must get back to the kitchens. Mrs. Dav—"

"Mrs. Davies can go to the devil. As can you, madam. You can drop your dreadful attempt to sound English as well."

Fear skittered down Elaina's spine. *What is he after if not a tumble in the hay?*

"Yes. Imagine my surprise when I came across this broadsheet in town resembling a certain maid in a certain captain's house. A maid wanted for the murder of who?" The soldier pulled the broadsheet from a pocket inside his coat, pretending to study the words upon it. "Ah, here it is. The murder of three British officers. I thought you looked familiar yesterday."

"I do not know what you mean, Lieutenant. That woman is not me, but I have heard of her. She has flaming locks of red hair and is a force unto herself. I do hope you find her. Now, if you will." Elaina stood and made a move to sidle past the officer.

He shoved her back down on the barrel and then bent over, one hand on his knee and the other waving the broadsheet in the scant few inches between their faces. "No, Elaina Spencer. It is Spencer, am I correct? As in Lord Edward Spencer's long-lost sister? Captain Spencer, who is housing a known traitor to the crown beneath his roof. His own kin, no less. You are the woman on the sheet. Your kerchief does nothing to hide that fact. As for being a force unto yourself, we have yet to determine that, but I hope it is as you say. I do love a good challenge."

Elaina glared at the man with her arms crossed, awaiting his demands.

"Now that I have your attention," he straightened and placed his arms behind his back. "You are under arrest. I have orders to leave, and you shall accompany me. You will not alert a living soul if you wish to save your brother's reputation." When he garnered no response, he added, "And protect the little heathen. Yes, I thought that might do it if your brother's life didn't mean all that much to you. How could it when you have put him in such peril?"

Heat flushed Elaina's cheeks at his words. Why had she put her brother in this position? The blasted man was not supposed to be home, is why. He was supposed to be off saving his king from the Bonnie Prince and her father-in-law, who should be here with his wife. Why was it men never did what one thought they ought?

"Arrest?" Elaina dropped her fake accent and denied her identity no further. "You said you have orders to leave. Then leave. Don't worry about me. I will disappear again soon, and you will never hear another word about me."

"I'm afraid that cannot be done, madam." The arrogant arse leaned closer to her. "I need the reward," he whispered before giving an annoyed huff. "I needn't explain myself to a prisoner."

"I need to tell—" Elaina stopped seconds from revealing that her family was also present in Edinburgh.

"Your brother?" the lieutenant mistakenly assumed. "He will know soon enough. God help him when the time comes to answer for the fact that you have been hiding in his house all this time."

"I haven't been here 'all this time,' Lieutenant." She sneered at the imbecile.

"Then where have you been, madam?" he crossed his arms, rocking back on his heels.

Elaina couldn't find words. Should she tell him she had been in the Highlands? That she had married? That she was not truly William's sister? He wouldn't believe her. He already had his jaw set in that way men did when they had their mind made up and could not be deterred.

He gave a wicked grin at her silence. "That's what I thought." He took her by the arm, dragging her to her feet. "Don't even think about screaming or your precious lad will no longer be able to wreak havoc on the household. Understood?"

Elaina nodded, and the officer readied his horse while Elaina stood dutifully by without a peep for William and Jamie's sake.

"Pull the hood of your cloak over your head," the lieutenant ordered as he led Elaina and their ride out of the south end of the stables, away from the prying eyes of the household.

She did as told and mounted the horse at his command. He swung himself up behind her and turned his horse toward Edinburgh, away from Duart Manor and the rest of her family that, thank the heavens above, the man didn't even know were huddled up in the servants' quarters.

Elaina kept her head down as they rode through the streets of Edinburgh toward the castle upon the hill. Though the day was so cold that the horse's nose had ice dangling from it, she began to sweat. They traveled at a slow yet steady pace, and as she watched the castle grow larger, the bile in her wame grew more sour. She truly thought she might cast up her accounts. She squirmed in the saddle.

"Nervous, are you?" the lieutenant asked.

"Why, not at all, Lieutenant. I quite enjoy riding to meet my doom."

"Should have thought of that before killing those men, my lady. How did the sister of a British captain come to be a cold-blooded killer, anyway? Your brother seems quite loyal to the crown. I thought him an exemplary officer until—"

"My brother *is* an 'exemplary officer,' sir. Never doubt that. He did not know that I was hiding in the servants' quarters until I came barreling through the door to save that woman and her boy from being sent to prison for only wanting to…" She bit her tongue and chastised herself for nearly giving away their secret. *Idiot.*

"Wanting to what?" Suspicion laced the question.

"Wanting to not starve to death, sir. She is a widow, and they had nowhere else to go. She is a friend of a friend."

"If only you had shown such mercy to the soldiers you killed."

Elaina huffed a sigh. "One death was an accident," she said to the lieutenant, trying to explain her actions to the man who probably didn't care. "He impaled himself on my knife as we tumbled down an embankment after fighting over my horse."

"Quite the sophisticated lady, aren't you?"

She could feel him laughing behind her and had half a mind to butt him in the chin with her head. She continued instead. "The other was an eye for an eye after he murdered my stable boy." Elaina did not mention her taking Robert Campbell's head. No need to give the man more ammunition. As far as she knew, the English remained ignorant of the incident. Besides, the soldier behind her had made up his mind to turn her in, and she couldn't run forever. Her time had run out. She only wished that she could have stayed hidden until the end of the war, and perhaps could have garnered a pardon. But they couldn't have stayed in Gleann Eader, for if they had, Rhona would have surely died lying in that crofter's cottage. She wouldn't have stood a chance. She might not stand much of one now. The physician seemed pleased with the outcome of the procedure, but he said Rhona was far from safe. Only time would tell. It would depend on how strong her will to live was. Her resolve. Her family was by her side. Certainly, that would spur her on. Give her something to live for. Elaina could only hope.

They traveled at a leisurely pace toward the large stone fortress that sat at the end of High Street. Around them, it was business as usual in the capital city. The residents took no notice of the middle-aged British soldier and his cloaked captive. Elaina wondered how many of them knew the rebel forces that had once occupied Edinburgh had made it all the way to Derby in England? Did they even care? They hadn't fought back when the British army retook the city. Hell, they didn't fight the rebels, either. The bunch of insignificant wishy-washy sheep. Elaina's breath caught in her throat, and her spine stiffened. She forced herself to breathe and to relax lest she draw his attention to the man and woman standing on the sidewalk gaping at them as they rode by on horseback down the middle of High Street.

Lady Caroline Taylor and her father Lord Taylor stood outside of a dressmaker's shop.

Elaina kept her head turned toward the road ahead but watched the pair out of the corner of her eye as they passed. Caroline made a move to step toward the street, but her father laid his hand on her arm. Elaina wondered just exactly what the good Lord Taylor was doing here. She knew him to be a secret Jacobite rebel. Or was he a spy for the English? She now held serious doubts about which side he served. He'd once stood in Laird Beinnmaree's castle having words with Prince Charles Edward Stuart, and now here he stood in English-occupied Edinburgh, shopping, of all things. She was so distracted by the sight of Lord Taylor and his lovely daughter that she didn't realize they had reached the entrance to the castle grounds until the lieutenant pulled the horse to a stop at the gate. He didn't bother to dismount as he spoke to the guard. Probably scared she would make off with his horse. He was a smart man.

"Delivering a prisoner," the lieutenant announced.

"Prisoner?" The guard studied Elaina with a fair amount of skepticism.

She stared daggers through him.

The guard gave the lieutenant a nervous glance, then cleared his throat. "Yes…well…carry on."

The lieutenant must have given the same expression as Elaina, and she stifled a laugh at the way the man's hand shook as he waved them through.

The lieutenant, however, didn't move.

"Do you know me, guard?" he asked the man.

"Uh, n-no, Lieutenant."

"Have you ever seen me at this castle before?"

"Uh, n-no," the poor man stuttered again.

"That's because I have not been here. Now, where in the hell am I going?

Where are the governor's offices?" the lieutenant all but yelled at the poor guard, who was cowed beneath the force of his words.

"S-sorry, Lieutenant. J-just through the gates. Th-the large square building on the right side of the circle."

The lieutenant urged his horse into motion without so much as a nod to the poor lad.

When they were out of earshot, Elaina hissed at her captor, "Must you always be so rude? Just barking orders at everyone as if—"

"As if what, my lady? As if I am an officer of the king's army? Well, I regret to inform you—"

"And you still bark." Elaina could not still her tongue. She was moments from facing her demise, at any rate. She might as well voice her opinion.

The lieutenant stopped his horse in front of the stone facade of what she took to be the governor's quarters and slid to the cobblestones, pulling her with him. He deposited her not so gently on her feet. She hid her smile behind the hood of her cloak at the confirmation that she had touched a nerve. Good. That meant he was not completely dead inside. Not that she could see any way to talk herself out of this mess.

He set her feet into motion, pushing her through a doorway, and instructed the guard just inside that they were there to see the governor of the castle.

"The governor is a busy man," the soldier leered at the lieutenant as if challenging him to question his authority.

"Then I shall wait," the lieutenant said, shoving Elaina down onto a chair. He leaned against the wall beside her and crossed his arms.

The soldier shrugged and went on his way.

The lieutenant was a patient man, for they stayed in that tiny room for hours. Elaina had dozed at one point after watching the lieutenant pace back and forth. The room was approximately eight paces by eight paces, and she had lost track of the number of times the man had traversed the short path. She eventually closed her eyes to the dizzying sight and woke to the sound of a different soldier announcing that the governor would see them, wondering exactly how much time had passed. Was it enough time for Calum and Ainsley to return and find her missing? Long enough for them to discover what had become of her?

The lieutenant marched Elaina in front of him down a short corridor and into a candlelit chamber. The walls were lined with dark tapestries except for one that held a fair number of books and a display of crude weaponry alongside several rough sketches of all the ways the English liked to garner information from their prisoners. Her hand flew to her mouth. She had heard the rumors, but to see drawings of such heinous acts hanging in a place of honor on a governor's wall made her break into a sweat and her knees melt. She felt herself sinking.

The lieutenant grabbed her arm, and she looked up to see concern clouding his icy blue eyes. "Are you going to faint?" he hissed as if it were not a fitting reaction to seeing a drawing of a naked man with a white-hot poker being shoved in places that things should not enter. "Sit." He shoved her down onto the only empty chair in the room.

A red-faced bulbous form Elaina took to be the governor of the castle occupied the other behind an oversized and rather worn excuse for a desk. Ink spots dotted the surface, along with a mishmash of used quills, crumpled paper, and sand that had yet to be cleaned up after the man's last drafted document. The man had steepled his fingers beneath his chin, taking in the interaction between captive and captor. "Quite finished, Lieutenant Perry?" he asked when the lieutenant had released Elaina's arm.

"Not quite," Lieutenant Perry said. "There is the not so small matter of the reward, sir."

"The reward will be given to you upon the prisoner's arrival at the Tower of London. Her journey will begin on the morrow."

"What is to keep the other officers from receiving the reward, with all due respect?"

"Do you hold no trust in your fellow soldiers?" The governor leaned even farther back. His chair creaked and groaned its protest under the exorbitant amount of strain being placed upon it.

"Forgive me. What is the reasoning that you will not pay me now for delivering the prisoner? Nothing states that she was to be taken to the Tower of London."

"You question me?" The governor rose to his feet as if the lieutenant were the only one who had ever had enough gall to question the rotund figure.

Elaina could have sworn she heard the chair breathe a sigh of relief. She, too, wondered why she would need to be delivered to London. She felt quite certain they held executions in Edinburgh. Not that she was in any hurry to take part in the act, but it was disconcerting, to say the least, to be transported that far and into the very lap of King George himself. Though, being on the road for that long would provide the opportunity for her family to come to her rescue.

"I did not realize I was questioning you, Governor, but your current actions are curious. If it is as you say and the prisoner must be delivered to London, then I will be the one to do the delivering. No offense to you or your soldiers, but I feel I must take care of the matter myself. Get up." Lieutenant Perry dragged Elaina to her feet.

"Do you not have other orders, Lieutenant?" The governor stepped out from around his desk and took Elaina by the other arm.

For a horrified moment, Elaina thought she might become the object of a vicious game of tug of war.

"I do have other orders, Governor, but fortunately for you and for me they are on the way to London. I will take care of certain matters, deliver the prisoner, *and* collect *my* reward. Now, if you will release her, I will be on my way."

"I'm afraid, that's not poss—"

"Gov'ner!" A young soldier who couldn't have been seventeen burst through the door and stood bent in half, hands on his thighs and panting for air.

"How dare you come barreling in here like some heathen? I should have you flog—"

The boy held up his hand. "Beggin' yer pardon, Gov'ner, but there is a riot in the yard. We were transferin' prisoners, and I think… Well, I think they have killed Captain Riley."

"Oh, bloody hell. Wait here." The governor pointed a finger at Lieutenant Perry before snatching up a pistol and running out the door after the young soldier.

Lieutenant Perry wasted no time taking Elaina by the arm and dragging her out of the room and down the hallway.

"Where are we going?" Elaina hissed, then stumbled on an uneven stone in the floor.

"Leaving. We are going to London."

"But he told you to wait." She started pulling him back the way they had come.

"He is not my commanding officer. I have orders I *will* follow, and *then* we are going to London. Would you rather stay here or enjoy a few more days of freedom?"

She didn't wish to die. All the drawings of women prisoners on the wall in the governor's office depicted every single one being burned to death. She thought she would rather hang if it were all the same to them. For a brief, disturbed moment, she wondered if she could request the way in which they were to end her life?

She stopped pulling against the lieutenant, mostly because she had no strength in her legs. They had turned to mush at the thought of being in the hands of those that wanted her dead. If she did travel with the lieutenant, she stood more of a chance of getting away from this man. She looked around at the towering walls of the castle. There would be no way to rescue her from this formidable place. No. She would go with the lieutenant willingly, but she would look for every opportunity to escape.

Chapter Twelve

"WE ARE STOPPING ALREADY?" ELAINA stared at the front of the inn.

"In a hurry, are we? That is quite the change in attitude." Lieutenant Perry pulled her from the horse, depositing her roughly on her feet.

"It's only…just…it's not even dark yet." Elaina glanced over her shoulder, expecting a barrage of soldiers to come rampaging down the street on a mission to seize the prisoner because they hadn't traveled quite far enough from the castle in Edinburgh.

"Night is well on its way, and believe me, there will be many an opportunity to sleep under the stars, freezing your arse off. But today, I am done, and I have business to attend to. Prepare for a longer jaunt tomorrow. While we are here, you are my wife."

"Wife?" Elaina hissed at him.

Instead of answering her, he snapped his fingers toward a mountain of a man. "Boy. You there. Yes, you." The lieutenant barked at a man who was in no way, shape, or form a boy. He carried a mighty large pair of ballocks and not much upstairs, it seemed.

The man turned and shot a blank stare at the lieutenant.

"Take our horse."

There was a moment's pause before the lieutenant shook the reins at the man as if he were a small child.

Elaina grimaced as the man reached to take the reins.

His other arm, she noticed, remained at his side—his fingers twisted and gnarled, one missing from the first joint and the smallest completely gone. He stared through the lieutenant and then turned his intense look to her. His face held no emotion and, more disturbing still, neither did his eyes. She could not be certain if he were tetched or just good at hiding his discomfit. She offered him what she hoped was an apologetic look, to which he continued his blank stare. With a nod to him, she followed her captor into the building.

Elaina slid the hood of her cloak from her head as a tinkling bell announced their arrival. The entry to the inn was just as cold as it was outside, but a wave of warm air blew out of the noisy dining hall and bathed her in a comforting blanket, and she found herself grateful that they had stopped. She hadn't realized how cold she was.

"Welcome, welcome." A man as large as a bear lumbered toward them with a broad smile painted across his face that did not reach his eyes as he took in the appearance of his two new guests. "The dining hall is just this way. Maggie!" The man called out to a delicate girl, who turned her tired blue eyes to him. "Seat the gentleman and his—"

"Wife, and we require a room as well." Lieutenant Perry stood with his gaze trained on the dining hall, all but dismissing the man.

"Yes, well. Ye are in luck. I have just two rooms left for the eve—"

"I'm starved. Make the arrangements and be done with it."

Elaina mouthed *"I'm sorry"* to the bear with yet another look of contrition, which he waved away behind the lieutenant's back. The man took up a quill and dipped it in the inkwell sitting on the rough surface of a table. He scratched something onto the page as Maggie waved the lieutenant to follow her.

Elaina's gaze lingered on the quill. If she could somehow scratch out a brief note to Calum, perhaps the innkeeper could see it delivered for her?

"This way, please." Maggie's soft voice could barely be heard over the din of voices rumbling from the dining hall.

"Gordie," the lumbering innkeeper said to Elaina.

She dragged her gaze away from the quill he still held in his hands. His eyes matched Maggie's. She must be his daughter, which was hard to imagine with her being so frail and him… Well, his size was quite intimidating and nothing like his demeanor. "If ye need anythin', lass. Anythin'." He glanced at the lieutenant's back. "My name is Gordie, and ye just need to call it."

Elaina offered him a nod and followed the lieutenant and Maggie to a table in the corner of the packed dining hall. Apparently, half of the king's army had decided to partake of a meal at the inn, and Elaina felt the unease worm under her skin as she took in the sea of redcoats.

"What if some of these men are from Edinburgh?" Elaina whispered to her captor when Maggie had left to fetch them ale. "What if I am recognized?"

"Then you are my prisoner." The lieutenant's gaze traveled over the faces in the room, searching.

"But you told Gordie I was your wife."

"Who gives one damn what he thinks? I'll not have you rooming by yourself and me having to sleep outside of your door. It's the best way. Just shut your mouth and keep your face to the table."

Elaina held no argument with that order, having no desire to be recognized. After several moments of sitting in silence and her ears being assaulted by the surrounding din, she gratefully took her mug of ale from Maggie, who left as quickly and quietly as she came.

"Stay put," Lieutenant Perry barked at her as he rose from the table. "Ross, ol' chap. Where have they been hiding you these days?" He rounded the table, shaking hands vigorously with another officer.

"Oh, hither and yon." The man cast a wary glance at Elaina.

"Captain Ross." Elaina bowed her head to him, earning her a glare from the lieutenant.

"Who is this?" The captain turned his suspicious gaze back to her companion.

"His wife," Elaina said before the lieutenant could speak. If they hadn't been in a room full of other redcoats, he might have killed her on the spot from the look she received.

"Your *wife*?" The captain seemed dumbfounded by the possibility.

Elaina studied Lieutenant Perry. He wasn't the greatest specimen of a man that a woman might seek for a husband, nor was he an ogre. Perhaps it was she the captain found so offensive as he stood there with his face twisted in a look of disgust.

"Wife," the lieutenant said, looking rather annoyed at her.

Elaina smiled adoringly at him. "Well, now that we have made it quite obvious that I am your betrothed, why don't you introduce me, darling?" She placed a hand on the lieutenant's sleeve.

He stiffened at her touch, the corners of his mouth drawing down even more.

Elaina suffocated a laugh. That would show him.

"Captain Ross. I would like you to meet E-Elsbeth."

"My pleasure," Captain Ross replied, although the look on his face told her otherwise. "May I join you? We've much to discuss, Perry."

The lieutenant's pointed glare sent her a warning, but about what, she wasn't sure. Was it to keep her hands to herself or to keep her mouth closed?

"Absolutely. It has been entirely too long since we last spoke." Lieutenant Perry waved Captain Ross to a chair and then snapped his fingers at Maggie, who, bless her soul, looked weary and drawn. The dining hall of the inn was packed, yet customers continued entering in droves.

Must be the weather bringing them in. Elaina glanced out at the darkening sky. The wind had picked up, and sleet was pinging off of the glass.

She found herself relieved that her companion had stopped for the night. Elaina kept her ears on the conversation at the table while watching the bustling room from under her lashes. She forced herself to eat, though her stomach clenched in knots at the number of British military present and still so close to Edinburgh.

"You can speak freely," Lieutenant Perry said, pulling her attention back to the table. "There is no one for her to tell. Her kin are all dead." He cast her a sideways glance.

Dropping her gaze to her plate, her mind sped through his last statement. He spoke as if he had already set a plan in motion to kill her brother and Jamie, even with her cooperation. It had not dawned on Elaina until now that the man might not be true to his word. Why was she so damned trusting? She'd trotted off with this blackmailer without a fight, as if she hadn't a care in the world. As if the English hadn't lied and played games with her for the past two years. William and Jamie could be in peril even now as she sat with a piece of lamb lodged in her throat.

"The Jacobites have retreated to Carlisle, and Cumberland is not far behind them," Captain Ross said.

The bite of lamb seemed to grow, and Elaina found it harder and harder to breathe. She concentrated on the act of pulling air in and out of her lungs, her gaze trained on the unappetizing plate of food in front of her. She knew her expressions were easily readable and didn't want to reveal the fact that the captain's sudden announcement had sent a knife of fear through her chest. *"Not far behind them."* What exactly did that mean? Were they in immediate danger? Were they days away from a confrontation? Weeks away from slaughter? She wanted to grab the captain and beseech him to be more precise.

"Well, certainly Cumberland will be victorious. This ridiculous rebellion has gone on far too long. I wish to return to the normalcy of our lives before the Scots reared their ugly little heads."

"Well, we shall quell it soon enough." Captain Ross took a draw from his ale while casting a disparaging look at their host.

Elaina watched the innkeeper from the corner of her eye, treating each guest the same. He slapped a friendly hand upon the back of a soldier while emitting a rumbling laugh that seemed to echo about the room and exchanged good-natured insults with what had to be locals. She wondered which side of the line did Gordie stand upon? There were plenty of Scots who sided with the English. Probably most of them in the lowlands. Was he one? Could she trust him to get a message to Calum?

She had a sudden gut-clenching fear that her husband *would* come after them. Of course, he would. There was no question of that, but she needed him to keep his distance. It was too risky. She didn't know what town they sat in at the moment, nor how near or far they were from either side of the conflict. What if they were within Cumberland's reach? William knew that the Laird Beinnmaree was at the prince's side. Certainly, Cumberland would know it as well, and he knew Calum. But Lieutenant Perry did *not* seem to know about Elaina's relationship to the MacKinnon clan, so she needed to keep it that way. For everyone's sake. It was too big of a risk to involve Gordie. She would have to bide her time.

Chapter Thirteen

ELAINA SAT STARING AT THE locked door. Not for the first time, a member of the king's army had locked her in a room at an inn, and knowing her luck, it probably would not be the last. She shook her head as the sound of the lieutenant's boots faded away down the stairs. His reasoning for her posing as his wife had been that he did not trust her to not attempt to escape and, as a result, he would have to sleep on the floor outside of her door. Apparently, however, he felt confident at the moment that he could merely lock the door and venture off to enjoy the company of the few remaining soldiers in town. Many of the men at dinner had been in another regiment that had headed out as soon as their meal was complete.

She glanced around the cozy room for two. A fire blazed in the hearth, and someone had turned down the modest coverlet on the bed. A shiver crawled down Elaina's spine at the sight of it. At least if the lieutenant was off drinking with the other men, there were no worries about him accosting her. *Until he comes back blootered out of his gourd, you fool.* The man was already feeling his drink.

The thought set her feet in motion, and she crossed the room to the window. Unlike when her own brother had locked her inside an inn, the lieutenant hadn't been thoughtful enough to ensure there was no way out. Elaina wrapped her cloak tighter around her and opened the window. The blast of frigid air took her breath, bringing tears to her eyes. She swiped them away and eased her head out of the opening, glancing up and down the street below. A handful of men had gathered about 200 yards from the inn and stood warming themselves around a fire, passing a bottle between them.

Elaina turned back to the room and extinguished the tapers, plunging herself into darkness. Standing on the precipice of captivity and freedom, she closed her eyes and offered up a swift prayer. Fisting her skirts in one hand, she placed her booted foot on the window ledge and eased her way out into the blustery night. The soldiers' laughter skimmed her ears as the winter wind carried their words through the streets. She gripped the frame of the window with her fingertips and closed her eyes against the dizzying sight of the black street below her. It seemed much farther away now that she was on the outside of the room, and she questioned her sanity. With a deep breath, she inched her way across the three-inch-wide slip of wood that continued on some forty feet to the end of the building. From there, she hoped to shimmy down the post at the edge of the porch, providing no one was about. *And if there is?* She would deal with that then. There was no guarantee she would even reach the end of the porch, and then that would be another matter unto itself. As if her foot thought her mind was giving a command, the toe of her boot slipped, and her fingers clung in desperation to the edge of the wood above her. Frantically, she fought to get her foot back on the ledge. When she succeeded, she clung to the side of the building, panting and trying not to cast up her accounts. She laid her head against the frozen wood, her heart galloping in her chest.

Below, a pair of soldiers sauntered by with a woman of the night clutched between them. Elaina closed her eyes as if it would hide her presence. When their voices faded away, she opened her eyes and glanced around. The street was empty save for the men by the fire whose number had dwindled to four. With a new sense of urgency, she slid her feet along the ledge, keeping her toes as close to the wall as possible. When she reached the post at the corner of the porch, she glanced around and shimmied down, silently thanking her father for letting her climb trees like a boy.

Elaina darted across the empty space between the inn and the building next door. Peeking around the corner of the next building, she locked gazes with a terrified Maggie. Two soldiers had her cornered against a far wall that connected the two buildings with each other. One of the men was rucking up the front of her skirts.

"Help m—"

The soldier's hand dampened Maggie's plea. He twisted her around, pressing her face against the wall and hoisting her skirts over her hips.

Elaina looked down the road toward the freedom that lay steps within reach.

She turned back to see the man had already released his breeches as his friend kicked Maggie's legs open.

"Hurry up. I want a go as well." The second soldier elbowed his mate.

With a shake of her head, Elaina ran down the alley, catching the exposed man in the backs of his knees and sending him tumbling to the ground, wanker flopping.

Maggie turned and kicked at him, barely missing the man's exposed parts.

The second soldier grabbed Elaina by her hair. "Stupid bitch. Now, I guess you'll get more of the same."

Elaina elbowed him, and he backhanded her, sending stars shooting through her eyes and tears down her cheeks. She lost Maggie in the foray but heard the scuffling of feet and her angry grunts, meaning she had not made her escape. Now they were both in a mess. Elaina fought but found herself pressed against the wall, the soldier's body crushing the air out of her lungs. Maggie managed an earsplitting scream before being silenced by a crack to the back of her head. Elaina watched as her legs crumpled beneath her.

Running footsteps sounded behind them, and someone yanked her captor from her body. She doubled over, gasping for air.

"What the hell do you think you're doing?" a familiar voice barked, and Elaina closed her eyes, her head drooping.

"Just having a bit of fun is all, sir," one man answered.

"These women don't enjoy your kind of fun, soldier."

Lieutenant Perry and Captain Ross. Marvelous. Elaina cringed at her own stupidity.

"What...what are you doing here? How..." Lieutenant Perry snatched Elaina around to face him, one hand still latched onto the redcoat and the other digging painfully into her arm.

"Do you know what you've done, you idiot?" Captain Ross slapped the man in the lieutenant's grasp across his head. "This is the lieutenant's wife. We should hang you."

"I-I... Sir, I didn't know." The man pleaded, terror twisting his features to look like a small child and not an almost rapist.

"Does it truly matter, son?" Lieutenant Perry said, surprising Elaina. "Rape is an incorrigible offense and one I do not tolerate. Even against a bloody Scot." He cast his gaze at Maggie, who had roused from her blow and sat hunched in the shadows, hugging her knees to her chest.

"Let's go." Captain Ross shoved his man forward.

"Just let me—"

"Absolutely not." Captain Ross swiped the man's hand away from his breeches. "You shall flaunt your deeds all the way to the pillory. You shall stand with your bits proudly on display until we decide exactly what to do with you."

Lieutenant Perry whistled through his teeth to draw the attention of the men still by the fire.

"Madam." Captain Ross's gaze fell on Elaina with a mix of suspicion and contempt. "I do not know what you thought to be doing on these streets in the dark without the escort of your husband, but I trust he will deal with the matter in a sufficient manner. I will see to these idiots if you would like to escort your wife back to your room, Lieutenant."

"Indeed." He tugged Elaina back toward the inn.

"But what about the girl?" Elaina asked, twisting to look back for Maggie, whom they had left alone in the alley.

"Her father will see to her. Your daughter needs your attention, sir. That way." Lieutenant Perry cocked his head to Gordie, who began to run, calling his daughter's name.

They made the trip up the stairs and to their room in silence. Lieutenant Perry wiggled the still locked doorknob, then cast her a glance as he released her arm and plucked the key from his pocket.

"Tricky one, aren't you?" he said as he crossed the room and closed the open window. "I suppose you heard the crime in action and thought to be a hero and save the girl? I'm sure you were not attempting to escape."

Elaina stared at him.

He stood between her and the fire still burning in the hearth. The light of the flames dancing all around him and his face shrouded in darkness gave him an almost demonic look.

"Bed," he commanded. When she hesitated, he snapped his fingers at her like she was a child. "You should know that act will not happen, my dear. You've already heard me say I do not take with rape. I have no interest in you in that manner. You are a means to an end and nothing more. I would rather have my cock removed with a dull blade. Believe me."

"How flattering and quite a relief, Lieutenant," Elaina said, unsure of whether or not she should take offense. "I would hate to have to castrate you in your sleep." She did as commanded and climbed onto the small bed.

The lieutenant sank onto a chair by the window and slid down, crossing his legs. "Sleep. 'Twill be a hard journey on the morrow. I don't want you slowing me down."

Sleep would be elusive this night. Still, Elaina turned to the wall and pulled the blanket over her head, trying to block from her mind just how close she had come to freedom.

Chapter Fourteen

T HE DEAFENING SILENCE WOKE ELAINA. She eased the blanket from her head and searched for the lieutenant. He stood by the window, peeking through a slit between the thin curtain covering the window and the frame itself. She felt the tension from his stance rippling through the air, filling the room.

"What is it?" she hissed, sensing something greatly amiss.

"Dammit, woman." The man whirled around, his eyes wide. He clutched his chest, sinking against the wall.

Elaina would have laughed had she not seen his unease only moments before. "What is wrong? What's happened?" She swung her feet off the side of the bed.

"I'm not sure."

"Well, what do you see?" Elaina rose and advanced toward the window.

"Stay there." The lieutenant recovered himself and held out a hand toward her. "I see nothing out there. Not a man, not an animal. Something's ami—"

The light rap on the door startling both of them, they whipped their heads simultaneously toward the sound. Their visitor tapped light as a feather, as if not to disturb those inside or out. If not for the unearthly silence surrounding them, they might not have heard it.

The lieutenant crossed to the door, snatching a pistol from the table on his way. "Who's there?" he hissed, one hand on the knob.

"Gordie. Ye must leave. Now!"

The lieutenant opened the door, and the large man came barreling inside. "If you are to retain yer life, ye must go." He panted as if he had run up the stairs, though the cumbersome man had made no sound.

"What—"

Gordie shook his head. "There is no time. Get the missus and follow me. Quiet as ye can."

Elaina snatched up her cloak, tying it around her and raising the hood. Gordie nodded his approval. She followed him, and the lieutenant brought up the rear as they wound their way down the stairway as quietly as possible. The area was dark, the candles extinguished, as if to hide anyone who wished to flee in anonymity.

Gordie held out his arm quite unnecessarily as he came to a stop, his giant form blocking any progress at the bottom of the stairwell. He peeked around the corner and whistled softly between his teeth. Though barely audible, the sound seemed to echo through the silence.

The quiet swelled around them. Never before had silence seemed its own being. An entity living and breathing, its fangs at the base of Elaina's neck, sending chills throughout her.

Their leader motioned them forward, and Elaina turned the corner to see a rectangle of gray light illuminated by only the difference between the dark inside and the eerie morning light of approaching dawn. They scurried through the door that Maggie held open for them.

The lieutenant came up short at the wagon sitting by the door, its bed piled high with used hay and manure from the stables.

"You cannot be serious," he whispered. "Where is my horse?"

"Ye shall have it, sir, but at this moment, this is the only way. The only *safe* way. Ye must hurry."

Someone had scooped a portion of the manure and hay from either side of the wagon bed. Gordie helped Elaina up and motioned for her to lie down. She curled onto her side as Maggie approached with a burlap sack. She dragged it up and over Elaina's body as if covering a corpse.

"Thank ye, mistress," the girl whispered. "Thank ye for yer help last eve. Godspeed and may the saints protect you." She covered Elaina's head, and someone began shoveling hay and manure onto her.

Elaina thought she would suffocate between the heavy burlap and the stench surrounding her. She dug a breathing hole to the side of the cart and sucked in the wintry morning air. She cleared another spot and put her eye to the gap between the boards. What she saw froze her breath in her lungs. She could not inhale nor expel the air she held. The wagon turned down the main street of the town, eerily void of any moving thing besides their conveyance. They passed the pillory where the accused soldiers had been chained the evening before. The snow was no longer white around the contraption. One man, his arms still held tight by the wood and chains, had slumped almost to his knees, but they couldn't quite reach the platform of the pillory. The weight of his body pulled against his arms grotesquely, as if his legs had given out from sheer exhaustion. But that was not the case. They had removed his head from his shoulders. The other soldier…the offender who had revealed his parts and tried to lay claim to the young Maggie still had his head. It remained locked in the stockade. His unseeing eyes stared out into the void with his offending member removed from its rightful home, extending out of his mouth instead.

Elaina swallowed the bile rising in her throat and fought with all her might not to vomit. Her gaze moved down the street, and she caught sight of another redcoat lying near the entry to a pub. And another. And another. Someone had slaughtered the soldiers throughout the night. Elaina watched as the people of the small town began to move about, men nonchalantly tipping their head to the mysterious driver of their cart.

"Och, Gordie. How goes the day?" one man said.

Elaina's heart lurched as their cart pulled to a halt in the street.

"Oh, a mighty fine day of it, 'tis," Gordie said. Both men acted as if they slaughtered English soldiers on their streets every day.

"Aye. Mighty fine day." The stranger grinned in response, and Elaina noticed the brownish stained rag in his hand as he wiped his knife clean. "The Lord's Day."

"Aye, 'tis."

The stranger studied his cart full of hay, manure, and stowaways. "Ye workin' on the Lord's Day, Gordie?"

A pause rang through the air, and Elaina tried not to breathe. God help her, she could never convince anyone of her innocence if they found her hiding in a pile of shite with a redcoat after the two had taken their meal in the inn the previous day as husband and wife.

"No more than you. Riddin' the town of shite is all," Gordie answered.

The stranger barked out a laugh. "Right ye are, old fella. Right ye are. See ye at church?"

"Aye, ye ken I'll be there."

The man in the street tapped the blade of his knife on the side of the wagon inches above Elaina's head, and the wagon lurched into motion, taking Elaina's stomach with it. She closed her eyes to the remainder of their trip through town, having seen enough of the retribution. The sound of the earth under the wagon's wheels changed timbre, and Elaina braved a peek with one eye. The surrounding trees grew denser and the road bumpier with it. Soon, the wagon turned onto a small path and eased to a stop. There was a creak and a lurch as their driver jumped to the ground.

"Now! Come on. Ye must hurry." Hands brushed Elaina's cover from the top of her, and she scrambled to the end of the wagon, blinking in the bright light. "Ye must go." The man yanked her to her feet and pushed her to a horse, shoving her unceremoniously upon it. "God go with ye." He smacked her horse on the rump, and her mare broke into a clip behind the lieutenant's.

Elaina looked back and Maggie, who had been silent the entire trip, lifted her hand. Elaina did the same and turned back to the lieutenant, wondering whose horse she was on.

Chapter Fifteen

THE LIMBS OF THE TREES stood laden with snow, and the scene would have been beautiful if Elaina's heart weren't frozen to the core. The pair rode in silence for some time, as quickly as the frozen ground would allow. When the sun had risen fully in the sky, the lieutenant stopped to rest the horses by a small stream. Elaina noticed a slight tremble when the man's legs hit the ground. He had been as affected as she. Uncertain that her legs would hold her, she followed him down to the water's edge and splashed icy water on her face.

"Do you want to talk about it?" Elaina asked.

"Trying to entreat the enemy, are you, madam? You know if you had not tried to escape, none of this would have happened."

"None of… This is my fault?" The shrillness of her own voice startled her.

"Yes, madam. If I had not had to come to your rescue, those men would never have been in the stockade, and all of those soldiers would still be alive."

"You bloody bastard." Elaina sat on her haunches and gaped at him. "What of Maggie? Are you telling me you would not have stopped her attack if it had only been one young Scottish lass trapped in an alleyway with two despicable soldiers hell bent on taking her innocence?"

"I doubt she was innocent, madam. Who is to say that they had not paid for services?"

The slap across his face stung her hand, and she was coming back for more when he grabbed her wrist. "You horrible lout of a human being. How dare you say such things? That girl did not want what was being given. If she had, I most certainly would have made my escape instead of trying to help her. Your men tried to rape her."

"They are not 'my' men." The lieutenant shoved her hand away and rose to his feet. "My men would not commit such atrocities. I don't stand for it."

"But you do when it comes to those of a different nationality than yourself?"

"No," he said, pulling a hunk of cheese and dry bread from their small provisions. "But no one truly knows the things that go on unless one is present for the entire interaction. You do not know what the lass might have done. She might have been flirting inappropriately—"

"There you are with your excuses again."

"And there you are, presuming to be all knowing. Just like a woman."

"You arse."

"Call me what you will, but at least I can say I am not a criminal."

"Kidnapping and threatening innocent lives would make you a criminal, sir, if this world was a fair one."

"It's not kidnapping if the person is wanted for murder." The lieutenant cocked an eyebrow at her.

"You threatened my nephew."

"Would you have come willingly if I hadn't?"

"I do believe you know the answer to that question full well."

"I have grown weary of this conversation. Eat." The lieutenant turned his back on her and moved off, looking over the horses' hooves and legs.

Elaina knew full well why he tended the horses so carefully. Stopping for fresh horses would be insanity. The violence and retaliation she had seen this morning had been enough to scare her. These steeds would have to get them to London.

The afternoon carried on much the same as the morning had. Silent. Elaina took the time to ponder escape plans. But escape to where? She didn't know where they were. Could she find her way back to Duart Manor? Safely?

The clouds cleared, and the change in weather brought with it the sun and its blinding rays that reflected off the packed sleet in glaring sparkles so that she had to squint against it to even see where she was going. Apparently, the horses couldn't see either, for hers stepped into a hole, and they both crashed to the ground in a thundering cacophony. Elaina's foot lay trapped under the side of the horse, and she kicked and shoved, trying to free herself as the horse scrambled to regain its footing. She broke free at last and rolled out of the way of its stomping hooves, then lay panting on the ground. Her foot throbbed.

"Well, this is marvelous." The lieutenant sat atop his steed studying the struggling horse and Elaina lying on the ground.

"No. I am fine. Thank you." Elaina glared at him before collapsing onto her back. This was just marvelous. Her horse had broken its leg. There would be no escape.

The lieutenant slid from his ride, withdrew his pistol, and shot the horse between the eyes.

It had to be done, but it turned Elaina's stomach. She examined her foot as the lieutenant rubbed a hand over his face.

"That steed didn't last long." He cast her a cursory glance. "Are you lame as well?"

"Why? Are you going to shoot me?"

"Tempting." The corner of his mouth quirked. "Here, let me see." He kneeled beside her.

"I'm quite all right. If it is all the same to you, I'd rather you did—" Elaina gasped, and her stomach lurched as he wiggled her foot back and forth and pushed on it.

"I don't think you've broken anything. But it will hurt for a time. Especially hanging off the side of a horse. We will see about having it looked at when we reach our destination."

"And that would be?" Elaina asked as he helped her to her feet.

"Wherever I decide to stop for the evening." He wrapped her arm around his neck and helped her hobble to the horse they would now have to share unless he chose to walk. Which he didn't.

Unfortunately, there was no stopping somewhere for the evening. No inns, anyway. Instead, Lieutenant Perry himself tended to her ankle, wrapping it in a strip of her torn petticoat while she sat shivering by a fire that was so small, she wondered why he'd bothered at all. The farther they traveled, the more paranoid the man seemed to become. For three days, they skirted even the smallest of towns, sleeping under the stars…when there were stars. Not a single town they ventured past had a substantial British military presence, so the lieutenant was having none of them.

The desperate need for food finally outweighed the man's unease, and he guided their horse down a muddy road to a small grouping of carts standing in a half moon near a town center. Their owners looked as worn as their wares. Four dirty-faced children clung to the skirts of a large woman standing beside a cart with loaves of bread of every shape and size balanced on its edge. Lieutenant Perry approached the cart and the children who, though standing protected behind their mother's impressive form, all stepped backward with not a small amount of fear in their eyes.

Elaina stayed behind the lieutenant. She considered fleeing, but she couldn't leave the man standing there amongst a town full of Scots after what they had witnessed days ago. The man may have been an arse and she his captive, but no one deserved to die like that. Not even a bloody redcoat.

Lieutenant Perry made his purchases with haste and turned to leave, but bumped into the next cart of furs, nearly toppling it. "Begging your pardon," he said, grabbing the cart to help steady it back on its wheels.

The commotion drew the attention of nearly all the townsfolk as it sent the cart's owner into a string of curses.

Elaina attempted to keep an amiable smile on her face as she studied those around her. No one made a move to detain the two visitors, but no one spoke to them either. Everyone eyed them with suspicion.

Lieutenant Perry mumbled more apologies before latching onto Elaina's hand. "Come."

He had no need to drag her. She wanted to leave as much as he did. She was becoming as paranoid as the lieutenant himself. Standing on the outskirts of the town, just inside the forest line, he tore a hunk of bread from the loaf he had bought and another from the wedge of cheese and handed them to Elaina before stuffing the remainder into the saddle's bags.

Once they had mounted and were on their way, Elaina tore the hunks of bread and cheese in two, handing a pair to the lieutenant behind her.

Silence reigned while they finished their lunch as their horse took them away from the village. Elaina thought she had never tasted such wonderfulness. So much better than dried venison and the handful of tasteless oats they had eaten for the past three days.

"That was an uncomfortable experience," she said over her shoulder.

Lieutenant Perry grunted.

All other attempts at talking garnered the same response. Elaina was uneasy about their stop in the village, but the lieutenant seemed to be scared to the point of losing his words.

The farther they rode, the more the man's posture deteriorated. For an English soldier who always seemed to have a broomstick up his arse, he grew increasingly limp in the saddle. Just when Elaina was thinking to ask if he was asleep, the man turned their steed to the sound of running water and all but shoved her off the horse.

She landed unceremoniously in the snow with an *oof.* "Well, thank God for a mountain of snow." She glared up at the lieutenant.

He didn't seem to care whether she had a sore bum, an injured foot, or three eyes as he slid from the horse and, without a word, wobbled his way to the water. He collapsed to his knees in front of it, nearly toppling headfirst into the stream.

Elaina shook some of the stiffness from her ankle as she watched the lieutenant splash water on his face. She shoved her way to her feet and hobbled the horse before coming to stand at the man's side. "What is it?" she asked.

He gulped water from his cupped hands, searched madly for his handkerchief, and then dipped it in the frigid water and rubbed that across the back of his neck. "Nothing. I don't feel well is all. I will be perfectly fine in—" He turned his head away and retched into the snow beside him.

Elaina pulled off her gloves and touched him on the cheek. "You are burning up. How long have you felt sick? Why didn't you say something?"

Her questions were useless because the man barely had time to catch a breath before vomiting again.

Elaina took her own handkerchief and dipped it into the running stream. She squatted beside him and placed the rag on the back of his neck, holding it there as the poor soul rested on his hands and knees, attempting to breathe.

"Poison. They poisoned me," he whispered, sitting back on his haunches.

"Who poisoned you? The old woman? I fear you are paranoid or hallucinating, for I ate the same food, and I am not ill."

"You are not an English soldier."

"I am traveling with you. Sitting quite familiarly in front of you on your horse. We are together. That makes me just as culpable and despicable in their eyes. Besides, if they wanted you dead, all they had to do was shoot you. There wasn't another British soldier in that town, as far as I could tell. Now, I'm going to leave you here in case there is anything else you would like to remove from your wame, and I am going to start a fire. You are in no shape to move forward today," she said as she rose to her feet.

He shook his head in protest so hard that he dislodged her handkerchief from the back of his neck.

Elaina bent over and picked it up, finding it warmed from the heat of his fever. She watched him for a minute and then sighed, dipping the rag back in the stream. "I'll hear no arguments, Lieutenant." She laid the rag back on his neck, sending shivers throughout his body. "You are burning with fever. Now, stay here for a moment."

Truly, the man had no alternative. He leaned forward and retched again.

Elaina set about attempting to gather enough wood for a fire. Though better for the most part, her foot had still swollen and stiffened, hanging off the side of the horse. The more she moved around, the better it felt. By the time she had gathered enough wood to start a fire, it no longer pained her much to walk. It hurt more to move it side to side, but not much more. That was the most she had walked in days, and it felt marvelous. She piled her findings under the edge of a shelf of rock jutting out of a small mountainside. She could lay him under the lip of the overhang and protect him from the elements and hopefully trap some of the heat from the fire…or she could take the horse and leave him to his own devices. Standing by the pile of wood, she chewed her cheek, contemplating. The thought was tempting, but he looked pitiful on his hands and knees in the snow, with his hat tumbled haphazardly aside. Not to mention the fact that she owed him a debt for having saved her from being raped.

With a sigh of resignation, she lit the fire, coaxing it into a decent blaze before returning to the lieutenant and helping him to his feet. The vomiting seemed to have ended for the moment.

He stumbled twice, nearly taking them both to the ground.

"You are going to have to walk, sir," she scolded him lightly. "I'm not sure I can drag you through the snow."

She got a grunt in reply, but he remained on his feet until she got him settled beside the fire.

"I'm going to get the blankets," she said.

No response.

Now she was more concerned. *Had* someone poisoned him? If he died suspiciously, and she in his presence at the time, would they accuse her of yet another crime? He could not die. She made her mind up on the spot. Yes, he had taken her to earn him the reward, but he had saved her from an atrocious act, *and* he was a human being. She untied the blankets and returned to the pitiful creature, who now lay on his side, shivering. Luckily, the outcropping had kept snow from piling up in that spot, so he only lay on the cold, hard ground, not the cold, wet snow. She draped the two blankets they carried over him and tucked them around him, bunching part of it under his head, which burned with fever.

Elaina sat back on her haunches, contemplating the situation. The blasted man could not die.

She spent at least an hour bathing his face with wet rags. At one point, she unbuttoned his coat, much to his chagrin, but he hadn't the strength to fight her. She shoved a cold cloth down his shirt, only to be met with the mutterings of curses and foul language. She couldn't help but snicker.

"You think this is funny?" the lieutenant muttered in between moments of retching that produced nothing but bile.

"Your situation? Never. Your choice of words? Yes." Elaina patted his head like a small child. Shoving most of the wood she had gathered into the fire, she built it up into a conflagration. "Now, sleep if you can. I must go, but I will return. Here is extra wood. You can feed the fire if it gets low."

"You cannot leave me here!" his voice rang against the overhead rock with the most strength it had held for the majority of the day.

"I'm not leaving you, you bloody oaf. I will return, but you need medicine. You are worsening by the minute." After mounting the horse to a steady stream of words that would have made her military-born and -bred father blush, she turned her back to him and retreated toward the small crofter's cottage she remembered passing hours ago.

She carefully picked her way back the way they had come. She didn't need this horse breaking a leg as well. A short time later, she sat watching the house from the edge of the snow-covered field. Gray smoke swirled from the chimney stack, but there were no other signs of life. She needed herbs and food. The man needed proper nourishment, not more dried venison and gruel. Mustard or linseed for a poultice would be nice as well. Night was inching closer, and if she were to find her way back, she needed to accomplish her mission quickly. She sighed and squared her shoulders. If she had to steal what she needed, she would, against her will, but the lieutenant could not die. Ask first…steal when desperate. Scots were known for their generosity, so maybe it would not come to that. If they were still in Scotland. She didn't know where they were.

The snow crunched under her horse's hooves and clouds swirled overhead, threatening snow yet again. Snow she could handle—it was the bloody sleet that seemed to be a nearly everyday occurrence that drove her mad.

She dismounted and tethered her horse to the bare branch of a tree before approaching the door of the simple stone house with its thatched roof. With a deep breath, she rapped on the door.

A faint rustling sounded from inside, but no one answered.

She waited a moment and rapped again, harder.

More noise ensued, but this time it was followed by a faint, "Who goes?" Barely audible, she couldn't tell if the voice belonged to a male or female.

She didn't know how to respond. "I-I. My friend needs help," she shouted through the crack between the door and the jamb.

Silence.

She stood for so long without a response that she turned to leave, as the words "Just bloody well come in," made it to her ears. Hesitantly, one hand reached for the handle, and she pushed it down. The door swung open to a dimly lit room. Elaina stood in the doorway, letting her eyes adjust.

"Close the damn door." The faint reprimand came from a pile of blankets in the back corner of the room.

She stepped inside and did as she was told.

"Take up the candle, lass, and come this way."

Elaina took two steps forward and lifted the only lit candle in the room, a large round candle meant to burn for days that had dwindled to next to nothing. The fire in the hearth had died down to low flames, but the room was still warmer than outside. She approached the mound of blankets with caution, her heart pounding in her chest. She breathed a sigh of relief when she reached her destination and looked down upon the emaciated figure lying on a small cot. His hair hung in strings around his drawn face. Cheekbones jutted out as if they were rock formations on the side of a craggy knoll, and his great beak of a nose turned under slightly at the tip where a small brown mole resided. She hoped it was a mole. But the stench was the most significant aspect of the man and his mound of blankets.

"Help me."

It was a demand. Not a plea. She was not sure that his lips moved with the utterance.

She asked, "Help you how? What is it you need? Have you family?" It was then she glanced around the room at the tumble of bowls and cups littering the table. One bowl rested on the floor against the table leg. Her gaze traveled back to the man beneath the blankets.

"Get me out of this heap of shite." The blankets hiccuped above what must have been his hand.

She doubted that the man could move the mound covering him. She pinched a corner of the top blanket between her thumb and fingers, glancing at his face to be sure this was what he wanted her to do.

He glared at her with a raised brow.

She took the look to be an order to get to it and attempted to breathe through her mouth to block out the stench that grew more foul with each blanket removed. The final blanket she grabbed with two fingers by the corner closest to the man's head.

Dear lord. She choked down a retch. When he'd said, "heap of shite," that was precisely what he meant.

"Dinna just stand there gaggin' like an eejit. Help me out of this mess. Aye, Una. I hear ye, ye auld witch. Dancin' with the devil ye are." His gaze darted around the ceiling, and Elaina couldn't help but look up as well to nothing but thatch and possibly a few insects burrowed in for warmth.

Removing the mound of blankets seemed to have freed the man's tongue as well as the horrific odor emanating from him.

"Where is the well?" Elaina choked out from the corner of her cloak she had pulled across her face. She needed air just as much as she needed water.

"The well?" His brow creased in puzzlement.

"The well," Elaina said slow as if talking to a small child. "Where you get your water from?"

"Ah…the well. Why did ye no' say that to begin with?" The man was delirious. "That way." He jerked his frail bird head in the direction of the back of the house.

"Stay here," she said.

"And just where in hell do ye think I would tarry off to? Are ye simple, lass? Can ye no' see that my carcass is stuck right where I lay? Do ye think I would lay here and shite all over myself if I had a choice in the matte—"

"Forgive me," Elaina interjected. She considered walking out the door and doing the best she could for the lieutenant with what little they had. But judging by the man's twisted legs, devoid of all muscle, he more than likely hadn't walked unaided in some time and had been in the bed for a dreadful length of time. But someone either visited or lived here because there had been wood in the fire and yes, the candle had burned low, but it was still lit, not to mention the clutter that covered every area of the room. Obviously, it was not the work of the man lying before her. Elaina grabbed one of the blankets that had been in the middle of the pile covering the man. She didn't want to use the cleanest and could not bear to touch the filth of the one she had just removed. She would burn it…outside.

"I will return with water and wood. Do you have more wood?"

"How would I know?" he barked at her with a scowl.

Pleasant man to be wanting someone to help him, Elaina thought as she draped the blanket over him. *Perhaps that's why his help left. His poor ungrateful attitude.* "Well, I shall find some," she said, instead of what she wanted to say, which would have been about as pleasant as the man.

Wrapping her cloak tightly around herself, Elaina grabbed a bucket from beside the door and made her way outside and around the house. She found the well with little problem. Snow and sleet had buried the wood beside a small outbuilding, so that was a little trickier to retrieve. She stood on her sore foot and kicked at the stack with the other, finally breaking through the ice. She stuck her head inside, spying a handful of hens huddled in a corner and a cow in desperate need of milking.

Stuffing a few pieces of wood under her arm, she picked up the bucket of water and lumbered to the house. She would have to come back for more of both. It might run the well dry with how much she would need to clean the poor man. She shuddered at the thought, but her conscience would not let her leave him lying there in his own filth.

After several trips, Elaina had the fire roaring and a large cauldron filled with water heating over the flames. Night had also set upon her. She would not be returning to the lieutenant this day. She had traded one patient's mess for another.

"Are you thirsty?" she asked her new patient.

"Are ye goin' ta get me out of this or not?"

She returned his scowl. "Do you want me to bathe you with freezing water? I might be more than happy to."

"Now ye threaten me?" he growled.

Elaina wanted to smother him. Instead, she turned and searched for a lantern. She finally found one behind a pile of rubbish and lit it from the fire. She stalked across the room and took up the bucket and headed out once more into the cold with the man's angry protests echoing behind her.

She fumed all the way to the outbuilding. Curses escaped her lips on a hiss of smoke the entire time she sat relieving the poor cow, who stomped and shuffled, almost knocking Elaina from her perch on the stool. "Sorry, old girl." She patted the protesting cow on her hindquarter. "I shouldn't take my frustration out on you. You can't help it. You haven't been milked in who knows how long."

Elaina took the time to fork some fresh hay in for the cow before she resumed her tirade on her return trip to the house and the filth that awaited her. Now, she thoroughly regretted leaving the lieutenant. Even though he was trading her life for a rank, he was still more pleasant company than what she endured now. She began to think she *must* be simple. It was the only explanation for why she remained at this godforsaken place enduring hell all so she could return to nurse the enemy.

She pushed the door open and slammed it shut with her foot before searching for the cleanest cup she could find. She ignored his curses and ungrateful mutterings as she ladled the warm milk into it.

Standing by his bedside, she stared down at the pitiful creature. She, too, might be in a foul mood if she had been lying in shite for who knew how long. "Would you care for a drink?"

He raised a brow at her.

She sighed and slid an arm behind his frail shoulders, easing him into a semi-sitting position. Mother of God. He, too, burned with fever. What was going on with the menfolk? She wanted to sink to the floor in despair. Instead, she held him steady, his bony hand shaking as he reached for the cup.

She helped hold it to his lips as he took a long drink.

His eyes closed and his brow finally released into a look of rapture instead of disgust.

"How long have you been on your own here?" Elaina asked.

"I cannae remember. Two…three days."

Elaina found that doubtful since there had still been a candle burning and a low fire in the hearth. "Who lives here with you?" She glanced around the cluttered mess.

"Rory." The man pulled the cup back to his mouth.

"Where did he go?"

"She. Rory is my worthless shite of a granddaughter. Said she was goin' ta town after some herb or somethin'."

A granddaughter? Could she have abandoned the wretched old goat? Elaina wouldn't blame her if she had. "What age?"

"Five and ten. Her mam died of the fever three years ago, and the little whore sought me out. Thought she could get something from me, she did. Been nothin' but trouble since she came. Cannae do nothin' right. Gets herself with child out of wedlock. Won't even tell who the bastard is that lay with her. She knows I'll kill him."

Elaina doubted the man could kill anyone. Well, maybe with his words or with his shite he could accomplish the task. "Perhaps she ran into trouble," she offered as she eased the man back onto the bed. "Let's hope no evil has befallen her."

"Just as well if it did. Good riddance."

"That is what you say as you lay in days' worth of shite. How do you think you would survive on your own? You cannot walk. How will you feed yourself?"

"You."

"Me? Are you mad? I came to beg for herbs from you for an ill friend, not to become your nurse or your slave."

"So, you too would just leave an old man to die?"

Elaina heaved a sigh. Is that what she had just done? Left the lieutenant to die? What had she gotten herself into? Two sick and dying men. Surely this man's granddaughter would return soon. "I will not stay forever, but I will stay long enough to get you clean and feed you a bite before I leave. I'm sure that Rory will return soon."

The old man grunted in response.

Elaina set about searching for something, anything, cleaner than what the man was lying in. She found a petticoat in a corner spotted with a brown substance. Possibly blood. The girl must have soiled it during her menses and discarded it instead of washing it. That seemed to be how she did things, by the look of the place. It would do, Elaina decided. She ripped the garment into rags and hauled the warm water from the fire closer to the bed. She stared at the frail remnants of a man. There was nothing left to do but dive in.

"We need to remove this…this…" There were no words for what the man wore. She hated to even touch him. How was she going to get the thing off without getting the shite on herself?

"Ye must be out of yer heid, if ye think ye are goin' to undress me. I should have kent that ye were a whore too."

Elaina took a step back and looked at him with her hands on her hips. "You sorry old goat. No wonder your granddaughter left you if this is how you treated her. I am only trying to help you. Any person in their right mind would shut up and accept help when it comes." As she ranted, she noticed the man's breathing had become a great deal faster. He heaved and panted, as if struggling to find air. "Calm down, sir. Sir…" She didn't even know his name. As she bent over him again, it was then she caught the scent of rotting flesh in and amongst the foul odor of shite. "Shite," she hissed and would have snickered had the man before her not looked so panicked. "Sir? Calm down."

"Just let him go."

Elaina squealed and stumbled backward at the sound of the girl's voice from across the room.

"His arse is covered in sores that he willna let me treat. I feel certain he has already accused ye of bein' a whore. He does most females."

The girl—Elaina could only tell from her voice because she was wrapped in an oversized fur coat and had a knitted cap pulled low on her head—moved about the room gathering things. Her speech and her movements were halted and awkward, as if she weren't certain what she was saying or doing.

"Rory, I presume?" Elaina asked and squealed again as the man's bony hand seized her wrist.

"Dinna let the whore near me! She did this to me!" he all but screamed with what little breath he had. "The fault lies on her head and that whore of a mother of hers."

Apparently, the man thought every woman a whore. Elaina didn't feel as special.

Rory crossed the room and stood at the foot of the cot. "He is dyin'. His blood has turned to poison. I smell it. He is rottin' away." A faint smile crossed her lips but for a moment. "Just as well he dies from his own shite. That is all he has spewed forth his entire life. He has shite on everyone who has ever tried to help him or love him. Let him lie. He will be dead before sunrise." The girl's gaze roved over the man with no expression on her face. Her gaze was empty. Void of any emotion…even anger…or relief.

Elaina stared down at the invalid still clinging to her wrist, his touch searing her skin like a brand. The act brought forth the reason for her visit to the farmhouse. "I must go." She blurted out to the girl and wrenched her wrist free of the hateful man. "I've a sick friend I must tend to. I came only to beg for herbs. Anything you might have for…for fever."

The girl looked at her as if seeing her for the first time. "Take what ye want.

Linseed in that jar. Mustard in that one. Might could have saved his life if he weren't such a…such a…"

"No words needed, dear. Could I bother you for a hen as well?"

"Ye'll no be takin' my things, whore!" the man bellowed.

Elaina looked down at him and shook her head. He was no longer her concern, and she could leave with a clear conscience, unencumbered by guilt. Unless she returned to the lieutenant and found him dead. Then she was not sure she could live with herself, having abandoned a fevered man in the middle of nowhere.

"Take what ye like, miss. 'Twill no' be long now. He'll no' need it where he's going."

Elaina turned and grabbed the two jars the woman had gestured to. She reached the door before turning back. A short-handled knife tossed haphazardly amongst the clutter on the table caught her eye, and she eased back, reaching for it. Her fingers wrapped around the bone hilt. She glanced up at the girl, but the lass had no interest in Elaina. She stood at the foot of the bed, staring down at the thrashing man. The girl looked as sickly pale as her patient. Well, she was with child, and the stress of her grandfather passing on in such a horrendous way would certainly take a toll, no matter how much of a lout he was.

Elaina slid the knife into the pocket of her skirt. "Thank you," she said.

The girl turned to look at her, expressionless. No fear, no relief, nothing. She nodded once to Elaina and turned away.

Elaina hurried away in the rapidly dwindling light. She hoped like hell she could find her way back to her patient and offered up a prayer that she would find him alive.

Chapter Sixteen

T HE FULL MOON, THOUGH OFTEN hidden behind scurrying clouds, had finally revealed its face and gave her enough light to find her way back to her patient. Elaina slid from the back of her horse with the dead hen in her hand like a prize she had won in battle, for that was exactly what the entire day and night had felt like.

The lieutenant did not move at the sound of her approach.

Damn him! she thought as she squatted down, setting the dead bird down near the fire on her way to him. He couldn't have died while she was enduring that hell, all to garner him something to help build his strength and settle his stomach. Afraid to touch him, she tentatively reached out a hand, her fingers brushing his cheek. His eyes flew open, arms flailing about, and he yelled something unintelligible.

Elaina stumbled backward, landing hard on her bottom. "Damn you!" she yelled at him.

"Damn me? Lying here freezing my arse off, dying of the ague, and you just abandon me. Leave me for the wolves to devou—"

Elaina regained her footing and loomed over the hysterical man. "First off, wolves did not eat you. You are perfectly intact, frozen arse and all. And obviously from the number of words flowing past your lips, you are not dying. In fact, you seem to be a great deal recovered. I'm thinking I should have just stayed here and avoided the trouble of procuring a hen and other things to help return you to the healthy, infuriating, hateful arse that you are."

The lieutenant then began coughing until she thought he would pass out. He had developed a damn cough during her absence.

"Oh, bloody hell," she fussed, raising hand to hip.

Blinking through tears brought about by his fit, he gasped, "I thought you had left me for dead."

"Why? Is that what you would have done? I do not leave the dying, Lieutenant, but I am leaning toward helping you along to the river Styx." The heat had left her voice, and she poked at the almost-dead fire with a stick, stirring the glowing coals and bringing it back to life. "Lovely cough you seemed to have developed. Might I feel your forehead without your howling at me?"

He collapsed backward onto the ground. "Fine."

Elaina rolled her eyes and came onto her knees, crawling closer to him. She laid the back of her hand against his forehead. "Yes, you are still feverish, though I think not as hot as before I left. I will blame your lack of gratitude on that. If I hadn't spent the previous two days with you, I might well believe that was the cause myself."

The lieutenant raised his brow. "Gratitude for what? Abandoning me in my time of need."

Elaina huffed a sigh. "I will ignore that remark since it is quite obvious I have not abandoned you." She pulled several jars from the pouch at her waist. "I'm going to mix a salve and rub it on your chest. I'll not have you dying in my presence."

"Scared of the dead?" His voice held a hint of teasing before he broke off into a coughing fit.

"I've seen plenty of dead, Lieutenant. I would rather not be charged with yet another crime I am not guilty of. Now, open your coat."

"I'll not." He looked at her as if she had sprouted a second head.

"You will if I have to truss you up like a Christmas goose." Elaina scooped the medicinals from the jars with a twig and stirred the mixture in a tin cup she had pilfered from the home of Rory and… She never had learned the name of the great horse's arse she had parted company with. *From one arse to another.* She sat the cup on the outermost coals and added a bit of snow to the mixture and stirred it with a stick, warming the salve. "Now, then." She turned to the man to find he had not opened his coat as she had asked. She took a step toward him, and he scooted backward across the ground. They exchanged glares for a moment before she lunged at him, snatching a hold on his sleeve before he could scurry away from her. "You are acting like a child," she said through gritted teeth as she fought to keep her grip on his coat.

He fought to free himself.

"That's it," she growled, and she sat on his chest.

The lieutenant kicked and squirmed underneath her.

"I am not going to make you drink the stuff."

"Kindly remove yourself from my person," he grunted. "I can't breathe."

"Stop fighting me. Do you want to die out here in the frozen wilderness, or do you want your bloody commission?"

"Why on earth would you be concerned with my actually getting my commission?"

"You threatened people that I love very much. It behooves me to think that if you succeed in your mission to turn me over, then those that I love will no longer garner your attentions and can live their lives in peace." He *had* threatened them and, therefore, she *should* leave him for dead, but lying there on the hard ground, he looked so pathetic she couldn't help but have a bit of compassion. "Just bloody shut up and open your coat before this gets cold." She waved the cup of salve at him.

The lieutenant huffed at her but he stopped squirming.

"You will not try to get away if I release you?" she asked.

He closed his eyes and shook his head.

She had won. With a smirk, Elaina slid from his chest to the ground beside him.

Lieutenant did as he was told and unbuttoned the top few buttons of his coat without opening his eyes, as if keeping them closed would alleviate any embarrassment he might feel.

She scooped up a bit of the foul-smelling mixture and slid her hand down the front of his tunic, smearing it across his chest. Her fingers encountered an indention on the right side. "You've been injured before," she said to break the awkwardness of the moment.

He cleared his throat. "Yes—" A violent coughing fit interrupted his statement. "Bloody hell…what is in that? I thought you were trying to save me, not finish me off," he whined between gasps for air.

"See? 'Tis clearing the airways already." Elaina finished her ministration and cleaned her hand with snow before filling the cup with more of the white stuff and setting it on the glowing coals for the snow to melt and the resulting water to warm so she could rinse it out thoroughly. She rose from her kneeling position by the fire. "Let me gather some wood, and we will see what we can do with this bird."

She scooted it closer to him with the toe of her boot.

He stared at it as if seeing it for the first time. "Where did you…"

"I told you I was on a mission to save your life." She turned on her heels and set about searching for firewood.

When she returned about an hour later, the lieutenant had risen from his frozen bed and cut the feathers and skin from the bird, erected a makeshift spit, and had the now-naked fowl impaled and in place, awaiting extra wood for the glowing coals. There was already the smell of roasted bird in the air, though only enough coals remained to warm its exterior.

"I thought you had left me again." The lieutenant raised his brow at her.

"Once more, you are mistaken, sir," she replied while adding some of the wood she had gathered to the coals, carefully building the fire back up into a full blaze.

Elaina plopped herself down, exhausted, starved, and freezing. She scooted as close as she dared to the fire while the hen roasted away, though she'd have loved to throw herself on the coals as well. It was a good sign that he'd felt well enough to clean the bird and cook it, though he was probably as starved as she, if not more so.

When satisfied with his job of turning the bird over the fire, the lieutenant dropped the bird in the snow to cool it off a bit before pulling it apart. He offered her half, which she gladly accepted.

"I owe you an apology," he said after a couple of bites. "You could have left me. You could have escaped and returned home."

"Yes. I could have." Elaina eyed him with speculation, tossing the bird from hand to hand. Finally, she dropped the still scalding hot meat in the snow. She didn't know how he was holding it or eating it.

"Why didn't you?"

"For one, I could have been easily found. Two, it is quite dangerous for a woman to travel alone, as you well know. Three, for what it's worth, I am not the cold-hearted mercenary the British army portrays me as. Yes, I have taken the lives of three men in my lifetime. One by accident, one murdered my stableboy, and the third… Well, let's just say the third deserved everything he got and more. As despicable as your act of threatening those I love to garner my cooperation is, it is not so despicable that I would leave you to freeze to death nor to get eaten alive by wolves. Although I considered it after the hell I had to endure to get you this bloody hen."

"What *did* you endure while away?"

"No." Elaina held up a hand, stopping his question on the frozen air. "I am not discussing it. You wouldn't believe it even if I did."

The sound of footfalls crunching frozen snow snapped them both to attention. The lieutenant pointed his pistol into the black night as Elaina reached for the knife she had pilfered, but she didn't draw it. No need for the lieutenant to know she was now armed.

A gray gelding emerged out of the black of night carrying a figure hidden beneath an enormous coat, with a sack slung over one shoulder. A tangle of red hair peeked out from under a knitted cap.

"Rory?" Elaina scrambled to her feet.

"You know this..." The lieutenant waved his pistol in the direction of the approaching girl.

"Yes."

Rory slid from her steed and plopped herself beside the fire as if that were where she belonged.

"What are you doing here, lass?" Elaina asked, squinting into the inky blackness that the girl had emerged from as if her invalid grandfather were following close behind.

Rory held her hands out toward the flames, rubbing her woolen gloves together as she scooted an inch closer. "'Twas an easy enough trail to follow."

"That's not what I mean. Well, that is partially what I meant, but—"

"Who the hell is this?" Lieutenant Perry barked from across the fire.

Elaina glared at him but ignored the question. "Rory, where is your grandfather?"

"Dead. Quit breathin' minutes after you left, actually. Flew into a screamin' rage and that was the end of him."

Elaina wanted to ask if she had helped with the act but was afraid to in front of present company. "Do we need to go bury him?" There was no way the girl had had time to dig a grave.

"I set the house afire." The girl's gaze remained steady on the flames, her eyes unblinking. She looked as if her soul, too, had left this world.

"I'm sorry, Rory." Elaina fell to her knees beside the girl and took her gloved hands in hers, the heat of the mittens warming her own frozen fingers.

The girl finally turned to look at her. "The bastard's dead. There is nothin' to be sorry about. 'Tis a time of rejoicin'." Rory didn't exactly look like she was rejoicing, though. She looked pale, even for a girl who was already the color of parchment paper. She resembled the surrounding snow. Perhaps she was in shock about the entire ordeal.

"Here. Eat something." Elaina scrambled back around the fire while the lieutenant greedily clutched his half of the chicken. "Oh, don't be an arse, Lieutenant. I will not share your portion of the precious bird with our guest, whom I procured it from, by the way. I wouldn't dream of it." She snatched up her discarded supper and rounded the fire to sit beside the young girl. How old did her grandfather say she was? Fifteen? At the moment, huddled against the cold, she looked like a small, lost child. Elaina tore off a chicken leg and held it out to her.

The girl grabbed the end of her mitten in her teeth and pulled it off her hand before accepting the offering.

"Who is this, and where did she come from?" Lieutenant Perry asked through gritted teeth.

"This is the girl responsible for your dinner. Any normal man would be a gentleman and say thank you instead of barking like a hound every time he opened his mouth."

The lieutenant glared at her before turning his attention to Rory. "Thank you," he snipped. He glanced back at Elaina. "Happy?" he snapped before dissolving into a fit of coughs.

"I suppose, if that is the best that you can do, and that serves you right." Elaina waved a finger in his direction as he fought to catch his breath. She earned herself a hard glare as he wiped the tears from his eyes.

Rory ate without looking at either of them. Nor did she acknowledge the lieutenant's reluctant gratitude. She kept her head lowered, concentrating on the food in her grasp.

Elaina placed a bite of chicken in her mouth before meeting the questioning gaze of the man across the fire. She shrugged and shook her head. She no more knew what Rory was doing here than he did. Why *had* she followed her?

"Have you no kin, lass? Is there somewhere we can take you?"

The lieutenant cleared his throat in protest.

Elaina cast him a withering glare.

Rory shook her head. "I've no one, miss."

Elaina leaned close and whispered, "What about the father of your child?"

Rory swallowed hard, then shook her head and continued studying the now bare bone she held in her hand. A tear ran down her cheek.

"Would you like more?" Elaina extended what was left of the bird they shared.

Rory shook her head. "I shall sleep." She lay down next to the fire with her head resting on her arm and closed her eyes.

Elaina sat for a moment before rising and returning to the lieutenant's side.

"Where did she come from? She cannot stay with us," he hissed.

Elaina took a deep breath and told him the story of where the herbs and the hen had come from. "And…she is with child, according to her grandfather. We cannot just abandon her here. Perhaps in the next town we might find a place that we can send her. A home for unwed mothers of sorts."

The man snorted. "And if not?"

"We will see when we get there. Surely there will be a church of some sort. Where *are* we going?" Elaina raised an eyebrow at him. "Are we in Scotland or England? I do not even know."

"Scotland at the moment, if I am not delirious enough to have forgotten," he smirked. "England is a day's ride, whenever I have recovered from this poisoning."

"If you had been poisoned, I'm sure they would have given you enough for you to die, not just lose your wame in the snow."

The two sat in silence as the wolves howled in the distance, sending shivers down Elaina's spine.

Lieutenant Perry glanced into the dark beyond the campfire.

"Don't worry, Lieutenant," Elaina said, a grin stretching her mouth although her chest squeezed tight with apprehension. "I'll protect you if they get near."

"As if I need your protection, madam. How am I to know you won't put that knife you carry through my heart as I sleep?"

"You don't, and how did you know?"

"I observe all things, *my lady*."

Elaina didn't tell him that there was no chance she would slit his throat. The fear of what would happen to Jamie and William superseded the fear of traveling with this blackmailing redcoat. She didn't know if he already had a plan or not.

To change the subject from the knife she now carried in her pocket, she said, "So, tell me about your mission, Lieutenant Perry. Where does this need to impress Cumberland come from? *Is* it Cumberland you are trying to impress by your acts of kidnapping and blackmail?"

The lieutenant cast Elaina a warning glare from the corner of his eye as he poked at the fire with a stick. He didn't look quite as intimidating, hunched and shivering in the night. A light snow had begun to fall, and it dusted the top of his balding head, his hat still discarded beside him. His color had improved. Perhaps the meal and the herbs were doing their job.

"All right. If you will not answer that, how old are you? Is that a safe enough question?"

"Why don't you sit there in silence before I tie you up and stick a rag in your mouth?"

"The nerve. Threaten me when I have saved your life," Elaina teased. "I thought it only women who balked at sharing their age. Besides, what would our company think if she woke up to me bound and gagged?" Elaina laughed as she scooted closer to the flames. It was as if the frigid night seeped through her clothing, her skin, and into her bones.

"How old are *you*, my lady?" the lieutenant asked.

"I asked you first, and you are not supposed to ask a lady her age." The fact that he kept calling her 'my lady' grated on Elaina's skin, but she didn't correct him on her title. To do so would reveal the truth that she was not William's sister, but a full-blooded Scot and a Highlander to boot.

"Four and thirty, if you must know." He cast her a cutting glance.

"Two and twenty."

The pair sat in silence, and Elaina wondered how much more information she could garner from the officer. She needed whatever she could get. A leverage of some sort. She picked at a string on her coat while studying her blackmailer, who, in turn, stared into the fire before him.

"Are you married, Lieutenant?"

He gave a start like he had forgotten she was present. "Not that it is any of your business, but no."

It can't have been his pleasant countenance that kept him from a mate. Elaina rolled her eyes at the grumbling man before her. The sickness had weakened him somewhat, but his spunk was returning. "Have you family?"

"Go to sleep, my lady. We've a long journey still yet." Lieutenant Perry curled himself into a ball close to the fire, tucking his great coat and a woolen blanket around himself.

Trusting fellow. I could put my knife through his eye even now.

"I can hear your thoughts, madam. Don't try it." He pulled his hand from beneath his blanket and pointed his pistol at her, eyes still closed.

Elaina sighed and glanced at their new sleeping companion across the dwindling fire. What to do with the lass? She supposed the situation would work itself out. Wrapping herself up in her own makeshift bed, Elaina drifted to sleep under the serenade of howling wolves, the pips and pops of the fire, and the feather-like brush of snowflakes falling upon her cheek.

Chapter Seventeen

"Well, now, ain't this a picture?"

The voice startled Elaina from her sleep, and she sat bolt upright and clutched the knife in her fist as snow fell from her head, tumbling down her face. She brushed it from her eyes and looked toward the voice through the pinkish gray of dawn.

Donald Murray's mouth gaped at the sight of her.

She gave a slight shake of her head, warning Caitir's father against revealing that he knew her identity.

"What's this about?" the lieutenant snapped.

Elaina turned to witness him trying to shrug away Martin MacKenzie's musket poking into his back.

"I think it would be in your best interest to move along," the lieutenant growled.

"Move along, he says." Donald Murray cast a grin that also contained a warning glance at the MacKenzie now staring wide-eyed at Elaina. "Two for one?" Mr. Murray stepped across the red coals left from their fire and nudged Rory's leg with his boot. "She yours as well? A happy trio *traveling* together?"

Elaina doubted that Rory truly slept through the nonsense surrounding her. At the touch of Mr. Murray's boot, she sat up, shaking snow from her knit cap, but refrained from making eye contact with anyone.

"That…that is my sister," the lieutenant stuttered.

His answer shocked Elaina, and she glanced back at him.

He raised his brow at her as if to say, 'What would you have me do?' Then he looked up at Mr. Murray again. "Now if you gentleman would scurry along—"

MacKenzie jabbed the barrel of his gun into the lieutenant's back hard enough for him to jerk forward. "I dinna see where ye have any leverage to be tellin' us what to do."

Mr. Murray said, "Where are ye and yer *family* headed? I find it hard to believe that in the state ole Johnny Cope is in that he would let such a fine specimen of a soldier set off on holiday."

"Well, he did, so bugger off." The lieutenant didn't look like such a fine specimen of a soldier at the moment. A cap of snow still dusted his head, and what was left of his hair had slipped from its queue and was hanging in strings around his face, which burned a deep crimson, a sign the illness that had crippled him was waning.

Donald Murray snatched Elaina off the ground by her arm, sending snow puffing out around them.

The lieutenant scrambled to his feet. "Take your hands off of my pr—my wife."

Elaina arched an eyebrow at him, which he returned with a withering glower. True, he couldn't very well tell them she was his prisoner. For all he knew, they would kill him and take her themselves for the bounty.

"Yer wife, eh?" MacKenzie didn't bother to hide his merriment at the man's words. "If I had a wife that young and bonnie, I'd be curled around her with one hand up her skirt and my c—"

"Sir!" Elaina could feel the heat creeping up her face. She had exchanged only a handful of words with the man ever and didn't know whether his words were part of his pretense of not knowing her or how he spoke all the time around unfamiliar women. She glanced at Rory, who sat still as the dead with her head down.

MacKenzie chuckled and cast Elaina a wink. And just why was the father of the woman Calum had broken his betrothal to being so blasted friendly?

The lieutenant made a move toward Mr. Murray and Elaina.

MacKenzie caught him by the collar of his coat, dragging him back. "Ye're ours now, ye bloody redcoat. Ye will be goin' nowhere with yer *wife* and yer *sister*. Gather yer things and come along. We've places to be. I'll take those." He relieved the man of his weaponry, and Elaina of the knife she still held clutched in her fist.

"Ye can gather yer things," Mr. Murray said from behind Elaina, giving her a little shove. "I'll nay give favors to a woman who would dare lay with a redcoat, let alone marry one." To Rory, he said, "Get up and on the horse, lass. I'll hold yer reins." He barked at Elaina, who had gathered their few belongings, "You. On this one."

"Where are you takin' us?" Lieutenant Perry asked as MacKenzie tied the man's hands together in front of him.

"Places. Ne'er ye mind." MacKenzie held the end of the length of rope around the soldier's wrists before mounting his horse, then jerked the line and pulled the lieutenant stumbling through the snow beside him.

The poor man was going to have to walk to wherever they were going. Elaina found herself hoping he was strong enough to make the journey. She shook her head at herself. What had she become? A sympathizer? Donald rode up beside her and held his arm out in front of her, slowing their pace until they were out of earshot of the others.

"So, where'd ye come across the likes of him, and why are ye pretendin' to be marrit to him?"

Elaina told Caitir's father the story of Rhona, then how the lieutenant had learned her identity and his failed attempt to collect the reward. She strategically did not mention the man's threats against Jamie. No need to feed the fire of distrust and revenge. Besides, he was now in the custody of the rebels. What could he do from his new position as captive?

"Hmph," Donald grunted, then a smile stretched across his face. "If the man wishes to play games, we can abide for a period. He may come in quite useful where we're headed."

"And where is that? Will the Laird Beinnmaree be present? I must get word to him about the condition of his wife."

"Aye. We can get word to Calum's da. But he'll no' be where we are bound at the moment. We are on a mission, lass, and ye have just provided us the leverage we need to succeed."

Puzzled by his words and lack of explanation, Elaina followed Donald Murray as he kicked his horse into motion to rejoin the group. The snow that had fallen through the night muffled the sound of the horses' hooves and seemed to oppress everything, including the riders. The silence made her ears ring, and she was grateful when MacKenzie started whistling a tune. That gratitude faded as a half hour passed and the tune moved faster, as did the horses—she suspected on purpose. They moved at a pace far too fast for the lieutenant.

"Stop," Elaina said after Perry had fallen for the fourth time. She dismounted and came to a squat beside the lieutenant. She felt his forehead, finding the man's fever was gone, but so was his strength.

"I'm fine," he grumbled, pushing himself to his feet where he wobbled a bit before straightening to his full height.

"He is weak. He has been ill. It is torture to make him walk." Elaina cast a withering glare at Mr. MacKenzie.

"Why such sympathy for the redcoat?" MacKenzie asked with a wrinkle of his nose, as if smelling something foul.

"Because…" The one word hung in the air as Elaina searched for more.

"Because she is my wife," the lieutenant intervened. "And I assure you, *darling*, I'm fine. No need to concern yourself."

"You are *not* fine. You are anything but fine." Elaina glared at him. "I am trying to help you," she hissed between her teeth.

"I don't need your help, my lady," the lieutenant hissed back. "Return to your horse."

"I'll not." Elaina crossed her arms and raised an eyebrow at him.

"Get back to yer horse," MacKenzie growled at her. "We've places to be."

Rory sat upon her steed beside MacKenzie and watched the argument unfold. Her gaze darted from person to person, the grip on her reins seeming to tighten with every word. Elaina shot her a sympathetic look, hoping the girl would understand that she was in no danger.

Returning her attention to the arse on the horse, Elaina said, "I'll not return to my horse without the…without my husband." She cast MacKenzie a look, daring him to say anything.

"You—"

"That's enough," Mr. Murray bellowed.

Startled, Elaina nearly fell backwards into the snow, but the lieutenant grabbed her arm, righting her on her feet. She had never heard Mr. Murray yell before. He was usually a calm sea in all storms.

"I've had enough. Enough of this bickering and enough of this charade. Elaina, return to your horse. Time is of the essence." Mr. Murray was now himself again, his voice on an even keel.

"With all due respect, Mr. Murray, if time is so important, then you had better let the lieutenant ride with me or we might never get to our destination."

"You know her?" The look on the lieutenant's face was almost comical.

"Aye, we do. So, we ken that she is no' yer wife. We should just shoot him."
MacKenzie glared at the redcoat.

"You'll do no such thing." Elaina laid a hand upon the lieutenant's arm.

"No, you will not," Mr. Murray agreed. "We need him, MacKenzie. Alive.
And we need to be movin', not standing here squabblin'. Lieutenant, mount the
horse." He nodded his head to Elaina's empty steed, who stood stamping his
hoof in the snow as if he too were eager to be on the move.

"But—"

"Just do it," Elaina interrupted whatever protest the man had about *not* being dragged through the snow until he succumbed to death. She removed the
lead that Martin MacKenzie had tied him with like an animal but left his wrists
bound. No need to take more chances than they already were. "Come." She took
him by the arm and led him to the horse.

He stood and stared at it.

"Can you not do it with your hands tied?" Elaina asked.

"I can," the lieutenant said. "But why?"

"Because you are going to die in the snow from sheer and utter exhaustion is
why. Because your pallor still has the grayish tinge of death to it."

"That's not what I mean, my lady. Why do you care? Let me die if it is my
fate."

Donald Murray urged his horse up beside them. "I will bloody beat you
to death if you do not mount that horse right now," he said through clenched
teeth. "Ye can bloody well make nice with each other on the ride to our destination. *Up.*"

Spurred into action, the lieutenant stuck his foot in the stirrup, gripped the
saddle with both hands, and pulled himself up.

"You too," Mr. Murray said to Elaina, jerking his head toward the horse.
"Make certain he does not flee or die on us." With that, he turned to Martin
MacKenzie and nodded him back into motion.

Elaina mounted the horse in front of the lieutenant as quickly as she could
and took up the reins, and they were off once more to God knows where.

The group traveled all day, stopping once more for water and a rest. The
trees closed in around them as Mr. Murray and Mr. MacKenzie led them off the
trail they had traveled all day and into a dense forest that threatened to suffocate
any remaining daylight. Night was close upon them when the black of the forest
cleared before them, exposing a sea of red uniforms. How a set of clothes could

make Elaina's heart stop beating was beyond her. It was not only the uniforms but the sheer number of them that constricted her throat.

"This…this is where you mean to take us?" Elaina asked Mr. MacKenzie.

"Aye, 'tis." His wicked smile was barely visible in the dwindling light.

Elaina glanced back at the lieutenant wearing the smug look of a man who thought freedom within his grasp. Although she didn't know what their plan was or even their mission, she was fair certain that it did not involve untying the man and letting him walk free. In fact, MacKenzie took the opportunity to drag the man from the horse and shove a rag in his mouth.

Now standing beside her horse and still silent as ever, Rory seemed paler, if that were possible, as she, too, watched the soldiers milling about the streets. She looked Elaina in the eye for perhaps the first time, and the fear in them made her look like a cornered wild creature. Elaina felt much the same.

"Now what?" Elaina asked.

"We sit and we wait." MacKenzie helped the lieutenant unceremoniously to the ground, his grunt of protest muffled.

"What are we waiting for?" Elaina hissed to Mr. Murray. "To be discovered? They will hang us."

"If we are lucky," Mr. Murray whispered, his expression turning unnervingly sober. "We have word that Auld Ruadh and the Calhoun are in there." He tipped his head toward a large stone building.

Elaina studied the structure and the guard standing attendance at the door, questioning everyone who requested entry. One man was no worry for the two Highlanders standing at her side. It was the several hundred roaming the streets and those holding vigil beside roaring fires that worried her. She craned her neck to look farther down the street. The row of tents and fires spread as far as she could see. She felt her knees and her will crumble, and she plopped down beside the lieutenant. Were they to use him as a barter for the lives of her friends? He didn't seem like a man the British army would just turn over prisoners of war for. Guilt tugged at her. The man had saved her from being raped, after all. Even if it was only to further his own cause, it was still a rescue. She owed him that much. She glanced sideways at him, but he stared straight ahead, watching every move of the men milling about just beyond the trees. He studied them…strategized. He was not a daft man.

They sat, watching for near an hour as far as Elaina could tell. Nary a word was spoken.

"Up," Mr. Murray hissed, startling them all. "We must retreat while there is still enough light to do so."

He grabbed Elaina's wrist and pulled her, groaning, to her feet. Her limbs were stiff from sitting on the cold ground. MacKenzie did the same with Rory. Both men struggled to pull the lieutenant up from the ground, and the man did nothing to help.

Mr. Murray finally grew impatient and placed the tip of a knife under the man's chin, drawing a drip of blood. "I will shove this dirk up through your mouth and into your brain if ye bloody well dinna get to yer feet. Ye think ye are the only redcoat important to us? The only leverage we have? Ye are quite mistaken."

The lieutenant huffed a sigh and rose clumsily enough to his feet, coming close to toppling headfirst into the snow.

MacKenzie shoved the lieutenant's feet into motion, and the group retreated far enough into the woods that they could no longer see the light of the British camp nor the light from the setting sun. They stumbled and grunted and cursed in the dark until a black mound rose from the shadows, making Elaina's heart increase its pounding in her chest. The shadow finally took the shape of a great rock, and they rounded the boulder into a small clearing. MacKenzie brought the group to a halt and seated them against the rock, standing watch over them while Mr. Murray lit a fire from the already prepared wood.

"What is this?" Elaina asked, her gaze scanning the clearing where cut wood stood piled to one side.

"A Jacobite camp. There were several dotted around the country," Mr. Murray said as he shoved another piece of wood into the fire. "When one group leaves, they prepare it for the next."

Well, that is something, isn't it? Rebel helping rebel. Then another thought struck her. "The Calhoun," Elaina whispered to herself, catching the lieutenant's attention.

He raised a brow in question.

"A man who has saved my arse more than once." She didn't know why she'd confessed that to the redcoat tied up beside her.

He raised his brow and grunted through the rag.

"The other?" she asked.

He nodded.

"A dear friend…" Elaina felt an unexpected tear flow down her cheek. Auld

Ruadh was indeed a dear friend and confidant, but also her uncle by marriage. The first of Calum's family to accept her and love her for who she was. Now, he sat trapped in what seemed an impenetrable fortress.

A rustling in the brush startled everyone to attention. MacKenzie and Mr. Murray pointed their weapons into the surrounding darkness.

A bundle of fur came stumbling out, nearly falling to the ground.

MacKenzie hurried to the man's side. "Well, what did ye learn?"

The man wrenched off his bonnet and sat hard on the ground. "Whisky?" His question held a note of desperate hope.

"Aye, we've no' much left, though." MacKenzie seemed reluctant to give up the flask.

The wizened old man snorted. "A nip or ye'r on yer own."

He drives a hard bargain, Elaina thought. Then she wondered what kind of information he would have been garnering. He looked so familiar. Where had she seen him before?

MacKenzie relented when Mr. Murray shoved him with the butt of his gun.

The man took a long drink. "Ah, much better."

"Now, what did ye find?" It was Mr. Murray's turn to be impatient.

"They are indeed in that building and near enough to death to have arrived there by now. It is a lost cause, I'm afraid. Too many redcoats. Speaking of… what's this?" The man wobbled his way around the fire to where the lieutenant, Elaina, and Rory sat in a row. His curious yet oddly familiar gaze went from one face to another and then returned to the lieutenant. He reached down and pulled the rag from the lieutenant's mouth, and that was when Elaina noted the left sleeve from his coat dangling in the wind. The man had but one arm.

"Ye found ye a captive, then?" the man called over his shoulder to MacKenzie and Mr. Murray.

"Aye," Mr. Murray said.

"And these two?" He nodded his head toward Elaina and Rory.

Mr. Murray walked up beside him. "That one is the fiery warrior on the mound." He called her by the name that the hill people had bestowed upon the legendary woman on a broadsheet, though not more than a handful knew she was, in fact, that warrior. "The redhead just happened to be with them when we captured them."

"The fiery warrior, eh? I thought the fiery warrior had flamin' red hair. Ye sure she's no' that one?" The old man cocked his head at Rory.

Elaina knew the man's face. She had seen it before. She had heard his jolly voice before. Even while asking all the questions, the man had a smile that remained on his face as if permanently etched there.

"Oh, I'm certain," Mr. Murray said. "Look at that one, shivering like a frightened kitten. This one"—he turned his attention to Elaina—"got her name not from her physical attributes but from her damned temper. That's MacGregor blood runnin' through her veins, and it shows itself near every time she opens her mouth."

Elaina did indeed open her mouth to tell Mr. Murray just what she thought of his description.

"Ollie?" The lieutenant's question beat Elaina's words out of her mouth.

Ollie…Ollie. "Ollie?" Elaina scrambled to her feet. "Now I know who you are. For the life of me, I couldn't place you."

"You know Ollie?" the lieutenant asked Elaina at the same moment MacKenzie asked the same question of the lieutenant.

Elaina shared a questioning stare with the lieutenant.

"Aye. I ken the both of them," Ollie said. "Though I dinna ken why they are together, and one in bindings and the other free."

"Well, if ye cannae see," MacKenzie said, sarcasm dripping from his tongue, "one of 'em is a bloody redcoat and the other isna."

Ollie didn't reply to MacKenzie's jab. His smile remained in place, but there was a slight shift in his eyes that told Elaina he was more dangerous than these men gave him credit for. But she too was curious as to his acquaintance with the lieutenant.

"Ollie was one of the soldiers with my brother when he died of his wounds after a battle," the lieutenant said, answering Elaina's unspoken question.

"Aye," Ollie said, a twinkle brightening his gaze as if he found something quite amusing. "And this lass, the fiery warrior without a heart that slaughters men at will—" He barked out a laugh at Elaina's glare. "This heartless lass sat and held his brother's hand. She let him think she was a lass named Abigail, comforted him and sang to him as he passed from this world to the next."

Elaina stared at him, not comprehending his words at first. Then she muddled them out and turned her gaze to the lieutenant.

He returned the look, his brow furrowed and his head cocked to the side. "You?!"

Elaina was not sure whether it was a statement or a question. "That was your brother?" she asked. "You…" She pointed her finger at the lieutenant and then at Ollie.

"Ye ran so fast, lass, that he couldnae thank ye proper for bringing his brother such peace upon his dying."

The lieutenant shook his head. "I asked every staff member in that building, and none of them knew who you were. All they could tell me was that you had come in with a small group of others seeking help and herbs. But there you sat with my brother's dead hand clasped in yours, singing a melody to make any heart smile."

Elaina's legs gave out, and she sank to the ground. She and the lieutenant studied each other for a quiet moment before he cleared his throat. "It seems I owe you a debt, madam."

Elaina did not feel that entirely necessary but listened with interest anyway.

"I release you from your captivity. I set you free."

MacKenzie barked out a laugh behind her. "Some payment, considerin' she sits here free among rebels and ye sit trussed up like a hen."

Elaina and the lieutenant offered MacKenzie the same glare. She didn't know MacKenzie. All she knew of him was that he was the father of the woman to whom Calum was once betrothed, so she was not sure she trusted him but felt certain that she did not like him.

"If you would hold your tongue, sir, and let me finish." The lieutenant shook his head and returned his gaze to Elaina. "I will help release your friends from captivity."

Silence weighed heavily on the campsite until Elaina finally found her tongue. "Why? Why would you help us?"

"I have no other way to repay my debt, and your men are more than likely being tortured for information. I would rather they were not."

"And just what makes ye think that?" Mr. Murray squatted beside Elaina and studied the lieutenant.

"Because one of the officers leaving that so-called hospital was General Compton. He is a man well practiced in the art of torture. If the English need information from anyone, he can get it."

Mr. Murray rocked back and forth on his heels. "How do we know we can trust you?"

"You don't. My word is all I have that I will not reveal you or your plans. I think I can get you into that building, but I need more information on where the men are inside and how many. Besides, I owe the lady two debts. One for my brother and one for myself. She could have left me for dead, and I thought she had for a time." He chuckled, casting a glance at Elaina. "But she returned for me and was nursing me to health when you arrived and graced us with your most pleasant company. Another day and I would have been good as new, but after my lovely walk and the rest of the journey, I do feel as if I could fall over and die at any minute."

"Here." Ollie shoved the whisky at the lieutenant. "Fortify yerself, man. We cannae be losin' ye now."

"We will return at first light and devise a plan. Now, eat and rest. We will all need our strength and our wits on the morrow." Donald Murray stood and distributed biscuits and cheese to everyone, including the lieutenant.

Rory, who had remained silent as ever through the excitement of the evening, looked more pale now. She picked at her food, only nibbling a bit here and there.

Elaina crawled over to her and whispered, "Are you well, lass?"

"Nay."

Elaina could hardly hear the response. "Is it the loss of your grandfather?" She couldn't imagine it being so, that horrid old man.

Rory shrugged. "It is a loss," she whispered, then she lay down on the ground and curled herself into a ball.

Elaina retrieved a blanket and covered the girl with it, patting her head as if she were her mother. She sat beside the girl until most of the men slept and the fire began to dwindle. Tomorrow would be a big day, and she didn't know whether they could trust the lieutenant or not. She wanted to believe him a man of his word, but only time would tell.

Chapter Eighteen

THE GROUP ROSE BEFORE DAWN and returned the campsite to its original state, readying it for the next set of rebels that would come along. Elaina looked around the clearing, counting heads. Ollie was gone. Her heart sank a little. They needed all the help they could get, and even a one-armed Highlander was better than none.

MacKenzie reluctantly untied their prize lieutenant, but not before voicing his concerns on the matter. Elaina felt somewhat the same, though she kept her feelings to herself. They then made their way back to the small town and once again stood at the tree line watching.

The lieutenant studied the door to the hospital once again, then looked down the street to the right of it before turning his gaze to the woods some forty paces away from the western wall of the stone building. He turned and took one step toward the east before MacKenzie scrambled into his path.

"I dinna think so." MacKenzie pointed the tip of his dirk at the lieutenant's neck.

The lieutenant raised his brow in return before glancing down at Elaina.

"Move, MacKenzie," Mr. Murray said.

MacKenzie cast a withering glare at him but stood where he was.

"I need to see the rest of this area if I am to devise a plan to stop what is happening to your friends in that building. I need you to move your arse, sir, so I may do just that." The lieutenant's words dripped with contempt.

MacKenzie pushed the dirk in a little farther until it almost broke the skin. "If ye make any move in the wrong direction, you will be dead before ye take yer next breath."

The two men glared at each other until Mr. Murray cleared his throat. With what appeared to be great reluctance, MacKenzie lowered the dirk.

"I will walk with him," Elaina said. "The rest of you stay here. We all needn't traipse up and down the tree line drawing attention to ourselves." She'd volunteered for the most part to remove herself from MacKenzie's company. The man grated on her nerves. Besides, Rory had already slumped down on the ground, looking absolutely horrid, so she certainly didn't need to be 'traipsing' anywhere.

MacKenzie finally moved his stubborn arse, and Elaina and the lieutenant began their trek around the outskirts of the small village. They walked in silence as the lieutenant studied the entire encampment, Elaina matching him step for step as they circled behind it and around the side. They had traveled the same path four times, but she had given up asking him what his thoughts were by the second round. All things would come in due time.

"We need more men," was the first sentence he had spoken in nearly an hour and a half.

"Well, we haven't any," Elaina said. "Those two are all we have."

"I don't trust the MacKenzie fellow."

"Nor do I."

"What I am about to do could be construed as treason." He looked down at her with a resigned look on his face. "I suppose there go my dreams of glory and retiring to France or some other country."

"I had no idea you had those dreams, Lieutenant."

"Do not most men have dreams, mistress?"

"Yes, but I didn't think you were most men."

"Should I be insulted or flattered?"

"That depends on what you are planning," Elaina said, offering him a smile. He was certainly turning to out to be a puzzling man.

As he came to a stop beside a dead tree trunk away from the others, he slid down to the ground and she followed.

"My father had only one arm," the lieutenant said.

Elaina stared at him, puzzled by his confession.

"The other he lost in a war with the French."

"I'm sorry." It was a pitiful response, but it was all she could think to say.

"He did not lose it from a sword, nor a cannon blast. Not even gangrene, though that nearly took his life. He lost his arm one joint at a time. One finger. One hand. Inch by inch, they cut my father to pieces in order to garner information about the king's next move. They tortured him. I cannot bear it. I cannot bear atrocities of such manner, and that is what they are doing, my dear."

Elaina shuddered at the thought but kept her composure. "That is the nature of the beast, is it not? War? Cumberland?"

"Yes. He will give no quarter to any person he believes to have wronged himself, his father, or their name, including his own men. And I will be giving him more than a fair reason to hang me."

"But you are willing to lay your life and career on the line to free the enemy?"

"In the end, mistress, we are all just men. When stripped down, we are all flesh and bone, and everyone deserves the dignity of a swift death. God does not always grant it, but, if possible, it should be given, especially in war."

"What is your plan, then?"

"I haven't one."

"That is quite encouraging, Lieutenant."

"Quite."

Elaina sat with her knees up to her chest while she studied the makeshift field hospital. The two sat for who knew how long. They needed a plan, and none was forthcoming.

A hand clamped over Elaina's mouth, and she kicked and flailed without success to free herself as her assailant dragged her over a log and farther into the woods. From the grunts and ruckus to her right, the lieutenant was receiving much of the same. When things came to a halt, she lay on her back with the grinning face of her brother-in-law, Aron MacKinnon, staring down at her. He put a finger to his lips before removing his hand from her mouth.

"What the devil—"

Another hand clamped down, silencing her as Ainsley's head popped into view. It was a good thing he had covered her mouth, because she could not contain the squeal that escaped beneath the weight of it.

Ainsley. She shoved his hand to the side and threw herself at him. "What in the devil are you doing here?" Then she remembered where they were. "God's teeth, are you out of your mind? What if you get caught?"

Aron finished binding and gagging the lieutenant and stood glaring down at him

"Oh, holy hell. Let him go, Aron," Elaina said with a smirk.

"Let him go? He kidnapped you."

"That may have been how it began, but there are Scots trapped in that building, being tortured, and he means to try to break them free."

"A turncoat, is he? Bloody fuckin' English. Can't trust their own m—"

"Shut your mouth and untie that man at once." Elaina took Aron by the arm, meaning to give him a good shake, but the man didn't budge. The amused look he bestowed on her made her want to stomp on his foot, and she would have done just that if Mr. Murray and MacKenzie hadn't crept out from the brush to join the group.

"Stop yer bickering. Are ye trying to get as all killed?" Mr. Murray growled through his teeth. "Do as she says. Auld Ruadh and the Calhoun are in there."

Elaina's stomach clenched at the look that crossed Aron's face at word of his uncle's captivity.

Moments passed while Aron chewed his lip as if trying to grasp exactly what was going on. Finally with a growl, he untied the lieutenant as his other uncle had ordered. His father's brother. It was his mother's brother who lay somewhere in that impenetrable building.

"Thank you, sir." The lieutenant bowed his head to Aron.

Poor Aron's furrowed brow turned into a wide-eyed, bewildered owlish look. He glanced down at Elaina, his gaze questioning.

She patted his arm with a sympathetic smile. The man would have to wait for an explanation of all that had taken place. There was no time for that at the present.

"Well, now that we have more men," the lieutenant said, rubbing his wrists, "we may be able to form a plan."

"And why should we bloody well trust anything that you say? You could be setting us all up for capture," MacKenzie said.

"If I wanted you captured, you daft imbecile, all I would have to do is yell." The lieutenant balled his fists as if he wanted to strike MacKenzie.

"The man has a point, MacKenzie," Ainsley, ever the voice of reason, said.

MacKenzie mumbled something under his breath.

"Where is Calum?" Elaina whispered to Ainsley. They needed him. *She* needed him.

"He and William are searching for you separately from each other," Ainsley replied. "William is with his regiment but asking discretely. Calum has taken up with John Roy Stuart's company, and they were tracking you until they met up with a band of lobsterbacks down around Balhernoch. Unavoidably detained," Ainsley said with a wink and a glance at Lieutenant Perry.

"Well. The most urgent matter at present is the men inside that building. What is your plan, Lieutenant?" Mr. Murray asked.

"I need to get inside of that place to get the lay of the land."

"Oh, ho, I dinna think so," MacKenzie interjected. "This plan gets riskier by the minute. We cannae just let him waltz right in and announce us."

"How do you propose to get inside?" Mr. Murray asked, ignoring MacKenzie.

"I'm not sure—" the lieutenant's words were interrupted by a crashing in the brush.

All heads turned as a figure stumbled out of the woods and into their little foray.

"Rory!" Elaina said a little too loudly, then she hurried to the girl's side. In all the ruckus, she had forgotten the lass was with them. The girl had lost her pale sheen and was now gray as the winter sky. "My God, Rory, what…?"

Rory collapsed into Elaina's arms, and both women sank to the forest floor. The girl's voice was little more than a whisper. "I…I…I drank a…a tea."

"Tea? Tea did this to you? What kind of tea?" But Elaina suspected she already knew the answer to that question.

"Tansy," Rory whispered, a tear sliding down her cheek.

Elaina was not so sheltered that she didn't know what young women used that particular plant for. "But wh—"

The girl had gone limp in her arms.

Elaina folded back the flap of the oversized fur coat Rory wore and swore under her breath.

Mr. Murray bent over the two women. "What is it?"

"She's pregnant."

MacKenzie inserted himself into the group, too close for Elaina's comfort. "Are you certain of that?" he asked. "Ye do ken that—"

"Stop talking!" MacKenzie's presence grated against her skin. Elaina closed her eyes against the sight of him and took a deep breath. When she opened them, she only looked at Mr. Murray. "She *was* pregnant. She drank a concoction to put an end to the situation."

"Idiot girl," Mr. Murray whispered without anger. He studied the limp girl lying in Elaina's arms for a moment before snapping his fingers and calling the

Chapter Nineteen

T HE SOLDIER TO THE RIGHT of the door of the stone building moved in front of it as the two men and two women climbed the stairs. "Halt."

Elaina sniffled into her handkerchief.

"Move aside, soldier," the lieutenant said. "This lass is near to dying."

"Of what?" The soldier's gaze roved over the entire group, sizing up each individual.

"She is bleeding to death. Move before I have you removed from your cozy post at the door and find something much less pleasant for you to do."

With that command, the man moved aside and allowed the group entrance to the building.

Once inside, the lieutenant turned to MacKenzie and spoke loud enough for the two soldiers in the hall to hear. "Take her that I might move ahead and find a physician to help her."

MacKenzie accepted Rory's lifeless body, his face marked with what Elaina took to be repulsion.

"She is your niece," Elaina hissed in his ear. "You might want to pretend to have a heart."

He glared at her as they fell into step behind the lieutenant, who marched down the hallway with the authority of a general, glancing about in each room they passed.

Elaina wiped at her tears and sniffled, finding it easy to cry with the thought of what might have happened to the girl. Any number of scenarios ran through her head, from her beloved having been killed in a battle to her having been raped. One thing was certain, though. Rory would have surely died if she had stayed with her grandfather. She might die yet, the foolish girl.

They met two soldiers in the hallway, and the lieutenant ordered them to bring a physician, yet he kept moving farther down the corridor, eyes scanning, calculating. MacKenzie moved with much less ease beside Elaina. His presence sickened her, and she drew great satisfaction from his unease, having decided the man was a snake. They had made it to the end of the corridor and stood with three directions to take, right, left, or up, and the lieutenant chose left. As they made their way down the hall, Elaina could just make out muffled, inhuman sounds.

Two uniformed men came sprinting down the hall toward them. "Come no farther!" they shouted. "You are not allowed down this hall. No one is."

"I'm searching for the physician."

"You'll not find him down this way. Turn and go back." The soldier pointed his bayonet back the way they had come.

Elaina thought for a moment that the lieutenant was going to argue the matter, but instead he turned on his heel and stalked back the way they had come.

"There you are," said a short robust man with round spectacles perched on his nose and a bloodied apron stretched tight around his oversized middle as he came waddling down the hall toward them. "This room." He cocked his head to an open door.

The four of them entered, and the squat man clicked the door shut behind them. "I was told that you are in need of my services," he said as he turned to face the group that he had amassed in a space that should have held far fewer people.

Elaina felt as if all the air had left the small room. The head of the bed was shoved up against one wall and there was very little walking room on the other three sides of it. MacKenzie lay the girl on the bed as if she were made of glass, his acting skills greatly improved. He stepped away from the table.

The lieutenant stiffened beside Elaina before he cleared his throat and launched into some rambling story about how he had found the three of them wandering the streets, searching for help before the girl had collapsed in the snow.

Elaina sniffled as she studied the room for possible weapons. The floor was stained with blood, and there was a small table to the side of the bed now holding Rory's near dead body. It was littered with assorted instruments but little else. No chair, no heat, no window. MacKenzie blocked the only entrance, so no escape either. Though it might not take too much to overpower the short yet robust man if the need arose.

"Turn, gentlemen," the man ordered. He spoke with authority that she had not seen a physician possess before.

Elaina stood by Rory's side and held her icy hand as he lifted layer upon layer of her skirts, each soaked with more blood than the one before.

"How long has it been?" he asked. When Elaina didn't answer, he looked up at her and said without malice, "I'm talking to you, girl."

"I'm uncertain," Elaina whispered from behind her handkerchief.

"Did you let her do this?"

Elaina shook her head in horror. "No. I had no idea until she collapsed. Thank God my uncle was there also."

"Don't be thanking God just yet, madam. Your cousin is gravely ill. I'm not sure I can save her. Don't fret. I will do my best." He lowered the girl's skirts and turned his attention to the two men who still faced the wall. "Gentlemen. Yes, you, step out of the room, please. Lieutenant, you are free to return to your duties." The physician glanced at MacKenzie. "I will send word when you are needed, Mr...."

"MacKenzie. Thank ye, truly."

For only a moment Elaina thought something amiss between the two men, but then the physician straightened and shooed the men from the room. Perhaps MacKenzie should not have given his true name.

Without a word, the physician tugged open a drawer on the little table and pulled out a handful of rags. Lifting Rory's skirts once more, he stuffed one inside of the young girl's privates and pushed another up against it. "We must staunch the flow. Do you understand?"

Elaina nodded.

"Stay with her. I will return momentarily. Let me go see if we have anything that will help the girl in this godforsaken place." He bobbed his head at Elaina before he wobbled out of the door, leaving the two girls alone.

Elaina stood staring at the door. He'd left her. In this room. She took the two steps necessary to reach the handle, finding it pushed with ease. She breathed a sigh of relief that he had not locked her in. To ease her nerves, she pulled the door open a crack before returning to Rory's side.

The poor lass. Elaina pulled her skirts down to cover her nakedness. Why had she not told anyone? She removed the girl's cap and tried to comb her fingers through her matted hair. Her freckles stood stark against her pale skin. She soothed and patted the girl in case she was in there somewhere, not wanting her to feel alone.

Soon the physician returned with a vial of salts and a cup of something. He stepped to the other side of the bed and waved the salts under Rory's nose, giving her a start. She blinked her eyes rapidly, as if attempting to clear her vision. "There. That's better," the physician said. "Now, young lady, I need you to drink this no matter how foul it tastes." To Elaina he said, "Lend me a hand."

They both slid an arm under Rory's slim shoulders and lifted her enough for the physician to force the concoction down Rory's throat.

She coughed and sputtered and fought against him, but she hadn't much fight left in her.

"I know this will be uncomfortable, so hold your cousin's hand." He nodded to Elaina.

Rory's gaze turned to her, but instead of the confusion Elaina expected to see, only appreciation graced the girl's face. She took Rory's chilled hand and squeezed it.

"I have to check to see if I have slowed the bleeding. Do you understand?" the physician asked.

Rory nodded, then closed her eyes as the man once again lifted her skirts to investigate.

A series of harrumphs and mutterings commenced from the opposite side of the table. Elaina looked up at the physician, who threw a bloody rag into the corner and then inserted another.

"I know it is a lot to ask of you, girl." The physician raised his gaze to Elaina. "I have soldiers that need tending to. Do you think you can remove this rag in a bit and insert another? Say a half hour? Keep at it. The flow has slowed already, but we need to watch it. If it picks up at all, tell the soldier outside the door to fetch me."

Elaina stared at him unblinking for a moment.

"Can you do it?"

"Y-yes, of course. Who do I ask for if I need you?"

"The general will do."

Elaina watched the squat man toddle from the room and wondered if that seemingly caring, thoughtful man could be the butcher the lieutenant had spoken of? The same man supposedly inflicting torture upon her friends and family, all the while saving the life of a girl he didn't even know? A chill slid down her spine. A Scottish lass too…not even an English one. Elaina's stomach sank, and she nearly collapsed to her knees. When she had answered him, she had done so with no effort to disguise her odd accent. He had not asked about it either.

"Are ye ill, miss?" Rory's quiet voice brought Elaina's attention back to her patient, the only person who mattered at the moment.

"No, my dear, not ill, just…*shaken* is all. How are you feeling?"

"Embarrassed."

Elaina pulled the girl's skirts down, as the general had left them up around her waist.

"Thank ye," Rory said with a weary smile. "That helps a wee bit, but I am mostly embarrassed that this happened at all. I should have stayed at my grandfather's house and perished, for I will surely go to hell for this, but I just couldnae…I couldnae bear the child, and I couldnae be alone." A tear slid down her cheek.

Elaina wiped the girl's tear away with her thumb. She looked like just that, a girl. Not a young woman, but a child, terrified and broken. "Shh, lass. Don't cry. I will not ask you any questions about how you came to be with child, but I dare say, I do not think you will go to hell. I am glad you came to me. Your presence may very well save the lives of people I care deeply for."

"I do hope that I am truly a help and no' a hindrance. If ye must leave quickly, dinna fret about leavin' me here. I dinna wish to slow ye down," Rory said, her voice still little more than a whisper.

"I will do my damndest not to leave you behind, I swear it," Elaina said, not knowing why she felt such a connection to the girl. She could not even fathom leaving her behind in that building full of strange men. "You rest. Gain your strength so that when we do make our move, you will be right there with us. You are a strong young lady, Rory… What is your surname?"

"Campbell."

Elaina involuntarily increased her grip on Rory's hand to keep from sinking to the floor.

The girl's panicked look seemed to push away the darkness edging into her vision. "What is it? What has happened?" She tried to sit up on the table.

"Nothing." Elaina offered the girl a smile that she hoped contained encouragement and not the incredible angst the mention of the Campbell name had brought forth. "I had a not-so-pleasant encounter with a Campbell once." That was as much as she wanted to tell the girl about the man who had nearly killed her on more than one occasion and who she held responsible for the loss of her own child, only months previous. That Campbell was dead. She had taken his head, which had in turn finally given her peace and satisfaction. If anyone was going to hell, it *might* be her, but it most assuredly *was* Robert Campbell. *May he burn for eternity.*

"Well, I've no' had such a pleasant time with the Campbells either, so dinna let the name give ye pause. There is no love lost between us. My grandfather was a Campbell."

That explains his horrific countenance.

"My mother was a Cameron. That is part of the hatred my grandfather held for me."

"No need to explain." Elaina patted the girl's hand. Ever since discovering the deception her adopted parents had hidden all of her life, she had been learning well the feuds between clans. The MacGregor blood that ran through her veins earned her no good graces from the Campbells. "Rest, Rory Campbell, so we may leave this place as soon as possible."

Rory nodded, her eyes drifting shut.

Elaina sighed and bent her head over the girl's hand. Her legs trembled with the strain of standing under the weight of all that had happened through the morning. The urgency of the situation with Rory, coupled with being inside an enemy stronghold, though free, was taking its toll. Elaina merely rested her head on the bed and prayed that Rory would recover and the men could concoct a plan to free the others.

Elaina gave a start and a little squeal when a firm hand came down on her shoulder.

The general chuckled. "A chair, my lady. I would rather not gain another patient today. God knows I have enough on my hands." He guided her to a chair someone had placed on the other side of the bed.

She collapsed onto it, exhaustion weighing heavily on her bones. She didn't know how long she had stood at Rory's side, nor how many rags she had changed, but the general confirmed that the bleeding had slowed considerably.

Taking up the stance that Elaina had vacated, the man spoke kindly to Rory, "There now. Much better. Do you think you could drink something, dear? Eat a bite? We need you to gain some strength before we let you loose on the world."

Rory nodded in response, her cheeks pink with color once again and not the sickly gray of the dying.

Elaina sighed with relief and leaned back in the chair, resting her head on the back of it.

The general patted her head like a small child as he moved behind her and toward the door. "A steward will return shortly with nourishment for your cousin, my lady. I will see you once more before you go."

Elaina sat with her eyes closed, head resting on the chair, and may have been near sleep.

"Mistress?" Rory asked.

"Yes?" Elaina raised her head and looked at her.

Rory had risen to a full seated position. "Why did that man call ye 'my lady'?"

Elaina sat straight up in her chair, warning bells clanging in her head. She wanted to stand and run, but the leaden hand of panic rendered her immobile except for the trembling that surged through her body. *Surely not. Surely the lieutenant would not.* She opened her mouth to respond, but Rory squealed with panic and dove off the other side of the bed as something was shoved in Elaina's mouth from behind. Then two sets of hands gripped her arms, dragging her unceremoniously over the back of the chair and toppling it with a loud crash. She struggled and fought as chaos erupted around her.

Rory screamed and clamored back over the table she had once rested upon. "What are ye doin'?" The young girl pried at the fingers of Elaina's captives. "Let her go! She's done no wrong. She saved my life."

"Committed no wrong? You naïve twit," one of Elaina's captives huffed as if Rory were simple in the head.

Elaina looked up into the sneering face of a British soldier.

"She is wanted for murder. You're lucky we do not detain you as well. But you are free to go. We have what we want."

"I cannae leave her." Rory shook her head with such vehemence that her matted, unruly curls bounced back and forth. "She saved my life," she said again, as if the guards had merely not heard her the first time and were not, in fact, ignoring her claim.

"Escort this street urchin to the door," the other soldier manhandling Elaina barked at a third in the hallway.

Elaina dislodged the rag from her mouth. "I don't know what you are talking about. Unhand me at once."

"Oh, ho, the lady denies the claim." One soldier retrieved the rag and shoved it so far back in her throat that she gagged on it and struggled for air. They attempted to drag her down the hallway as the other officer took Rory by the arm and marched her in the opposite direction.

Elaina dug in her heels, but they merely lifted her off her feet. She kicked and fought to no avail, then stopped when she caught sight of the soldier standing in a doorway at the end of the hall just before it made a sharp turn toward the area with the animalistic sounds they had heard earlier.

The lieutenant stood watching the commotion with an expression that looked chiseled from stone, his gaze flitting from the two soldiers carrying Elaina to her face. There was no change in his expression as they passed, but she held his gaze and tried to sear him with as much hate as she could. She continued to throw daggers over her shoulder before they rounded the corner. But then a sight caught her eye at the far end of the hall, toward the door leading out into the free world. Martin MacKenzie slid something into the pocket of his coat before casting her an expressionless glance over his shoulder as he exited behind a still struggling Rory.

Chapter Twenty

S HE HAD LOST THE FEELING in her hands some time ago. Raising up on the tips of her toes, she attempted to relieve some of the pressure from the ties binding her hands over her head to get blood pumping back through her fingers, if only for a moment.

The door opened, and two soldiers accompanied the general into the room.

"There has been a misunderstanding. Tell them. Tell them I was here with my cousin. Tell them that you saved her. This is all a mistake."

The general stared at her for several moments. "Unfortunately, there has been no mistake. Your accent says as much. That poor wretch is not your kin. And even if one could give you credit for saving the life of a common whore, one would not, for you are a traitor to the crown of England and Scotland, and the crimes you have committed against your country overrule any good you might have hoped to accomplish with your little rescue."

"You are mistaken," Elaina said with a sigh, her words ringing hollow to her own ears.

The general motioned to one of the men who rounded behind Elaina, then a blast of cold air hit her as he cranked open the only window in the room.

The other soldier strode to a bucket sitting in the corner.

Elaina closed her eyes to what she thought was coming.

"Now, my lady. Where is the rebel prince?" the general asked.

"I don't know. Just as I do not know why you insist on calling me by a title that I do not own. I am not a member of the upper crust of society, I assure you."

"That is not what our informant has told us."

Elaina opened her eyes to find the general's cold stare upon her. A shiver crept through her body as she remembered what the lieutenant had said about the man who tortured prisoners for information. Was she looking at him? She asked the man, "Your informant is wrong. I have no knowledge of where the prince is, nor am I a lady."

The general gave a nod, and the soldier sent the contents of the bucket slamming into her face, the force of the water and its frigid temperature taking her breath.

And it begins, she thought when she finally regained her capacity to breathe. Her heart sank as the soldier deposited the empty bucket on the floor and picked up another. Three. Three buckets of water. Certainly, she could withstand three.

"Once more." The general was certainly a man of few words.

"Once more," Elaina said, sarcasm decorating her words as she tried to fling a string of hair out of her face. "I. Do. Not. Know where the prince is. I cannot give you access to him. I have just as much knowledge as you, in fact probably less."

The bastard nodded, and his minion impaled her with another bucket of frigid water, thrown with such force that she felt as if it passed through her body. It took her longer to gather her composure that time and now her teeth chattered, which only enraged her.

"Do you deny that you are Lady Elaina Spencer, sister to Captain Spencer, the third Earl of Strafford, and the woman wanted for the murder of three British soldiers?" The general stood with his hands behind his back and his sidekick next to him with a fresh bucket of water.

Elaina laughed. "I am Elaina MacGregor MacKinnon, daughter of Thamas MacGregor, slain chief of the MacGregor clan. Elaina Spencer, daughter of the late Captain Edward Spencer and sister to Captain William Edward Spencer, third Earl of Strafford, no longer exists, and I have only killed one murdering scum of a British soldier in cold blood, a member of the Black Watch purely by accident, and the most evil member of the Black Watch there ever was…so far."

She turned an icy glare on the soldier holding the water bucket, who gave an evil grin before slamming the contents of the bucket in her face without a cue from his master. The force of the icy water took her feet out from under her and brought back memories of another time that she stood in almost the same precarious position.

Damn them. She coughed and sputtered while fighting to find her feet. When finally she did, it took another moment to regain the ability to open her eyes, and another moment to garner enough breath to speak. "Y-you will have to improve your interrogation s-skills, General, if you are to outdo y-your predecessors. I have withstood much more than some bloody cold water."

"A murderer and a foul mouth." The corner of the general's mouth quirked.

"And y-you consider yourself what? A savior? At least I didn't torture the ones I killed, and they bloody well deserved it."

"War is war, madam. We all do what we must to survive. Leave her hanging for a bit. I've others to attend to. I'm certain she will be hanging somewhere else before very long." The general turned on his heel and left the room.

Elaina resisted the urge to spit on the soldier before he left. The last time she had done such, she'd received a broken nose in return, and her eyes had swelled shut. She would rather like to keep her sight. She might need it. Certainly, Mr. Murray and Ainsley would come to her aid…somehow…in a building swimming with British soldiers who rather liked to torture Scots.

She sighed and fought to stop her chattering teeth, but the wind through the open window chewed through her bones. She turned her head to see how far away it was. Perhaps she could catch it with her boot and close it. The sunlight had all but disappeared from the sky, and the never-ending barrage of sleet seemed to have returned. But there, across the way at the edge of the forest, stood a figure, his wavy hair whipping in the gathering wind. Elaina could not tell where his gaze was focused until Ainsley raised a bow above his head in salute, and her heart soared.

Chapter Twenty-One

Hours later, the general's method of torture became her saving grace. She struggled to stay awake and on her feet despite the cold that had crept deep into her bones, and she would have sworn that every one of her teeth was cracked and broken from clashing together with such force. A sound at the window brought her around, and a figure draped in a black cloak tossed in a long sack that landed with a soft plop before he crawled through. When his feet touched the floor with nary a sound, he flung off his hood and gave her a bright smile.

"M-Mr. M-Murray."

"Ye seem disappointed. Would ye like me to leave?"

"If y-you do, I w-will have your head. I w-was expecting Ainsley is all."

"Aye, well." Mr. Murray crossed the room and cut the ties holding her to the ceiling, and she collapsed into his arms. "He is attendin' to other matters. Now, stand still and hold out your hands."

Her entire being trembled from the cold and the pain of being hung from the ceiling like a calf for slaughter for God knew how many hours.

"Well, quit movin' so," he scolded.

"Easier s-said than d-done, Mr. M-Murray. Can you not hit a m-moving target? I-I would have thought y-you better with a knife." She crooked a smile at him.

He chuckled as he severed the ties binding her wrists and massaged her hands.

Elaina gritted her teeth against the stabbing sensation of her blood returning to them. "Surely, we've no time for this. W-we must be going." She nodded toward the still-open window.

"Here." Mr. Murray pulled a black woolen cloak out of the sack he had tossed in and wrapped it around her shoulders. "We will be exiting through a different route."

"Are y-you out of your mind? F-freedom is mere steps away. To exit a d-different way would be s-suicide."

"Take a wee nip." He handed her a flask. "Warm yerself, lass. We need your hands steady if ye are to stay alive. I brought ye gifts." Mr. Murray pulled a bow and a quiver of arrows from the sack that just kept giving.

The whisky from the flask burned as it seared down Elaina's throat and into her belly. "Y-you really are out of your m-mind. You want me to go out there with that when we could g-go out the damned window?"

"Believe it or not, we had enough sense to devise a plan of action. We are awaiting a signal. Then the rooms we seek are at the far end of the hall to the left. No pistols. They will attract unwanted attention. You will follow me and watch the hallway to the right and kill anyone who comes around the corner."

"What k-kind of signal are we waiting on and who c-can we expect to be alerted to our actions?"

"You will know. Now, warm your hands." Mr. Murray stood by the door, waiting for whatever was supposed to happen.

"How did you know what room I was in?" Ah, the whisky was doing the trick. Her teeth had at least stopped chattering enough for her not to stutter. "I thought I saw Ainsley earlier at the wood's edge." Elaina rubbed her hands vigorously on the woolen cloak he had adorned her with.

"The lieutenant."

"What? That traitor? He is the one who turned me over to that-that *monster*." Elaina all but spit the words.

"'Twas no' he. He swears it. He was just as surprised as ye when he saw them marchin' ye through the buildin'. If it were he, do ye think he would have supplied us with the information we needed? Where to find ye and where to find Auld Ruadh and Ru—"

An explosion rocked the building, and Elaina ducked to the ground as if attacked by cannon fire.

Mr. Murray held up his hand, slightly cracked the door open, and put an ear to it.

How he could hear anything was beyond Elaina. Her ears rang with the aftereffects of the blast.

A moment that felt like a lifetime passed before he gave her a nod, then eased the door open and slipped through the gap, out into the hallway. She followed shortly after, nocking an arrow in her bow. He pointed in the direction she should watch as if she did not know her right from her left. She rolled her eyes as she followed him down the long corridor. Her gaze flicked between the direction they moved in and behind them, the way they had come. The muffled sound of orders being barked met her ears, and she set her sights on the end of the hall, preparing herself. The deep thud of boots against a door brought her attention back behind her, and she glanced long enough to see Ainsley, MacKenzie, and, *good heavens*, Rory stumbling through a splintered doorway, Ainsley with an ax in his hand. MacKenzie shot her a look that sent chills down her spine before he began helping Ainsley demolish another door. Elaina backed up slowly and steadily, following Mr. Murray, but with her sight once again trained down the hallway they had just traversed. With a few grunts and lots of racket, the door beside them splintered open and Mr. Murray disappeared inside.

Elaina put her back to the doorjamb where she could watch behind them and see inside the room. The sight brought her up short. Ruske, the Calhoun, the beast of a man, lay sprawled out naked with his arms and legs tied to four corners of the table. She kept her eyes from the most intimate parts of him. Blood matted the side of his head. His eyes were swollen shut. Burn marks littered his body like a pox. Where no burn marks existed were slits, pink lines etched upon the white of his skin with a dried crusty substance dusting most of them.

Donald Murray seemed in shock himself as he stood by the beast's side. He touched the crusty substance and brought it to his tongue, then glanced up at Elaina. "Salt."

They had burned him, beat him, cut him, and rubbed salt into his wounds. *Dear God*, she thought, willing herself not to vomit.

"Ruske?" Mr. Murray said.

Elaina thought the man was surely dead, but he groaned in response. She didn't know whether to be elated or horrified. Glancing back at the direction she was to be guarding, she stifled a scream at the sight of the lieutenant mere feet away and running straight for her.

"Look lively, my lady. The natives are growing suspicious." He cocked his head toward the direction he had come and then disappeared into the room with Mr. Murray and the Calhoun.

Her racing heart beat against her chest as if the organ were trying to break itself free. *Get ahold of yourself. He is obviously not the person who betrayed you.* But Elaina had a sinking suspicion who the culprit was, and it did not sit easy on her soul.

The lieutenant tried to help Mr. Murray hoist the giant off the table. Ruske's arms hung limply, and Elaina realized they had been pulled from their sockets.

She didn't have time to dwell on the matter, however, because a redcoat chose that moment to come careening around the corner, and she let her arrow loose, imbedding it deep into his thigh. He collapsed to the ground as she sighted another arrow. She was certain he'd been close enough that the tip had penetrated the bone. If he were a smart man, he would stay on the ground.

With another swift glance behind her, she saw Ainsley and MacKenzie exiting a room two doors down. The wilted clansman in their arms never raised his head. His red hair, dull and matted, hung in strings about his face. They dragged him toward the splintered door at the end of the hall.

Auld Ruadh.

The redcoat she'd impaled with her arrow had stopped screaming at the opposite end of the hallway. Instead, he pleaded for help, and Elaina didn't even have to look to recognize the voice that answered. She turned her gaze back down the hallway.

The general glanced over at her as she raised her bow. "Don't do it, madam." He held up his arms. "I am unarmed. How would it look to shoot an unarmed man?"

"Probably as disgusting as it is to torture one, General." The arrow landed directly in his round belly.

He dropped to his knees, his cries of pain intermingling with those of the man already on the floor. Her second arrow pierced his right shoulder, and when he bent over screaming, she could see the point sticking out of his back. She had taken aim and was waiting for him to raise his head so she could shoot him through the eye, ending their short time together.

"Elaina!"

The panic in Ainsley's voice brought her around in time to see Martin MacKenzie with murder in his eyes and his dirk fisted in his hand as if to plunge it into her back.

A shot rang out, and MacKenzie fell dead in the hallway. The lieutenant remained standing behind him.

Elaina grabbed the wall for support.

"No time for that now, my lady. The noise will bring soldiers. Go. Your friends are being loaded into a wagon. Run!" The lieutenant shoved her around him and down the hall, into Ainsley's waiting arms. "Go!" He sprinted away from them with his pistol still smoking in his hand. He yelled, "I've killed one!" to the sound of boots pounding the far hall.

Elaina stopped before disappearing into the night and let her final arrow fly, sending the general sprawling backward, as far as his fat form would let him. The feathered end of the arrow pointed at the ceiling. Her aim was true. She had hit her mark.

Ainsley dragged her stumbling through the dark, all but carrying her, and shoved her up into the back of a black rectangle. A pair of arms caught her and hauled her the rest of the way in as the wagon lurched into motion, sending her tumbling into *the chest of…*

The person giggled and sat her upright.

"Rory?"

"Aye, mistress," Rory whispered.

"You are feeling better, then?" Elaina asked.

"Some. Thanks to you." Rory squeezed her hand.

"No. Not to me. I could have gotten everyone killed. How stupid was I to think I could waltz into the lion's den and they would not discover the truth of my identity? The general…the general saved your life." How could one man be two different people? One part saving lives and the other ending them. Not just ending them but ending them in a most horrific manner. The wagon lurched, one side of it dipping as if hitting a large rut or as if it had run off the road completely.

The dark mass beside her let out a groan.

"Shh," she whispered to Ruske as the wagon bumped and banged over the frozen ground at a much more rapid pace than it ought to go.

"Who is it?" He turned his head toward the sound of her voice.

"Elaina MacKinnon," she said, brushing some of the matted hair from his face.

"About damn time ye returned the favor, lass. Ye certainly took yer time about it."

Elaina snorted, wiping a tear from her cheek. She would never hear the end of it if he knew she was crying. Ruske had saved her hide on not one but two occasions, both times from the clutches of the Campbells. "You be quiet. Rest. We will have help for you soon."

She prayed she was not lying, then turned to the lump on the other side of her and tucked the blankets around him as well. She lay her lips upon his forehead and let her tears slide into his matted and stinking hair. Fear's icy hand squeezed at her heart when the man did not move nor make a sound. She prayed God would spare Auld Ruadh's life.

"Thank you, Lieutenant," she whispered into the night, for even if Auld Ruadh died, at least he would be with those who loved him and not in that beastly place.

Chapter Twenty-Two

THE SUN WAS NEAR TO rising by the time the jolting wagon pulled into a sparse rebel camp. Men and women who looked no better than Elaina felt watched the new arrivals as they passed by. They had arrived none too soon. Elaina and Rory lay huddled together between the two patients, trying to keep everyone from freezing to death. That would be a terrible turn of events. Escape torture and certain death only to freeze to death on the way to freedom.

The sky shone a grayish pink in the east as the sun tried to peek its way between the ever-present slate clouds. The wagon pulled to a stop in front of an old kirk, and Ainsley leaped from the back of his horse and ran inside. When he returned accompanied by four men, Elaina's heart jumped into her throat at the sight of one. Tall and broad, although with a bit more hair than when last she'd seen him.

She threw herself off the back of the wagon and into Calum's arms, burying her face in his neck. "I knew you would come for me." She snuggled her cheek against his newly grown beard.

"Never doubt it, hen. I would go to the ends of the earth. I would go to hell and fight *an t-seann diabhal* himself to bring ye back to me."

"You haven't much faith in my soul, have you, if you think you would have to follow me into hell?" She laughed and tugged at his beard. "What's this?"

"Warmth." He rubbed his chin against her cheek. "Do ye no like it, then?"

"I love it. 'Tis quite red." It was a bright contrast to the dark brown curls peeking out from under his slouched bonnet. "Red. Auld Ruadh…"

Elaina scrambled out of Calum's arms and to the ground beside two clansmen and Aron and Mr. Murray as they removed Calum's uncle from the wagon.

Her feet skidded to a halt, and she stared in horror before turning to the far side of the wagon and retching onto the frozen earth. Auld Ruadh was a shell of his former self. Emaciated and gaunt, his reddish hair held far more silver than it had before. God help her…and him. They had gouged out his left eye. Calum slipped his arms around her as Ruske was unloaded and carried into the kirk as well.

"It is just awful," Elaina whispered to Calum. "I cannot bear it."

"Nor can I." His voice was hard and cold, but the kiss he placed on the top of her head was gentle and full of compassion. He led her inside what once was a stone house of worship but now held the injured from the last battle.

"What of Bridgette? Does anyone know her whereabouts?" Elaina asked about Ruske's wife, who had been Elaina's only confidante and friend during her time as a prisoner in the Campbell keep.

"She is there." Calum dipped his head to the black-haired lass leaning over Ruske's body, weeping.

"I must go to her. You go to your uncle. I am uncertain if he is even alive." Her voice broke on the words.

Calum kissed her on the forehead, his whiskers soft and his touch soothing. He squeezed her hand before loping off to his uncle's lifeless form sprawled on a wooden bench. Men with various injuries occupied several such seats in the kirk, and women scurried about tending to them.

Elaina lay her hand upon Bridgette's back.

She turned and threw herself into Elaina's arms. "Oh, God, Elaina. What did they do? Why would they…" Bridgette's questions disappeared into wrenching sobs.

"Madam, ye may want to take yer friend outside for this," a stocky gentleman said to Elaina over Ruske's prone body. Another man was pouring laudanum down the patient's throat. "I am going to put his arms back in their correct place. I'll need a hand, Murray. Ye too, MacEwan. Ye will have to help hold 'im."

Elaina nodded, casting Calum an encouraging glance across the room before wrapping an arm around Bridgette's waist. She spied Rory standing just inside the door to the kirk, looking somewhat dazed at the surrounding bustle. She grabbed the girl's hand as she and Bridgette passed. "Come. I think we need a drink. And if there is any food to be had in this place, I need some of that too."

Elaina made introductions as they walked out into the dismal winter day.

The sun had only teased them with its presence earlier. The sleet had won the battle yet again. Would it never stop?

Bridgette led the way through the haphazard camp. After procuring a flask of whisky and three bannocks, the women found a quiet corner in a three-walled tent enclosure. Out of the weather, they collapsed onto the ground. Men and a few women lay or sat about under the protection from the sleet. Their body heat permeated the chill in the covered space, warming it to a bearable temperature.

"How did he come to be captured?" Elaina asked, trying to savor the stale bannock. She wanted to devour it, but they had few supplies, it seemed.

"There was an ambush on the way to Carlisle. Several were captured. How can men be so cruel to another human? What kind of animal does that to a m-man?" Bridgette burst into tears again.

Elaina let her weep and wiped away a few tears of her own. "I cannot answer your questions. This is a cruel, cruel world we live in. There is nothing pretty about war."

"I wish we had never come." Bridgette sniffled, wiping her tears on a dirty piece of fabric she used for a handkerchief.

"I understand that sentiment," Elaina said. She wrapped her arms around Bridgette and rocked her like she would a child, letting her friend relieve all of her grief and frustrations on her shoulder.

Rory watched the interaction for a few moments while chewing her lip, then found something of interest on the hem of her oversized fur coat.

Elaina looked up to find Ainsley zigzagging his way through rebels who were sitting and chatting and others who were lying prone, attempting to catch a few moments of sleep. He dropped his lanky frame beside Elaina.

"How did it go?" Elaina asked, not sure she wanted the answers after taking in Ainsley's almost green pallor.

"They are back in place. They are attending to his burns and cuts now. That was enough for me. I'm not sure why I keep getting the job of holding people down." He accepted the flask of whisky from Bridgette, while casting Rory a brief glance.

Her pallor that had grown pale with Ainsley's words now flushed crimson up to the edge of her knitted cap. She, once again, found something of interest on her coat.

"Speaking of holding people down, how was Rhona when you left Duart Manor?" Elaina asked. "How did the procedure go?"

"Well enough, I suppose, but we didna wait around long. Left Caitir and Isobel in charge of things. God kens they have their hands full wi' wee Jamie." Ainsley gave a snort and a shake of the head. "We had to turn around once and take the lad back. Slowed us down three hours. Had to catch the wee mongrel before we could return him. No' an easy feat. Had packed him a sack of dried fruits and meat. Stole Mrs. Davies's best knife as well. He will be a fine warrior when he comes of age."

That didn't surprise Elaina in the least. What she wouldn't do for a smelly little boy hug at this moment. "The prince? Is he in this camp as well?"

"Nay," Ainsley said. "He and the rest of the clans have gone toward Inverness."

"Inverness? They have retreated out of England?"

Ainsley nodded.

"And Cumberland?"

"He is the reason for the retreat to Inverness. He is pursuing the Jacobite army with a vengeance."

His words sent chills down Elaina's spine.

Calum entered the enclosure, stepping across those who slept with determined strides. "Mistress Calhoun?"

"Please, Bridgette will do," she said as she rose to her feet.

"Very well. Bridgette, ye may visit yer husband. I must warn ye, he is quite drunk. The physician was successful in reinserting his shoulders, but they will need time to heal, and he may not regain the full motion of his arms. Only time will tell. The physician is more concerned with the burns. If they cause fever…"

"I understand," Bridgette said. With a nod to the group, she hurried from the tent to return to her husband's side.

"How can anyone be so brutal?" Elaina asked, sickened at the thought of what the English had put Ruske through.

"War makes animals out of men," Calum said. "It hardens them. They do what they must to win. To survive."

Elaina turned to the lad next to her, who bested her by more than a head. "I don't believe I thanked you properly, Ainsley, for coming to our aid and for helping to free these men. You as well, Rory."

"No thanks needed. They are my clansmen. Highlanders. My brothers," Ainsley said.

Rory merely dipped her head to Elaina.

"Did ye rid this world of the bastard who stole my wife? The lieutenant?" Calum asked.

"Nay." Ainsley cast Elaina a glance. "If not for him, the rescue would not have been a success."

Calum studied the three of them, confusion furrowing his brow.

"Not only did he help to save Auld Ruadh and the Calhoun, but he saved my life as well…from Martin MacKenzie." Elaina said.

Calum stared at her for a moment before his entire body tensed into stone and his eyes grew dark with fury. "MacKenzie?" he growled.

"Aye," Ainsley said. "He was going to knife her in the back."

Calum's hands clenched into fists, his knuckles white with the strain. "I'll kill him," Calum growled

"It is too late for that," Elaina said. "The lieutenant took care of that little matter. He shot him."

Calum looked from Elaina to Ainsley to Rory in disbelief.

Rory nodded her affirmation.

Calum let out a long breath as the tension eased from his shoulders. His gaze came back to rest on Elaina. "I am deeply sorry, Elaina. I should have stayed at the manor. I shouldna have gone into town."

Elaina shook her head and placed her fingers against his lips. "None of this was your fault, Calum MacKinnon. It is over, and I am none the worse for it. Now we know the truth of MacKenzie, and he is gone from this world and can never harm us again."

"Aye, that may be true, but Freya and her mother, Osla, are still out there. We must be ever vigilant. Now, it seems ye've much to tell me about yer little adventure," he said, wrapping her up in his arms. "But first, I need to get ye somewhere safe and warm, with food and a bed."

Elaina tilted her head back and searched his hazel eyes, which were clouded with worry. "I am safe, Calum. No need to fret any longer." She stood on her toes and laid a gentle kiss upon his lips, hoping to erase the all the doubts that lingered in his gaze. Pulling away, she whispered, "I've never kissed a man with a beard before, 'tis quite interesting."

"No? How many men have you kissed, Mrs. MacKinnon?"

"Never you mind. Come here."

Ainsley grunted. "That's enough for me, thank ye kindly. She needs rest." He gave Calum a pointed look and nodded to Elaina before he too left the tent.

She ran her fingers through his beard, cupping his jaw. Back in his arms at long last, her heart was happy, even if the cruelties of war troubled her thoughts.

Their lips met again, and Elaina was lost in the softness of his beard against her chin, in the way that his hand ever so gently stroked her cheek, as if she were made of the finest porcelain and he was afraid she would crack under the weight of his fingers.

The whistles of the men surrounding them in the tent brought her back to their present surroundings. A surge of heat in her cheeks made her bury her face into Calum's plaid. His laugh rumbled in his chest, and he squeezed her to him, alighting a kiss upon her head.

Elaina chanced a peek at Rory, who also looked embarrassed but with an amused grin decorating her pink face.

"There is a place nay far from here where I ken we would be welcome and could gain a bit of privacy." He growled the final words toward the surrounding men, piercing them with a steely glare.

That only fueled the fire. The men that dotted the floor of the makeshift shelter merely laughed under Calum's baleful glare. At this moment Elaina was thankful she knew as little Gaelic as she did so that she could not understand the obviously tawdry remarks the Highlanders hooted and hollered.

"Rory?" Elaina turned a pleading look on her husband as she snatched up the girl's hand, drawing her close to her side. "She cannot stay here alone. And what if—"

"She will go with us, *mo chridhe*. Dinna fash. Ye can tell me how ye found this scrappy young lass on the way. I've heard ye were a great help in rescuing my uncle, Rory. I owe you a debt."

Elaina wasn't sure that Rory's face could flush any redder.

She ducked her head away from Calum's compliment. "Ye owe me nothing, sir. I would have died myself if no' for yer wife."

"It seems there are debts flying all around." Calum stood and pulled Elaina to her feet, thereby pulling Rory up as well.

"Where are we going, Calum?" Elaina's feet did not want to move. Too many encounters with the enemy ran through her mind.

"There will be no redcoats where we are headed," Calum replied to reassure the two uneasy women.

"Let us go see about our patients before we take leave." Elaina tugged on

Calum's arm and linked her other arm with Rory, then the three made their way back to the kirk and its ailing men.

The sun had risen somewhere behind the scuttling clouds, its form hidden but its presence creating a pale gray hue that covered the dismal surroundings about her.

"Ye two go ahead while I gather the horses." Calum pecked Elaina on the forehead before shooing the two women toward the stone kirk.

Elaina stopped at a crackling fire on the way where a black cauldron hung over the flames. A woman stood beside it, her face drawn over the sharp edges of her cheekbones. She attempted a smile as Elaina and Rory approached. "Are ye in need of nourishment?" she asked.

"I know two injured men who are, if you would be so kind," Elaina said.

"There's nay much nourishment in this pot, but we've no' much else." The words exhaled on the woman's breath, and she looked as if she might collapse from exhaustion where she stood as she filled two metal tankards and handed them to Elaina.

"Let me help," Rory said, taking one of them out of Elaina's grasp. "I feel useless followin' ye 'round everywhere." She sniffed the contents of the tankard as the women entered the kirk. "Whew." She turned her head and coughed. "I'm no' sure I'll be helpin' if I deliver this reekin' brew."

"That bad?" Elaina took a small sip of the one she held. Her resulting coughing fit drew the attention of the injured. She wiped at her watering eyes. "Are you comfortable with the Calhoun? His bark is worse than his bite," she croaked out between gasps for air.

"Aye. His wife seems a good lass." Rory eyed the couple across the room.

"She won't let him bite you." Elaina chuckled. "I'll see to Auld Ruadh."

Rory glanced at Elaina as if sensing the hesitation in her voice. "He doesna look like he will bite either." She nudged her with her elbow.

"No, he doesn't. Not hard anyway."

Rory disappeared toward Ruske and Bridgette.

Elaina approached her uncle. "I brought you some…" She looked down at the tankard in her hands, not sure what to call the liquid within. It did not resemble soup much. No broth. Just hot water and a few bits of root vegetables floating through along with something that could scald your insides. Rations were low. Extremely low. She handed the cup to Auld Ruadh, whose hand nearly shook the contents all over himself. "Here, let me help." She sank down onto the ground beside him, reaching out to steady his hand.

"They only took my eye, no' my wits," he growled at her, snatching his hand away.

Elaina arched an eyebrow at him. "I know you are starved, but you needn't bite my head off. I still need it."

Auld Ruadh gave her a penitent look with his remaining eye. Someone had made a patch for the other out of a piece of MacKinnon tartan. "Och. Ye ken I didna mean anythin'. I'm just no' an invalid. Ye should be helping the Calhoun. He's worse off."

"I sent Rory over. Besides, he has his wife to see to him. So, you have me. I'm sorry to disappoint."

Auld Ruadh gave a deep sigh and reached for her hand, giving it a squeeze. "Ye ken I love ye, lass."

"I know. I love you as well." Elaina's eyes welled with tears at the thought of how close she had come to losing her confidant. The man who was her voice of reason when in turmoil. Caitir was good at keeping her in her place, but Auld Ruadh calmed the storms that arose in her life.

"Now, stop." He growled again. "If ye have to cry, dinna do it in front of me. No tears on my behalf. It's only a bloody eye. I have another. That one wasna working so well, anyway. They did me a favor, is all."

Elaina snickered. "Drink your…whatever that is."

"Goat piss? That's what it smells like."

"Pretty much what it tastes like as well."

"When have you ever tasted goat piss?" He cocked an amused brow at her.

"We put it in all of our soups in the colonies. It's considered a delicacy."

"Truly?" Auld Ruadh stared at her.

"No. Not truly. Drink it up, or I *will* feed you goat piss. Calum is taking us… Well, I don't know where we are going, but I want you to remain on your best behavior." She leaned forward, taking his head gently in her hands, and pressed her lips against his forehead. She felt him swallow hard. Leaning back, she said, "Do you want us to take you with us?"

"Nay, lass." He gave the slightest shake of his head, as if it pained him to move it. "I'm in no shape to travel. Bumping around on the back of a horse might do me in. I'll stay here with the rest of 'em and build my strength. We've much more to accomplish."

"Not anytime soon." She nailed him with a pointed look. "You rest and heal. Let the rest of them worry about Cumberland."

"Bit bossy, aren't we?"

"It'll get worse if you don't behave. I'm going to speak to Ruske before we leave." Elaina leaned over and kissed the grizzled old man on the cheek before she pushed herself up off the floor and crossed the room, speaking to each of the injured men as she went.

Ruske had raised himself to a seated position by the time she made it to his side. The man's face contrasted with the dark blanket he was wrapped up in. His ghostly pale form was covered with a sheen of sweat, but he managed a smile when she walked up.

"You needn't get up on my behalf," Elaina said, sitting beside him on the bench.

"I'm tired of lyin' 'round anyhow. Been doin' it for days now." Ruske winced as he adjusted the loose fabric over his body.

"I am so sorry," Elaina whispered.

"Why? Was it ye who ambushed us and beat us over the head? Was it ye who did this?" He waved a hand about his torso. "No. It wasn't. It was the bastard lobsterbacks, and I mean to make them pay. Every last one of them."

William's face flitted through Elaina's mind, and she prayed that her brother and Ruske never crossed paths. She didn't know if she could convince him not to hurt William if they did meet up.

"Well, I am sorry, nonetheless. I'm sorry we didn't find you sooner."

"Aye. That would have been nice. Took yer time about it. Payback I reckon for the Campbells."

"You rescued me from the Campbells."

"Yes, but before. Ye ken? Ye were in their clutches for way too long. Speakin' of, ye owe me one more debt."

"One more?" Elaina looked him over, thinking he must be delirious. "I rescued you from the redcoats when you and Calum got yourselves arrested. You would think that you would be more careful after nearly being hung for a crime you didn't commit."

"Aye, ye would think that, wouldn't ye?"

"You saved me from Robert Campbell in the gardens at Dalmunshire Castle. We are even."

"Tsk, tsk, tsk. How easy we forget."

"I haven't a clue what you are talking about."

"Who do ye think found ye roaming the halls of the Campbell keep where ye no' should have been? Who do ye think put yer arse back in bed where it belonged?"

"That was you who knocked me on the head?"

"Who'd ye think it was, a faery?"

"Well, I thought it possibly Erroll at the time, but I was wrong about that, to say the least."

"Aye, betrayin' rat bastard."

"No worries. Caitir stabbed him in the eye with a dirk during the little skirmish between the MacGregors, the Campbells, and the redcoats."

Ruske chuckled, his features softening as if conjuring up a fond memory. "Ah, good for her."

"I never thought about it again, I suppose," Elaina said, absently rubbing the back of her head. "Did you have to hit me so hard?"

"That's all the thanks I get for saving yer arse?"

"I may owe you another rescue, but you have reminded me I also owe you two knocks on the head. Twice you have clonked me on the skull and knocked me unconscious."

"Well, if ye would keep yer arse out of trouble, I would quit havin' to save it."

"You two stop bickering like children," Bridgette said from her seat on the other side of Ruske.

"Ah, we're just layin' odds on who is goin' to have to save who next." Ruske pecked his wife on the forehead.

"It better not be either one of ye. Are ye no finished, Ruske? Have ye no been through enough? Let us go home and live to fight another day," Bridgette pleaded. She picked his hand up from his lap and, light as a feather, ran her fingers over the burn marks.

"There may no' be another day, love. If the Jacobites are no' victorious, none of us may survive. We need all the men we can muster, and I'll no' let a few wounds be my undoin'. Look around ye, lass. Our numbers are dwindlin'. Men are givin' up and returnin' to their farms. But there will be no farmin' if the reckonin' comes, and there will be a reckonin' if we are no' on the winnin' side of history."

Bridgette looked away, her eyes brimming with tears. She swallowed them down before turning back. "Ye are one of the most stubborn men I have ever known, Ruske Calhoun."

"Would ye still love me if I wasna?" He pecked a kiss on the end of her nose.

"No, I dinna suppose so, but here, drink up. I brought ye more whisky. The men said ye'll be mighty sore when ye sober up."

"I'll no' have it. I want to feel the pain," he growled, his teasing voice taking on an unsettling tone that made Elaina's skin crawl. "I want to remember what they did to me, and I'll no' suffocate it with drink. May it raise a fire in me that cannae be put out by anything other than death."

Chapter Twenty-Three

H AVING PROCURED THREE HORSES, CALUM gathered Elaina, Rory, and Ainsley before setting the steeds in the direction of wherever it was Calum had in mind. Elaina traveled with a fair bit of guilt, hating to leave their injured comrades. And how could she sleep in a warm bed when the rest of the men slept on the cold, hard ground and starved?

"Why do ye no' quit frettin' and tell me how ye found yer friend here?" Calum cocked his head back toward Ainsley and Rory, who rode in silence behind the couple. "And why are ye soaked through to yer underthings and havenae told me? Ye'll catch yer death."

Elaina realized she still wore the black cloak Mr. Murray had given her and when Calum had hugged her, that was all he felt. Not the soggy woolen mess underneath it, until he had lifted her into the saddle.

"Oh, where to begin?" Elaina snuggled up against his comforting form.

"The beginnin' is a fine place."

"Yes, well…" Elaina filled him in on all the lurid details of her horrid adventure. When she reached the part of her story that involved the first town she had stopped in, the road had widened, and Rory and Ainsley now rode abreast of Elaina and Calum.

Ainsley cleared his throat and shifted uncomfortably in the saddle before the group fell into strangled silence after Elaina told them the horrific details of the Scots' revenge on the British soldiers after a couple of them had almost raped the innkeeper's daughter, and then her and the lieutenant's harrowing escape.

Elaina cleared her throat. "Yes, well, enough about severed members and their resting places. After that is when the lieutenant took ill, and that is how I happened upon Rory." She relayed that tale and how terrible Rory's grandfather had been but skirted around the details of how they actually got inside of the military hospital, only telling Calum that Rory felt ill and fainted. If the girl wanted to talk about it, she would. It was not Elaina's story to tell. She wasn't sure just exactly how much Ainsley had comprehended of the issue. He had not accompanied them into the hospital when Rory was treated. Besides, it was no one's business but Rory's, the poor girl.

Elaina glanced over to where she continued her ride in silence alongside Ainsley. If she hadn't heard the girl speak before, she would have sworn the girl was mute. Not a single peep escaped her lips. She kept her gaze lowered, watching the ground in front of her horse.

"…and that is how I am now soaked to the bone," Elaina said upon completing her tale.

Calum sat stiff as a board behind her, and Elaina could feel the anger radiating off of him in waves.

Ainsley, apparently, felt the rage as well. "The general now rests in the pit of hell, however," he said with a note of pride in his voice. "She made sure of that. Dinna cross that woman, Calum. She is a dead shot."

Calum chuckled. "Have nay fear of that, young man. I like my member just where it is."

A strangled snort came from Rory's vicinity.

Ainsley and Calum's heads turned at the same time. It was the first sound she had made since they'd begun their ride.

She glared at them and shrugged her shoulders before turning her gaze back to the road in front of them.

"Well, at least we ken she has a sense of humor," Ainsley said.

Rory's face flushed pink, and she buried her chin farther into her coat.

⁂

Elaina jerked awake with a start as their horses came to a stop. She blinked at the building in front of her with its full front windows that looked in on a group of diners. Familiarity crept into her sleep-muddled brain, and she turned her face toward her husband's. "This is where you have brought me?" She could hear the panic rising in her voice.

"Ye are trembling, *mo chridhe*. What is the trouble? Ye have been here before?"

"Y-yes. Lieutenant P-Perry…" Elaina couldn't finish her thought, for Gordie's hulking frame filled the doorway.

Calum gripped her tighter around the waist, pulling her back into the curve of his chest.

"The lieutenant…did he hurt ye, Elaina?" he growled in her ear. "Did he—"

"No." Elaina shook her head with vehemence as the look of recognition passed across Gordie's face. "But the man that stands before us thinks I am Lieutenant Perry's wife."

"Well, let us set him straight, shall we? And put yer mind at ease." Calum swung with ease from the back of the horse and approached Gordie. The two men spoke in low tones, standing in front of the door to the inn.

Elaina glanced around at the small village. Not a redcoat in sight. Word must have gotten around quickly about the retaliation put forth by the citizens of the town. Something touched her leg, and she stifled a scream and came damn close to falling off the other side of the horse.

"Whoa. Easy there." Calum's large hand wrapped around her ankle, pulling her more upright.

"I'm not a horse." She raised an eyebrow at him.

"Then stop being skittish as one, and let me help ye down. There are nay but friendly faces here, *mo chridhe*. Ye are safe."

With a sigh, Elaina let him help her down from the steed and was not a little surprised to find that her legs did not want to hold her.

Rory scrambled down as Ainsley took two steps in her direction to offer the same courtesy. She kept her gaze cast to the ground, managing on her own.

Ainsley gave Elaina a grin and a shrug, taking no offense at the girl's timid manner.

Calum steadied Elaina with an arm around her waist.

The same man who the lieutenant had been so callous to on their first visit took the reins of two of the horses, and a small, ragged child of about eight years or so took the remaining one. The man gave no sign of recognition, though his eyes lingered on her for a moment before he and the child led the horses away.

Once inside, Gordie led the group up the stairs, opening three doors adjacent to each other.

"Madam, if you please." He extended a small bow to Rory.

The girl flushed and pulled her oversized fur coat tighter around her before giving him a small nod and disappearing into the first room.

Gordie then offered the middle room to Elaina and Calum, and Ainsley, the one to the left of it.

"Let me just start that fire for ye." Gordie made to move toward the hearth, but Calum laid a hand on his arm. "I have it, Gordie. I'm certain ye've other things more important to tend to."

"Aye, well…if ye're certain?" Gordie seemed torn between the hearth and the door. At Calum's nod, he broke into one of his welcoming smiles. "Good enough, then, I shall check on my Maggie and be certain she is mixing something up to fill yer gullet." He turned and lumbered from the room.

"I'm going to check on Rory while you do that," Elaina said as Calum fiddled with the kindling already in the hearth, awaiting a spark to bring it to life.

"Ye are concerned about her. What has happened to the girl?" Calum swiveled on his heel to look at Elaina while his deft hands still sifted and stacked the kindling tighter.

"I have no idea. That is part of the problem. I don't know what to do for her because I don't know what has happened."

Calum nodded with a frown etched upon his face. "See to the lass, *mo chridhe*, but return to me quickly."

Elaina crossed the room and kissed him on the forehead.

Calum grabbed her, pulling her down onto his bended knee, and took her mouth in a crushing assault that washed all thoughts from her head.

When he pulled away, her fingers grazed her bruised lips, and she fought to open her eyes. "What was that for?" she whispered.

"I thought ye had been gone so long from my arms that ye forgot where and what a kiss was meant to be. I was only reminding ye."

"Well," Elaina's voice rasped, and she cleared her throat. "You accomplished that task well enough."

Calum chuckled and pecked her softly this time. "Go. See about the girl."

Elaina patted his chest before rising onto legs that once again wobbled, but for a different reason. The man was intoxicating. She rapped lightly on Rory's door, and a moment later it was opened by Rory, still wearing the oversized coat.

"I came to see your room and how you fare after our journey?" Elaina said. "I haven't had an opportunity to speak to you about how you are feeling."

Rory opened the door wider to allow Elaina entrance. "I am feeling well enough. Tired is all."

Closing the door behind her, Elaina was pleased to see that a fire already burned in the hearth and someone had added a few logs. Her room was still quite chilled, which she assumed was the reason for the coat. "Does it suit you? The room?" She stood by the fire with her frozen fingers held out over it. She might never be warm again.

"Aye, verra much," Rory replied, standing by Elaina and doing the same. "'Tis too much. I should have remained at the camp with the others."

"Nonsense. I could not abandon you with a bunch of strangers."

"Ye were willin' to send me to a home of unwed mothers."

The statement was no more than a whisper, but it hit Elaina with enough force to nearly knock her over.

"You heard?"

"Aye."

"Well, that was before. A lot of things have happened since then. You helped with the rescue, and you've been through a great deal of trauma. You needn't be sleeping on the cold, hard ground. Rory, you deserve more for risking your life and your health to help free us. You should have been resting, not storming the enemy's stronghold."

"It is not as if I really did anything. Just helped cut knots and aided yer uncle to the wagon. I actually did very little."

"You did more than anyone would expect of you, Rory. You were ill, and yet you still came to the rescue. You are a brave woman. Now you need food and rest. Let me repay you for my freedom."

"Why do ye care?" Rory spoke to the fire.

She had removed her mittens, and Elaina studied the hands of the young girl that were roughened by work and not needlework. Rory picked at a scab on the back of one while awaiting Elaina's answer.

"That is hard to say. I have a heart for lost things, I suppose."

Rory glanced up at her then, her mouth set in a thin, straight line. "I dinna need pity."

Elaina realized she had not truly ever looked at the girl. Most of their time together had been spent in the dark or fighting for their lives in one way or another. She had eyes the color of golden whisky and hundreds of freckles decorating her delicate face. She was too pale, still. "'Tis not pity that I offer you, Rory." She turned away from the girl's intense gaze to study her own hands. "We are not so different, you and me. We have both known pain, and we both know what it is to feel alone in this turbulent sea of life. You probably more so than I, having to spend such a long time with your horrible grandfather, but I understand your feelings all the same. I do not offer you pity. I offer you a place to belong. A place where people will care *for* you and *about* you. A place where you needn't be afraid."

The crackling of the fire grew as the logs drew in the heat from the kindling, and they too started to burn. Fear and hate were much like these all-consuming flames, but Elaina vowed that love and camaraderie could do the same. Hatred and abuse could spread and overtake everything surrounding it. But the flame of humanity could burn just as brightly and just as hot.

A knock on the door drew the two women back to the present. Rory swiped a tear from her cheek that Elaina pretended not to see as she opened the door to Maggie and the silent giant who had taken the horses.

"We've brought baths for the lot o' ye." Maggie hauled in a hip tub while the man carried in two monstrous buckets of water. "This is my brother, Nathaniel. Ye need no' be afeared of him. I ken he is a giant, but he is a kindly giant." She turned a loving gaze on the man who only looked at her as if awaiting his next orders, which she then gave. "I think we need two more buckets, Nathaniel."

The giant dipped his head and, picking up the buckets, exited the room.

"Ye have one in yer room as well, Mrs. MacKinnon. I am fair glad to see ye again so I can extend my gratitude for yer savin' my virtue."

"I'm not sure I did any saving that night." Elaina huffed a laugh. "If it hadn't been for the lieutenant, I don't know what would have become of either of us."

Maggie raised her brow at Elaina. "The man who claimed ye were his wife? Ye talk of him like he didnae take ye from yer people and try to use you for his own gain."

"How do you know so much of my story?"

"A soldier stopped in two days after ye left, lookin' for ye. That is when we learned the truth of what was and wished to God that we had nay spared the man's life."

Elaina stood astonished at the girl's words. "A soldier? What did he look like?"

"Tall. Verra handsome for a bloody redcoat. Blue eyes like the sea."

"Yes. That would be my brother, William." Elaina's eyes filled with unexpected tears.

How dangerous it was of him to have come hunting her. She needed to get word to him that she had been found and saved. To Maggie she said, "Yes, the lieutenant took me captive to gain the bounty on my head to buy himself a commission. But the man also put his life and his career in danger to save me and two of our own. You cannot always judge a man's character by the clothes that he wears. Lieutenant Perry acted gallantly on behalf of his deceased brother. He brought honor to his name, and I wish him only well. You must promise me that if he comes this way again, you will not retaliate against him on my behalf because he has gained my forgiveness."

Nathaniel lumbered through the door with the buckets.

"Rory, I will leave you to it." Elaina nodded, making her way to the door.

"I'll have clothing for both of ye as well," Maggie said. "We have much family here, so it will be easy enough to find ye something dry and clean to wear. For now, I have left ye both shifts and a cover. If ye will just deposit yer dresses outside the door, I will fetch them and bring ye something to fit and launder the others."

"Ye dinn—" Rory started.

Maggie held up her hand. "I ken I dinna have to, but we want to. So, it will be done, no arguments. And when ye have dressed, we will dine." She and Nathaniel took their leave.

Elaina offered Rory a smile. "I suppose we should get on with it. The faster we wash, the sooner we eat, and I'm famished."

Rory nodded her agreement.

Elaina closed the door softly behind her and stood for a moment with her hand pressed to the door.

"Are ye good, hen?" Calum whispered.

Startled, Elaina replied, "Yes, I am good."

The smile he gave warmed her heart. "Then come to me, for I have missed ye so."

"And I you."

Calum took Elaina's hand and pulled her into their room. Closing the door behind them with his foot, he then turned the lock with a soft click. "Now," he said. "Let us get ye out of yer wet things before ye catch a chill."

Elaina laughed. "It's a little late for that." She shivered at Calum's fingers grazing her neck as he untied the cloak.

He leaned forward, his breath tickling her ear. "I shall have to warm ye then, by any means necessary," he whispered. He turned her around and began undoing the buttons of her dress. "Do ye remember the first time we met?" he asked as he slid the damp bodice of her dress to the floor and made to untie her skirts.

"Which first time are we talking?" Elaina laughed at Calum's strangled curse as he tugged at the ties of her skirt, which refused to be undone. "The time I was covered in shite or the dinner at the Taylors' where you learned my name and tried to command me unsuccessfully to bend to your will? Hey!"

Calum's dirk sliced through the troublesome ties, dropping the skirt on top of the bodice. He made quick work of her stays and petticoats, then spun her around in nothing but her shift to face him. "That's better," he whispered, "but ye're about to rattle yer teeth out of yer head." He scooped her up in his arms and carried her to the hip tub by the fire, steam rising from its contents.

Elaina felt a bite of disappointment that he had not deposited her on the bed.

He slid her feet slowly to the floor as if he, too, regretted his choice of destination. "Now," he said, his voice low and husky, "ye cannae bathe in yer shift. Ye should remove it. Slowly."

Calum's gaze followed Elaina's fingers as they moved to untie the neck of her shift. His breathing came more rapidly than usual, and his fingers twitched at his sides. It was then that Elaina noticed he stood in his shirtsleeves and trews only, his feet bare, the neck of his shirt gaping open, and the light from the fire making the fine hairs on his chest shine more copper than usual.

She swallowed hard as she tugged at the other end of the string tying the shift at her neck. Then she tugged again. "Merde!" she hissed.

It was Calum's turn to laugh. "Blasted wet knots. Here, let me help."

Elaina closed her fist over the knot. "Do not cut the strings on my shift, Calum MacKinnon."

Instead, he dropped to one knee and his hands slid up under the hem of the offending garment. She gasped and closed her eyes at the jolt of desire that rushed through her as his warm hands gripped both of her ankles. His hands slid higher, his touch a whisper against her skin. She swayed when his hands gripped her buttocks, forcing her to grab the edge of the hip tub to keep from tumbling over backward. A soft moan escaped as his lips skimmed her most intimate place.

He groaned and his tongue left a trail of fire up her belly and between her breasts as he slid the shift over her head. "I was determined to go slow, *mo chridhe*," he whispered against her neck as he crushed her to him, his desire making itself known against the hollow of her stomach.

After feeling him fumble with the fall of his trews, she pulled him closer to her, her hands helping to make quick work of his clothing. He turned her then and placed her hands on the edge of the hip tub.

"You… You were saying something about the first time we met?" She lost her voice as his hand slid between her legs, opening them farther.

"Och, aye. Do ye remember what ye called me as ye sat on my floor covered in shite and still taking my breath away, if only from the smell of ye?"

Elaina snorted. "I called you a porcupine in a dres—"

He slid inside of her, cutting off her voice. His arm snaked around her, pulling her back toward him. The steam rose off of the bath in an intoxicating dance that contrasted with the chill of the room. She arched back into him, and his other hand cupped her breast.

"What…what about porcupines?" His teeth grazed her ear.

Their bodies stood locked together in an intimate embrace, neither of them moving.

"I'm trying to gain my senses, Elaina. I cannae think when I am inside of ye." His breathing came more labored as he slid a hand down to the place of their joining. "Do ye…do ye ken how a porcupine makes love to a hen?"

Elaina snickered.

Calum groaned.

"That might be quite the feat," Elaina whispered.

"Aye, ye are right about that." Calum's teeth latched onto her shoulder. Not enough to hurt, just enough to send a jolt through her, and her body squeezed around his. "Let me see if I can successfully accomplish the task."

———✦———

"Tilt yer head back, *mo chridhe*," Calum whispered, and he poured a pitcher of lukewarm bathwater over her head, rinsing the lavender-infused soap from her hair. His hand followed the path of the water with a gentleness with which one would wash a babe.

"I won't break," she said with a sigh. There was no point in arguing the fact that she could very well bathe herself, for she had already broached that subject.

"It's the least I can give ye for what ye have just given me." His smile had exposed the dimple she loved so well, and his curls hung loose and damp around his shoulders. Elaina closed her eyes, grateful for his soothing touch. In truth, she wasn't certain she had the strength to raise her arms, what with the excitement of the past two days and the intensity of their reuniting. When he had finished, he wrapped her in a light blanket before carrying her to the bed and tucking them both under a heavy fur.

"Do you know where they were headed? William's regiment?" Elaina whispered to Calum as she lay wrapped snugly in his arms. The scent of their lovemaking mingled with the smell of burning wood that had, at last, taken the chill off the room.

"Is that all ye can think to say after I have pleasured ye no' once but twice?" he asked her. "'Tis quite a feat. Ye should be touting my male prowess."

Elaina poked him in the rib, causing an unmanly squeak to escape his lips.

He wrapped up both of her hands between them with one of his. The other curled a bit of her hair around his finger. "Nay, *mo chridhe,* I dinna ken where yer brother is."

"What about Cumberland? Do you know where he is?"

"Why all the questions, hen? Ye are no plannin' to fight him yerself, are ye?" He squeezed her hands, his gaze searching her face.

"Is there no way to end this peaceably?"

"Ye ken there is not. It has gone too far. One side or the other must be victorious."

"I knew it was too much to hope for."

"I will do all I can to protect William, I promise ye. I owe the man a great debt. He shall not fall by my sword, but ye need to prepare yerself, Elaina. People that ye love *may* die. Many of them. Ye have seen the brutality firsthand at the hospital where you met the lieutenant, and now with Ruske and Auld Ruadh."

"I cannot comprehend it, Calum." Her voice quivered. "I don't want to think about it."

"Then dinna fash it, Elaina, for worryin' never solved anythin'."

A light knock on the door startled them both.

He smiled and pecked a kiss on her forehead. "That would be dry clothin'. They will be expectin' us downstairs."

Chapter Twenty-Four

Elaina and Calum stepped from their room to find Ainsley pacing the hallway.

"A man could starve waitin' on the two of ye. How long does it take two people to… Never ye mind." His face flushed, and he stomped off toward the stairs, nearly toppling Rory as she exited her room. "Whoa, steady, lass." He gripped her arms to keep her on her feet.

"Dinna touch me," she hissed.

Ainsley removed his hands as if her arms were hotter than a blacksmith's tongs. "Beggin' yer pardon." His words held no animosity as he gave the girl a bow of his head before hurrying on down the stairs.

"I…" Rory's gaze followed him for a second before she turned her attention to smoothing the green wool of her skirts. The orange bush that once peeked out from under her knit cap was plaited neatly down her back. The strands, dark, almost brown, were still wet, but the few strands that lay in soft waves by her face were as orange as a ripe pumpkin. Seeing her with her hair pulled away from her face and her out of that comically oversized fur coat made her seem much younger, smaller, and more fragile.

"Come, let us get some food in you before you faint." Elaina extended a hand toward the stairs. "Then you need rest."

"I think we all need some of that," Calum said, following the women down toward the dining hall.

The smell of baked bread and roasted meat met them halfway down, and Elaina struggled to descend at a womanly pace. Her stomach growled, the sound of it all but echoing off the walls.

Rory snorted in front of her.

Elaina felt her face turn crimson, and she whipped her head around to look at Calum to see if he had heard her stomach and Rory's response. He studied the faded paper on the walls with his lip between his teeth. "I fail to see what is so amusing about a woman starving," Elaina said.

"I thought it was my wame doin' all the talkin'," Rory said. "It's a relief to ken that someone else's is just as noisy."

Gordie met them at the bottom of the stairs. "Come, come," he waved them into the dining hall, his face etched with worry that had not been present when they first arrived several hours ago.

"Lochiel," Calum greeted a man standing by the window, staring out at the street.

The man turned from the window, recognition lighting his face. "Ah, MacKinnon. I was told I could find ye here."

The men shook hands, pulling themselves toward each other as men were wont to do and slapping each other on the back.

"What troubles ye?" Calum asked.

"First, introduce me to yer family, and let us sit and break bread. I might could eat horse dung at this point."

"I ken someone else who might could do the same. Donald Cameron of Lochiel, may I introduce ye to my wife, Elaina, and our ward, Rory. I see ye've already met our lad Ainsley there."

The admiration for the ease with which the words 'our ward, Rory' rolled off her husband's tongue made Elaina forget she wanted to stomp on his foot for mentioning the fact that she might eat horse shite. Rory seemed not a little shocked at the words as she stared at Calum, her expression unreadable. She might not appreciate his calling her their ward. She might not want to stay with them at all. Later, when they were alone, Elaina would ask her if she had family she wanted to be delivered to. Surely, they could arrange to have her escorted back to her clan, if she so wished. Whichever one that might be. But for the time being, they were here with friends, food upon the table, and Calum by her side, and the world seemed a bit brighter, if only in her mind, for outside the day was as gray and dreary as the one before and the one before that.

After a few minutes of everyone attempting to act like decent members of society and not animals devouring everything in front of them, Calum turned his attention back to Lochiel. "Seein' as ye're here and no' with our prince, somethin' must be amiss?"

Lochiel washed the bite of venison in his mouth down with a long draw of ale and nodded. "There was a skirmish. Yer father and yer brother are missin', and we've nay idea where they have taken them. It is no' to where they have taken the others. We have searched and released those prisoners and given Hawley hell in the meantime."

Two of their own just rescued and now two more had been taken prisoner. It seemed like a sadistic game of cat and mouse, with the Scots being the mice and none too quick.

Calum chewed his cheek and stared at Lochiel, giving an overall sense of being calm, but his hand had dropped to the hilt of his dirk, and his knuckles shone white with his grip. "We need to gather the clansmen," he said after several tense moments when all eyes rested upon him. If something should happen to his father and his brother, Calum would be the clan chief. As it stood now, he was in charge.

"Now that I've found ye and yer...group"—Lochiel's gaze roamed over those seated at the table—"I might have a plan. But it would only be with yer permission. 'Twould be dangerous."

"I'm certain Ainsley and myself are up to the task," Calum said, removing his dirk from its sheath and laying it on the table.

Ainsley did the same.

"There will be no' two of ye. Only one. I will leave it to ye to decide which it will be. If it is no' to yer likin', we will attempt another way."

"I've no' heard the first way yet," Calum said with a raised brow. "Tell me, and I shall make my decision."

※

Elaina found herself standing in the solicitor's office, squeezed between Calum and Ainsley, crammed into the small entrance while awaiting their announcement. An announcement with no appointment and a rather intimidating Lochiel doing all the talking. She could scarcely draw breath in the small room with two rigid-backed waiting chairs and little else. She found herself relieved that she had insisted Rory take to bed and rest. It was all the poor girl could do to stay awake after getting a warm meal in her belly. She had been through quite the adventure over the last few days. Lord knows she didn't need to be here for this.

Calum squeezed her hand in reassurance. "Are ye certain, *mo chridhe?*" he whispered.

Elaina reassured him with a nod as the door leading into the rest of the building swung open and the tall stately gentleman who had answered their inquiry led them single file down a narrow hall. The passage was devoid of any adornments on the walls but polished to a high shine with the smell of linseed oil lingering in the air. It brought back memories of her childhood in the colonies and playing in her father's study. The doorman ushered them into a spacious room filled floor to ceiling with books on every wall but one, which held a window with a view that traveled through the town and down the street to where the two soldiers had been killed during her first visit. What had the solicitor made of that day? Elaina stood looking out the window, trying not to relive it, when muffled voices sounded outside the closed door, as if whoever were about to enter were arguing or scolding someone.

Typical, she thought, turning toward the door and affixing a warm smile on her face as it was flung open and a short man bumbled in like a tumble of rocks. Words of welcome to his waiting guests spilled out of his mouth before his body had crossed the threshold. Entering more slowly and looking like he was about to be force fed a steaming bowl of shite, was a younger man with the same brown hair as the first but a much different demeanor.

The young man adjusted his shoulders and looked up from his shoes. "Mistress Murray?"

"Halloo again, Raibert. Mr. Drummond." Elaina nodded at the bewildered pair whom she had met months ago at Dalmunshire Castle.

"Mr. Drummond." Calum drew the attention of the squat man, whose brow also furrowed in puzzlement. "I was told that ye could help us."

"Brandy?" Mr. Drummond spewed out while his gaze rested on Lochiel.

"Nay," Lochiel answered for all. "I understand that yer lad here has an invitation to the ball to be held in two days' time at the home in Carlisle of Lady MacPherson, a known Whig and loyal supporter of the Hanoverian usurper. He shall be accompanied by Diana Campbell." He waved a hand at Elaina.

"Diana? What? Mistress Murray? Well…you see—"

Lochiel held up his hand. "I dinna care about anythin' ye are about to say. *Diana Campbell* will attend with yer son.

"I…but…"

The windbag was never at a loss for words, so Elaina found his stuttering and sputtering in the presence of Donald Cameron highly amusing; she fought to hide a smile.

"Yer carriage will retrieve Mistress Campbell from Hampton House in Carlisle at exactly half-past eight on the day of the party. If anyone catches wind of this, Mr. Drummond, I will ken from where it came, and I dare say ye will no longer be practicin' law. Ye will be feedin' the worms from below ground." With his last words hanging on the air, Donald Cameron of Lochiel turned and walked out the door.

Elaina looked from the open door to Mr. Drummond and then to Raibert, who stood ashen-faced. His father might not be the only one feeding the worms if this charade did not go well. She bobbed him a quick curtsy before following Ainsley and Calum out of the room.

"Well, that went well enough," Ainsley said as they walked back up the street toward Gordie's inn.

"It helps when ye have a piece of blackmail to hold over their heads," Lochiel said with a short laugh.

Elaina wondered what that bit of blackmail information might be, but decided it was best to know as little about anything of consequence as possible. That way they couldn't torture it out of her if she were caught.

Chapter Twenty-Five

RORY PLACED A BEAUTY MARK on Elaina's right cheekbone.
"There." Rory took a step back and surveyed her handiwork.
Elaina stood once again in those dreaded Campbell colors, a tartan she had sworn she would never touch again. *Be careful what you say…and think,* she reprimanded herself. The gown itself was a deep blue with the tartan cloth draped in elegant fashion across one shoulder and gathered at her waist with a Campbell brooch before flaring over the bottom of her gown, near to her feet. She found herself curious as to where a Cameron would find access to Campbell colors. Though she had agreed to the ruse, her stomach now churned with the ferocity of an ocean amid a storm. "Calum. Who is Locheil to you?" She turned to face her husband. Introductions had been made, and she had agreed to this absurd and dangerous mission without knowing anything of the man who spoke with a gentleness of a father but yet with the command of a man of power. Now she held her doubts about the entire mission.

"Dinna let Lochiel's tame demeanor fool ye," Calum said, taking Elaina's hands in his. "Ye have made the commitment to go through with this plan, and I understand yer reluctance and unease, now, but the time to decline has passed."

Apparently, her thoughts were as easy to read as ever. "But—"

"But nothin'. I dinna want ye to go, *mo chridhe,* but ye have given yer word to one of the most powerful clan leaders within this entire rebellion. The consequences of attempting to back out now wouldna bode well for any of us. Donald Cameron of Lochiel, may be gentle of voice but he is also a Highland chieftain who has burned the homes of many of his own men to *encourage* them to join the Cause. He is a ruthless and determined man. He is also loyal and honorable.

Remember your word stands above all else in this world. Honor is far more powerful than circumstance."

As if called up by Calum's speech, Lochiel poked his head through the doorway. "'Tis time."

Elaina nodded and sucked in a deep breath. *Honor above all.* She touched the white powdered wig with its elaborate curls cascading to one shoulder and eyed herself once more in the mirror. She hoped the extra application of rice powder and makeup was enough to hide her identity, should anyone she knew other than the Duke of Newcastle be present at the party. She prayed the duke held the information she needed to free Calum's father and brother and that he would reveal it willingly.

Elaina descended the stairs and accepted her cloak from the doorman of Hampton House. Lochiel had only said it was a friend's house, not which friend nor where the inhabitants happened to be at the moment.

Calum and Ainsley escorted Elaina down to the waiting carriage. "Are ye certain ye want to do this?" Ainsley asked, worry creasing his brow.

"If either of you asks me that again, I'll…I'll… I don't know what I'll do, but it won't be pleasant." Elaina cast a stern look at both men. "Stop your worrying. All will be well. Now, I must go." She gave each of them a kiss on the cheek before accepting the coachman's offered hand and then made her way into the carriage with an ashen-faced Raibert. As the carriage door clicked closed, she leaned across the seat and patted Raibert's hand. "I am sorry that they have dragged you into this nonsense. I wish there were another way."

"As do I," he mumbled, his gaze fixed out of the carriage window. They rode in silence for several minutes before the lad turned his attention to Elaina. "Why me? Why not my father?"

"Your father is a married man." Elaina cocked her head sideways. "And you are the one with the invitation."

Raibert harumphed at that.

"Raibert. Raibert, look at me."

He reluctantly turned his gaze to Elaina.

"I don't know what form of blackmail Lochiel has swinging over your head, but it must involve the Cause or we wouldn't be sitting in this carriage. I also know that this party will be full of loyalists. That is why we will be there. I need an important piece of information that I believe can only be garnered at this party. Now, I'm don't know where you stand on the issue of the Hanoverian nor the Pretender, nor do I care. I only care about your safety and the safety of those I love. I will do my best to protect you and to do no harm to your reputation."

"That hardly seems possible," he said. "With all due respect," he added with great haste.

Elaina sighed and studied her gloved hands. "That is fair," she whispered.

The silence that followed weighed heavily on those in the carriage for the remainder of their trip to Lady MacPherson's home. When their conveyance pulled to a stop in front of the lady's stately manor, one of the house servants helped Elaina from the carriage.

Elaina turned, blocking Raibert's exit. "No," she said. "I have changed my mind. Give me the invitation. I will go alone. I will say that you have fallen ill. Go home, Raibert. Stay safe."

She reached up and snatched the invitation from the lad's gloved hand before she pushed the carriage door shut in the young man's face. After ordering the coachman to ride him around for a few hours and then return him to where they found him, she spun around and faced the brick facade of the lady's home. Candlelight glowed through the expansive windows to the right of the door, their light shining like eyes in search of rebels on the prowl.

With a deep breath, the rebel climbed the short steps to the door, straightened her shoulders, and handed the doorman her invitation.

He ushered her in out of the frigid night while eying the invitation. "This invitation says Raibert Drummond. I dare say you do not look like a Raibert, unless your parents had an unfortunate taste in names?" He raised his gaze to her in question.

Elaina pasted on the most charming smile she could muster at the moment, as her head was telling her to turn and run. "I'm afraid my dear friend has fallen ill. He insisted I attend and extend his regrets to the lady of the house."

The doorman seemed placated with that little lie, and he took her cloak before seeing her to the ballroom.

Elaina stood just inside the doorway, her stomach giving a sudden lurch as if she stared off a great precipice instead of gazing at a buzzing swarm of party guests. She swallowed the bile that had risen in her throat and took two steps inside. The musicians struck up a lovely minuet, and couples began moving elegantly about the floor. A footman passed by, and Elaina nabbed a crystal glass of champagne as a regal woman with a pile of dark curls cascading here and there approached her.

"Lady MacPherson." Elaina bobbed a curtsy in front of her host, who looked exactly as she had been described in detail hours earlier. "A lovely party for such a worthy cause."

"I am pleased you think so, Mistress…?" One of Lady MacPherson's eyebrows rose in an elegant arch, a false smile pasted upon her face.

"Campbell. Diana Campbell. I am so sorry that Raibert, that is, Mr. Drummond, could not attend himself. He fell ill just this evening but insisted I still attend. He sends his warmest felicitations, greatest of apologies…and this." Elaina held out a blue velvet pouch heavy with coin.

"Oh, well." Lady MacPherson's smile changed from awkwardly false to almost as awkwardly giddy with a shrill cackle accompanying it. She took the bag, weighing it in her hand. "Thank you and Mr. Drummond. The orphans are very blessed this night indeed." She turned and took two steps before she seemed to remember her manners. She looked over her shoulder at Elaina, the false smile present once more. "I pray Mr. Drummond's illness is not too serious?"

"I do not believe so, my lady. I think he shall recover rather quickly."

"Good. Good. Excuse me while I see to…this." Lady MacPherson jiggled the velvet pouch in her palm. "Mingle, eat, drink! I am certain there is someone here you know if you are a friend to Mr. Drummond."

"I am certain there is," Elaina said as she spied a familiar head across the room. Just the man she was looking for.

Lady MacPherson took her leave, and Elaina made her way around the room, avoiding eye contact with anyone. Her sights were set on her squat round target, who was chatting away to another gentleman.

As she closed in on her prey, someone took her by the elbow and turned her toward the dance floor. "A dance, mistress?" he whispered close to her ear.

Startled, she looked up and a knot lodged in her throat as if she had swallowed her heart.

"Now, now." Lieutenant Perry somehow kept her on her feet and began leading her around the floor. "The rice powder is a nice touch, my lady. It's too bad that your face still haunts me in my nightmares, so I could recognize your features anywhere." The smile he gave her held no emotion, but he could have chosen more flattering words.

"I am pleased to know that you still think of me." Elaina batted her eyelashes at the man. "And tonight, I am Diana Campbell, if you please."

The lieutenant barked out a laugh, drawing unwanted attention from some of those dancing around them. "That goes hand in hand with your disguise. What are you up to? Are you spying this evening, madam?"

"Why, Lieutenant, you offend me." She cast him her most innocent smile. "I merely wanted to show my support of Lady MacPherson's generous nature and help the poor little orphans. Is that not why you are present as well?"

"I am present as I am a friend of the hostess, *and* she asked me to help with security, *Mistress Campbell,* in case any deplorable Jacobites should attempt to interrupt the festivities. They are camped not far away, you know? You should be careful roaming about the city unescorted. Uncivilized heathens could be anywhere."

Elaina cocked an eyebrow at him, but the dance ended before she could voice a proper retort.

He led her off the dance floor, still attached to her elbow.

"Are you planning to arrest me here, Lieutenant?"

"I haven't decided yet." He motioned a servant over and retrieved two glasses of champagne, handing one to Elaina.

"There is someone I must speak to before you do, if you don't mind." She took a drink of champagne, and it hit the back of her throat, causing her to erupt into a coughing fit as a familiar figure approached.

The lieutenant pulled out his handkerchief and handed it to her, then gave their elegant interloper a bow. "Lady Caroline," he said.

"Lieutenant Perry, a pleasure to see you again," Lady Caroline said, but her blue gaze remained on Elaina.

"Are you acquainted?" The lieutenant looked from one woman to the other.

"Yes," Elaina croaked, attempting to gain her composure. "We have met, but it has been some time since our paths have crossed."

"Quite some time," Lady Caroline agreed. "So long in fact, if you will forgive me, that I cannot seem to pull your name from my feeble mind."

"Let me introduce you," the lieutenant all but sneered, and Elaina cut him a disdainful look. "Mistress Diana Campbell at your service."

Without missing a beat, Lady Caroline nodded. "Yes, yes, that is it. Do forgive me, I've a terrible time with names. It is so wonderful to see you again." Lady Caroline cast Elaina a genuine smile. "I was afraid we might never meet again." She laid a soft hand on Elaina's arm.

Elaina placed her hand upon it and squeezed. "I hold our memories dear, Lady Caroline."

The three of them stood in an awkward silence.

Elaina could sense that there was more Lady Caroline wanted to say, but apart from present company, who seemed to be going nowhere. He desperately needed to bugger off, and she opened her mouth to tell him just that when the object of her entire reason for attending sidled up to the group.

The Duke of Newcastle stood staring at Elaina with reproach twisting his brow for a brief moment, then he turned his attention to a startled lieutenant. "Dear sir, would you be so kind as to find me a man with a whisky?"

The lieutenant looked from the duke to Elaina and back as if in turmoil as to whether he should obey a duke or stay with his captive.

For a moment, Elaina was afraid the lieutenant would try to take her with him.

"Tonight, sir," the duke barked.

"Forgive me. Yes, ladies." The lieutenant hurried off with a lingering glance on Elaina as if scolding her to stay put.

"What in the hell are you doing here?" the duke hissed when the officer was finally out of earshot.

"I came to talk to you," Elaina said. "I need a favor."

"A favor, you say? Have you not been in enough trouble as it is? Is it not enough for you to have a price on your head? You just come waltzing in here with that wig and some rice powder thinking that no one in the world would recognize you? You truly have lost your senses." He stood red-faced, glaring at her and apparently awaiting some kind of answer.

Elaina stood with her mouth gaping open. The duke had never spoken to her as such. "I must be an idiot, as you say, because the three of you have recognized me right off. So, let me ask my question of you, and I will attempt to be on my way before the lieutenant returns. Where are the prisoners, the Laird Beinnmaree and Aron MacKinnon, being held?" She probably should not have asked such in front of Lady Caroline, but there was little time.

"You…that's…that's what you came here to ask me? You want me to disclose the whereabouts of Jacobite prisoners to you? So you can what, attempt to free them? God help me, but you had better get your head on right, my dear, before they hang you from the gallows. Leave while you can. Board a ship to the colonies and never return. All the favors I have offered your family have run out. Your mother funneling money to your Highland family was one thing. I truly thought nothing would come of a Jacobite rebellion. I thought we had squashed that notion in '15. Yet, here we stand in the middle of a bloody war because some untamed creatures dislike paying their taxes to a German king. Well, I am here to tell you they will not win. They will lose, and they will lose royally. When they do, there will be hell to pay, and I will be nowhere near their side of the line." The ruddy-faced duke paused for breath, his words having spewed forth like venom. "I hate to inform you, Elaina, that I, in fact, stand behind King George and the fact that you are in this room, addressing a duke and inquiring after Jacobite prisoners, is more than disturbing. It is *treasonous.*"

Elaina stared at the man she had considered a family friend. A man who had helped her mother funnel money to the Jacobite Cause, and now he had the gall to accuse her of treason. She wanted to slap his face, but she stood with her fists clenched at her side, attempting to calm her fury.

"Lady Caroline, I've been looking for y—" Harry Everson's words died on his lips as his gaze came to rest on Elaina. "Sweet mother of God. Why is all of Edinburgh at this bloody party? Are we not standing on English soil?"

The question was ground out a bit too loud, drawing eyes toward their gaggle of people.

Harry, of all people, took her arm and turned her away from prying eyes. "Are you mad?" He had the gall to shake her arm as if scolding a small child.

"Kindly remove your hand from my person," Elaina said through clenched teeth.

Harry snatched his hand away.

"I must be mad. I thought I might still have a few friends and that I might garner aid in helping my family, but apparently, I was not only wrong, but I was dead wrong. Shall you turn me over to the authorities, your Grace?"

"No!" Caroline stepped between Elaina and the duke as if her petite figure could protect Elaina from the gallows. "You cannot. What has happened to you?" she scolded the red-faced duke. "She does not deserve this treatment. Do you not know what she has been subjected to? Near beaten to death, learning her family were not who she thought, losing a babe…" Caroline's voice choked on the last words.

Elaina's neck broke out in prickly heat as she fought to keep her own tears at bay.

"You will not turn her over to the authorities," Caroline said.

"I won't have to," the duke mumbled and nodded toward the doorway where two redcoat soldiers stood with a broadsheet in their hand, studying the image and scanning the crowd.

Lieutenant Perry appeared at her side.

"You," Elaina said.

"Once again, not I. Lady MacPherson loves her money, and there is a bounty on your head. I suggest you leave. Now."

"This way." Lady Caroline crooked her arm through Elaina's and steered her toward one of the many doorways that exited the ballroom. "Harry." She jerked her head at her cousin.

Harry made his way toward a different set of doors.

"Slowly. Do not draw attention," Lady Caroline whispered.

Elaina fought to keep herself moving at a leisurely pace. When they reached the hallway, Lady Caroline pushed her into a near run. Elaina gathered her skirts and hurried to keep up with her escort's longer legs.

Caroline glanced about, taking in the doors closed to various rooms. She stopped and tried one but found it locked. "Dammit."

It was the first time Elaina had heard her swear, and she let out a nervous snort of laughter.

Lady Caroline cast a grin over her shoulder. When the expression froze on her face, Elaina glanced back. The two soldiers were standing in the hallway. Lady Caroline didn't have to drag her. They began running for all they were worth, turning a corner just as a soldier called out for them to stop.

Lady Caroline did not seem to know where they were going any more than Elaina did. The pair searched wildly for an unlocked door. It seemed Lady MacPherson was not only fond of money but also paranoid, keeping all of her doors locked. Lady Caroline finally found some luck and pushed Elaina through an open door and nearly down a staircase where she fought to keep her feet under her. They all but trampled some of the help carrying laden trays of food up toward the party.

"Pardon," Lady Caroline said in a clipped tone as if it were perfectly normal for two women to be rushing down the servants' stairs.

Elaina's cumbersome wig had slipped down her head and partially blocked her vision. She shoved it back out of her eyes as the two women stumbled into the sweltering kitchen area. The help stood gawping at the scene playing out before them.

"The exit, kindly?" Lady Caroline's question rolled out smooth as silk, though she was panting for breath as much as Elaina.

A young girl lifted a hand holding a paring knife and pointed at a door off in one corner.

"Thank you." Lady Caroline grabbed Elaina's hand and tugged her in that direction. They stumbled out into the frigid night air, and Elaina immediately missed her cloak.

"Caroline! This way," a woman's voice called out from the end of the narrow close that they had stumbled out into.

Her words, too loud, echoed off the stone walls that seemed to close in on Elaina.

They both turned and ran toward the voice, taking turns catching each other as they slid and stumbled on the uneven cobblestones. One could have knocked Elaina over with a feather when she realized the woman was none other than Jeanette, the woman Harry adored and had been willing to confront Calum about while at Lady Caroline's ball, where the Duke of Cumberland had also been in attendance.

Elaina's feet came to a standstill, and she watched Lady Caroline continue toward Jeanette. Was she leading her into a trap? Why would they help her? They were acquaintances of Cumberland. Close enough acquaintances for him to attend a ball at a private home.

When Caroline noticed Elaina's absence behind her, she and Jeanette came running back to her. "What is it?" Caroline asked.

Elaina felt herself taking a few steps backward. "Why are you doing this?" she whispered. "Am I to be accosted when I leave this close so the two of you can collect a nice, hefty ransom?" She attempted to sound fierce, but she could not bury the fear in her voice. Fear that had followed her every single day for over a year. Fear that she was tired of holding. She felt herself collapsing to the ground.

"Oh, no, you don't." Lady Caroline grabbed her arm and, between her and Jeanette, they dragged her to the end of the close where a black carriage awaited with the door swung open.

Elaina began shaking her head. "No," she whispered, tears falling.

"Stop it!" Caroline's comely face appeared in her line of sight. "Snap out of it, Elaina. We are not here to harm you. Look at me. Laird Beinnmaree is being held in a secret room under Lord Crighton's stables just north of Buteland Hill."

The words shocked Elaina so that the tears froze in her eyes. "What? How do you know?"

"Because my father is Lord Taylor, and I'm not as naïve as most think that I am. Now go." Lady Caroline shoved Elaina toward the open carriage.

Harry leaned out, took her hand, and dragged her up into the carriage, nearly onto his lap. The coachman stared straight ahead as if he carried off hysterical women running out of closes every day. It was just a mundane part of the job.

"Wait." Elaina leaned out of the open carriage door, blocking Jeanette from entering. "Why, Caroline? Why are you helping me if your father is Lord Taylor, friend to the Duke of Cumberland?" She said nothing of her father being present at Gleann Eader when Prince Charlie had arrived on Scottish soil.

Caroline paused, casting a glance at Harry, who had leaned out over Elaina's shoulder, his hand outstretched to Jeanette. She closed her eyes and sighed. "Because I love William. I am in love with your brother, and he loves you very much. You are one of the most precious things in the world to him. To hurt you is to hurt him, and I will not do it. Now get yer arse in that carriage before they bloody well find you!"

Elaina had no time to comprehend her words and offer a response because Harry wrapped an arm around her waist and dragged her inside the dark confines of the carriage. Then he helped Jeanette in and slammed the door shut. He pounded on the roof with his fist, and the carriage jerked into motion, sending Elaina tumbling onto Jeanette.

"My apologies, my lady." Harry righted her onto the seat.

"I'm not a lady, and it's quite all right." Elaina straightened her skirts.

"Well, I am sorry again, Mistress MacKinnon, but you must hide. Now. Under the seat." Harry grabbed her arm and tugged her unceremoniously to the floor and under Jeanette's legs. The two of them whipped a fur over their legs and effectively hid her from view just as voices sounded outside of the carriage and the conveyance pulled to a stop.

"Nay. I've nay seen anyone lookin' like that this night," the coachman said loudly enough for the occupants to hear.

"Nay. Me neither, but I ain't seen much but the back of me eyelids all evenin', cap'ain," his helper said.

"We have orders to check all carriages." This soldier was just outside the door.

Elaina covered her mouth and held her breath, squeezing her eyes closed as if that would keep her from being found out.

"Kiss me," Jeanette hissed from above her, and the blanket moved minutely as the two leaned toward the center of the carriage.

The carriage door was flung open. "Oh…p-pardon me," the soldier stumbled out.

"Have you not even the decency to knock?" Harry said, and the blanket moved again as Jeanette leaned back in her seat.

"I-I'm sorry, sir, but I've orders to search every carriage."

"That's all fine and dandy," Harry all but spit out. "But bloody well have the decency to knock on your next unsuspecting victims. Who are you looking for? Are you so afraid that the villain will vanish into thin air that you must invade the privacy of every conveyance in such a rude manner? People do not vanish, sir. Let me see that." From the sound of it, he jerked a broadsheet from the soldier's hand.

"Hold it closer to the light, darling, so I may see as well." The words slid from Jeanette's tongue like silk. "A woman? All of this for a woman? Whatever could she have done?"

"She is wanted for the murder of three British officers, madam," the soldier said from outside the door.

"What a terrible woman. And you believe she is here? At this party? In amongst us all?" Jeanette sounded believably frightened.

"I'm afraid so, madam."

"Harry, did you hear that? Our very lives have been in danger, and you scolding this man for doing his job. He is only trying to keep us from harm."

"I do apologize, sir," Harry said. "I hope you catch her. She must be as mean as the devil himself."

Elaina considered kicking him.

More apologies were made from both inside and outside of the carriage as Elaina grew ever more impatient to be on their way. The longer they sat, the more her throat closed off. She couldn't breathe under this suffocating fur. *Merde.* She was going to sneeze. She searched around with one hand, holding her nose with the other, and gave Jeanette's ankle a squeeze.

"Good evening and good luck, sir," Jeanette said in a quick dismissal, and the door slammed shut.

The sneeze escaped just as loud as Elaina had feared. A muffled "God bless you" came from outside of the carriage.

Jeanette giggled. "Thank you," she called out as the carriage lurched into motion.

"Oh, thank God." Elaina lay flat on her back, half under the seat, half out, sucking in fresh air after Harry had pulled the fur back. "I thought I might die."

"I thought I might piss myself," Harry said, wiping sweat from his brow with his handkerchief.

Jeanette gave him a disapproving look. "Harry."

"I beg your pardon, La…Elaina." Harry caught himself in time not to call her a member of aristocratic society.

"Come, Harry, help her up from the floor. We are out of danger."

Harry obediently took Elaina under the arms and helped to haul her up to the seat beside him.

"I cannot thank you enough," Elaina said, shoving the wig back once again. "I must look a frightful mess." She patted the wig as if that would help it stay in place.

"I have no comment," Harry said. "But hold still. I dare say you don't need this atrocious thing anymore." He began pulling pins loose and gently removed the wig from Elaina's head, tossing it onto the seat beside Jeanette.

"My dear, who cares what you look like as long as I do not have to see you hanging from the end of a rope after all you've done for Harry and myself."

Done for them? She had done nothing but bully Harry into confessing his feelings all those years ago. That was when she noticed Jeanette's hand cradling her rounded belly.

"Are you wed, then?" Elaina looked at Harry, her voice squeaking with the words.

Harry cast her a sideways glance.

"Of course you are." She turned back to Jeanette. "And you are to have a baby!" Elaina gushed with joy, but then the danger of the situation overcame her. "Why would you risk this all for me?" She swatted her once-nemesis on the arm. "Do not ever do that again," she all but yelled at Harry.

"Don't fret so," Jeanette said.

"'Tis over and you are safe. We did it for Caroline as well as a thank you to you. Without your boorish behavior to myself, I would have never gained the hand of this beautiful creature." Harry kissed Jeanette's hand.

"I am glad that my overbearing personality has helped someone along the way and not just caused trouble to follow me in my wake. Congratulations. Where are we headed?"

With that question, the carriage began to slow and eventually came to a stop. Elaina prepared to dive under the seat again.

Harry placed a hand on her arm and creaked the door open just a hair, peeping through the crack. "Just as I thought. We have arrived at your escort."

"My escort?"

Harry swung the door open all the way, and Ainsley's beaming face appeared in the opening, his nose red from the freezing temperature. "I ken I'm a poor excuse for yer husband, but we thought it better that I save yer arse this time. No one ever notices a stable boy." When Elaina could do nothing but stare, Ainsley gave a snort. "Are ye comin', or would ye rather cause another ruckus and have the entirety of the British army at our throats?"

Elaina shook her head.

"Here. Wrap her in my coat." Ainsley shed his fur and handed it down to Harry.

Elaina tried to protest but to no avail.

Harry shoved her arms in the sleeves of the too-big coat, dressing her as if she were a child. He took her by the shoulders when he had finished. "The best of luck to you, my lady," he said and kissed her on each cheek.

Speechless, she merely nodded at his words. She truly had done nothing to deserve the kindness they had shown her this night, and there was no time to explain away the mistaken title that he still used for her.

Jeanette pulled Elaina into her arms. "Stay safe. You mean the world to Lady Caroline and Lord Spencer. It would injure them greatly to lose you…as it would us. Now, off you go." Jeanette pushed her toward Ainsley, whose steed danced with impatience.

Elaina climbed from the carriage steps to the back of his horse. "Thank you, truly," she said to the two faces peering out of the carriage door at her as she arranged herself behind her new escort.

They waved her off, and Ainsley clicked the horse into motion.

"How did you know?" Elaina asked him as they rode over the snow-covered bridge and into the black night.

"I followed ye. I kent ye could no' be trusted to keep yer heid. There is always some sort of trouble."

"You've become quite brave with your words, Ainsley MacEwan." Elaina tugged at his ear.

He huffed a laugh. "No' brave. Just the truth. I've kent ye long enough to know."

She lay her head upon his back. "Yes, you have, and I thank God for it every day," she whispered into the dark.

Chapter Twenty-Six

"Edinburgh? Damn Beinnmaree for getting himself cap-tured." Lochiel slammed his fist on the table, causing everyone in the room to jump.

Everyone except for Calum, who stood unruffled as ever, leaning against the ornately carved hearth with his arms crossed. The only sign that anything was amiss was the way his gaze roamed over Elaina from head to toe, over and over, as if looking for signs of injury, though she had assured him that she had not been hurt. Ainsley leaned against the door frame, much like Calum.

Rory sat still as a mouse in a chair across from Elaina, her fingers worrying each other until Elaina thought the skin might rub right off.

Lochiel turned on Elaina, pulling her attention back to him. The sitting room at Hampton House was spacious yet cozy with its blue damask on the walls and plush rugs under their feet. Elaina's blood ran cold, and she shrank under his severe glare.

"And ye said this was Lord *Taylor's* daughter?"

Elaina sat by the fire in a large sitting room at the guest house she had set out from hours and hours ago, it seemed. She squirmed, not just from Lochiel's severe glare but from the damned shoes that were pinching her feet. She could think of nothing better than shirking the bloody things and tossing them into the fire. Whenever anyone had spoken of Donald Cameron of Lochiel, they'd called him gentle. The look plastered on his face at the moment appeared none too gentle, and Elaina swallowed hard under his scrutiny. She must have swallowed her tongue, for she couldn't find it, so she forced a nod instead. Her gaze darted to Calum.

He offered an encouraging smile and a wink.

Lochiel's frustration dissipated a bit, that or he drew down his mask, concealing it once more. He leaned back in his chair. "Well," he said with a sigh. "I suppose we should be thankful that he is not in Edinburgh Castle, nor the Tolbooth. It will be easier to win his freedom than if we had to fight an entire battalion. Let's pray they dinna move the two of them before we can reach them. We need eyes on that building. Ainsley."

Ainsley stepped forward as if a soldier called to attention.

"Ye will ride ahead. Leave this night." Lochiel picked up the quill laying on the desk in front of him and dipped it in the inkwell. "This is a list of stops sympathetic to the Cause. Ye may trade out horses at these stops. Show them this letter. We will follow at a safer pace with the women. Ye should be able to reach Edinburgh in a day's time. We will be two days behind ye. Keep yer eyes and ears open."

"Aye," Ainsley said.

Lochiel shook the sand from the document and handed it to Ainsley, who studied it for a moment before folding it and inserting it in a pocket inside his coat.

Elaina stood and approached him. "Travel safe, Ainsley MacEwan." She patted him on the chest.

"Ye ken I will." He took her face in his hands and kissed her on the forehead. "Ye do the same. I dinna wish to have to save yer arse again, though God kens I've had enough practice it should be an easy enough task."

Elaina swatted him on the arm.

Ainsley chuckled and drew her to him, squeezing her so tight she could feel the letter crumple between them. He gave her another kiss on the top of her head before releasing her. "I willna let ye down, Lochiel."

Elaina's heart dropped as she watched him go.

Calum appeared at her side. "Dinna fash, *mo chridhe*. We will be with him again in two days."

Elaina nodded and laid her head against his arm. She could not help but worry. There was a bloody war raging out there. Spies everywhere. British soldiers everywhere. Besides, it was a great responsibility to care for another's child, though she felt as if Ainsley were her own. She had let his family down once before when she couldn't prevent the death of his younger brother, Angus. She did not want it to happen again. But Ainsley was a young man now. Free to make his own decisions, though he would forever be that young, shaggy-headed boy who'd stolen her heart years ago.

"'Tis late. Let us retire, for we leave at first light." Lochiel's chair scraped the floor as he stood.

Elaina turned to leave, catching sight of Rory, who was so quiet Elaina had forgotten she was present.

Rory's gaze lingered on the doorway Ainsley had traveled through. She turned at Lochiel's words, blushing crimson as Elaina met her eye.

The poor girl would forever have a time hiding her emotions as easily as she flushed. Elaina took the few steps necessary to reach her side, pulling her to her feet. She linked her arm with Rory's and patted it as she led the lass from the room.

"Ye worry for him?" Rory asked as they made their way to their rooms on the second floor of Hampton House.

"Very much," Elaina said with a sigh.

"Ye treat him as a son, and he thinks of ye like a mam, but he is no' yer son." Rory turned a confused look on Elaina.

What a life she must have led if the thought of caring for someone was such a puzzlement. "We do think of each other in that way."

"He is yer nephew, no?"

"No," Elaina replied. "We are no blood kin. He and his brother worked for me when I was an earl's sister. His brother, Angus, was murdered by British soldiers." The images of the snow soaked with crimson came flooding back and with them the crippling loss she had felt that horrible day. She paused in the hallway, attempting to gather her emotions.

Rory's grip tightened on her arm, offering comfort. "I'm sorry," she whispered. "Just let me…" She searched in vain for her handkerchief.

Calum laid a firm hand on the small of Elaina's back, and his handkerchief appeared over her shoulder.

"Thank you," Elaina said.

He kissed the side of her head, leaving his hand where it lay.

Elaina cleared her throat. "I'm not usually so emotional," she apologized to Rory.

Calum made an unflattering Scottish noise in the back of his throat.

Elaina elbowed him.

He laughed and pulled her tight to his side. "Forgive my wife," Calum said to Rory, who stood studying the two of them. "She has yet to realize what a big heart she has. She insisted that the lad, Angus, that his body be returned to his family. Some horrible things happened along the way, but also some wonderful things. She gained a family, and I gained a wife. We also gained a son when we visited Ainsley at his parent's home. They were poor and starvin', with too many bairns. Ainsley wished to continue with us and not be an added mouth at the table for his parents. We could no' be happier to have him with us. He is truly a blessing to our clan…to our family."

That little speech did nothing for Elaina's tears, except increase the flow of them down her cheeks. She had not realized that Ainsley meant so much to Calum too. Possibly as much as he meant to her. Her heart felt as if it would burst. She didn't think she could love her husband more. And he'd said *she* had a big heart.

Elaina turned to Rory to find a tear slipping down her cheek. "What is it?" She laid a hand on Rory's arm.

The lass shook her head. "I just…I've never known people to care so for others. My family…" She shook her head, making the soft curls around her face bounce. "I do no' consider them family, the people who raised me. They were cruel and heartless. I cannae understand this loyalty and caring that ye show for each other and for people who are no blood to ye." She broke off in a hiccup of tears.

"Did ye no have a clan, lass?" Calum asked, laying a hand on Rory's shoulder.

She scooted out from under his touch and clung tighter to Elaina's arm.

"I'm sorry," Calum said. "I didna mean—"

Rory interrupted with another shake of her head. "Forgive me. It is a reflex I cannae control. Anyone who has ever touched me has caused me pain. No. I have no clan. Excuse me." She dipped her head at Elaina and Calum and fled the few feet to her room at the end of the hallway. Her door closed with a firm click.

Calum stared in the direction the girl had fled. "Well, we have some work ahead of us."

Elaina turned her gaze up to him. "What do you mean?"

"If we are to make her feel welcome into our fold. The lass has no' had an easy go of it, and someone, I fear, has hurt her verra badly." He eased Elaina toward their room.

"Yes, I believe they have." She walked through the door and turned to face Calum as he closed the door behind him. "Do you feel as I feel about her?"

"If ye are askin' if I feel she is already a part of our family…yes."

Elaina nodded. "You seem to have a pretty big heart yourself, Calum MacKinnon."

"She did help save yer life. What else could I feel?"

"Don't forget Auld Ruadh and the Calhoun." Elaina turned to the dressing table and absently picked up a brush, twirling it in her hands. "And after only knowing me a few days. I wonder why?" she said, turning to look at her husband, who had moved to stand behind her.

Calum slid his arms about her waist. "Look at ye, *mo chridhe.* Ye look like a woman who needs saving."

"You look like a man who might have to find another place to sleep." Elaina poked him in the ribs, making him jump.

Calum laughed and pulled her close.

She wrapped her arms around him and lay her head against his chest with a sigh of contentment.

"Who kens the reason that God brings people into our lives, Elaina? Some stay and some go, but all who pass through bring us somethin' we need."

"What did Robert Campbell bring except pain and suffering?" she said, unable to suppress the sarcasm in her statement.

"The bastard did ye great harm, there is nay doubt about that, *mo chridhe,* but before that he did help ye to cope with the death of yer adoptive parents, even though it was he who took their lives. Could ye have come to terms with it cooped up like a prisoner under yer brother's watchful eye? Campbell gave ye the freedom ye needed to get out under the sky, to breathe the mountain air. I'm no' sure one could heal while continually surrounded by four walls. He also brought ye to yer family. Without the pain he inflicted upon yer person, ye would never have been brought to the Grahams at Balquhidder. If they had no' tended the wounds upon yer back, they would never have seen the mark upon yer leg, and ye would still be considered English, your truth forever hidden in the veils of time. Where would Ainsley be? Starvin' in the mountains? Rory? Would she be lyin' dead because there had been no one there when she fainted from blood loss?"

"But he killed our child." She buried her face in his chest.

"Nay. I fear our son wouldna have lived with or without your battle with the Campbell. Ye were already havin' pains, Mam said. But I do believe that riddin' the world of that monster helped ye heal from that as well. It brought ye peace that ye had no' had before. It all works for the good, Elaina."

They stood in silence, wrapped in each other's arms as she tried to process all that he had laid before her.

"Where would I be if ye had no' had to find the killer of yer family? We might never have found each other."

"Hmm," Elaina hummed against his chest. "You would be married to that witch, Freya, I suppose."

"I couldna marry her with or without meetin' ye, *mo chridhe*."

She felt him shudder under her embrace and smothered a laugh in his chest. "I suppose we have to find the good in her at some point, but tonight I am exhausted. Take me to bed, Calum."

Chapter Twenty-Seven

THREE DAYS LATER, THE GROUP arrived in Edinburgh under the cover of darkness after having stopped by the camp and retrieved the Calhoun, Bridgette, and Auld Ruadh. Though many of them were eager for news on Rhona's recovery, none felt it safe for the motley crew to chance a visit to Duart Manor. News would have to wait a day or two.

Instead, they took rooms at separate inns so as not to draw suspicion. Lochiel, Calum, and Auld Ruadh met up with Ainsley for a briefing on the prisoners' whereabouts. At first light they made a walk of the town, passing by the building they believed still held their laird and his son. Ainsley had not seen nor heard of any movement of the two prisoners from the stables. There seemed to be three guards on duty at all times. The British army had regained control of Edinburgh, and there were far too many soldiers for Elaina's liking.

The men had abandoned their traditional Highland dress, attempting to blend in as much as possible. Ainsley had performed his duties well. He knew what time the guards changed posts, who the guards were, and their route to and from the home where the laird and his eldest son were held. That night, the men concocted their plan for the rescue of the two MacKinnon men.

———◆———

Elaina, Bridgette, and Rory walked down High Street with baskets on their arms, speaking amiably about the dreich weather. The passersby took no notice as far as Elaina could tell, though she felt guilt and fear twisted her face into horrid shapes. When she glanced at their reflection in the glass of a store window, she saw three women out for a stroll to market. She had felt certain that the world could tell they were rebel women hell bent on releasing Jacobite captives from Royal imprisonment.

Elaina felt her gut seize as their prey appeared from around the next corner. The three soldiers approached, and she studied them to be certain they were the ones they sought. Ainsley had said one was tall and the other two stair-stepped beneath him. The second tallest had a scar down his right cheek.

"Ladies." The scarred one bowed as they came upon each other in the middle of the walk, the women blocking their path.

Elaina couldn't think for a moment, couldn't move, but Bridgette dipped her head in an ever so elegant fashion. "Gentlemen." Her eyes traveled over the man in a most intimate fashion, and the shock of it nearly caused Elaina to snicker. She swallowed it down and bobbed her head as well. Rory remained as quiet as always.

"And what a fine group of women," the soldier with the scar commented.

"Aye, a fine one at that." He leaned in as if to have a closer look.

It was this soldier that unnerved Elaina. He was tall and blond, with a keen eye. The other two seemed overtly friendly, while this one studied every face as if committing them to memory. This one was a thinker. The other two seemed like randy men. He seemed like a dangerous adversary.

"We must be on our way, gentlemen," Bridgette said, making a move to step around them, though her gaze lingered cloyingly on one of the friendlier soldiers.

"What's the rush?" the short fellow without the scar said.

"Do ye no' have somewheres ye need to be?" Bridgette asked, flashing the men her dazzling smile. "Dinna ye need to be savin' the city from those horrible Jacobite rebels?"

"Rebels?" the scarred soldier asked. "We routed those bastards already. Sent them runnin' home to their mammies' tits, we did." They laughed and slapped each other on the backs as if they themselves were responsible for the recapturing of the entire city.

"Well, if that's the case," Bridgette said, "we were thinkin' of stoppin' off at the inn for a nip of something to warm our bones. Would ye care to join us, or have ye better places to be?"

"Nay." The scarred one answered for all of them. He looked Bridgette up and down like he would like to devour her in one bite. "There is nowhere better to be than in the company of such fine lasses. What do ye say, lads? Give it a go, then?"

The one that looked like he held all the brains in the group looked down the street expectantly.

"Come on, Barkley. We don't have to be there for another hour yet. He is all about the bloody rules, that one," the spokesperson said and bowed to the women, extending an arm toward the small inn that nestled itself beside a cobbler's shop just down the way from the stables housing the laird and his son.

Bridgette slid her arm coyly around his, and they waltzed off, her basket swinging.

"Do what you want," Elaina said to the tall one. "We are goin' to have a drink with or without you."

Elaina and Rory hooked arms with each other and followed Bridgette and the other officer.

Bridgette winked and cocked her head at the brainy one, urging him to come.

He gave one last look down the road and sighed, falling in step with the rest of the group.

When they had all received their tankards of ale and settled in with Bridgette nestled between the two randier men, and Elaina and Rory bookending them, the one with the scar leaned closer to Bridgette and asked how they all knew each other.

"I am the lady's maid to a countess," Bridgette said.

"And I am the nanny in the same home." Elaina smiled at Bridgette and then cocked her head toward Rory. "She works at the manor next door."

"One big happy family." Bridgette glanced at all the ladies with a devilish grin.

Elaina hoped Calum and the others were having just as much success with their mission. They would know soon enough, she supposed. She did not like the way the tall soldier kept glancing over his shoulder toward the door as if either expecting someone or thinking of going on about his day, not interested in what the others thought these women had to offer.

Rory shocked Elaina nearly right out of her chair when, after his third look at the door, she leaned closer to him, her elbow on the table and her chin cradled in her hand. "Are ye expectin' someone?" she asked. The smile she gave him made her blue eyes sparkle. It was the first time the girl had not shied away from a man like he was the devil.

"What's wrong with you, Barkley?" the shortest one asked. "You prefer the company of trews to the company of skirts?"

The two men snorted with laughter.

Elaina believed they had started their imbibing before taking up with the ladies. All the better. Let their senses be addled. That's what they needed. She wondered how much time had passed. Had it been enough?

Her question was answered soon enough when she heard the sound of pounding hooves growing louder and louder. Moments later, at least two dozen horses barreled past, some saddled and some partially so. They were followed a short time later by a mob of red-faced soldiers yelling obscenities in between gasps for breath.

All three men in the tavern jumped to their feet and took three steps to the door.

"Not so fast, gentlemen. Ye didna say goodbye," Bridgette called out.

The three men turned to find themselves staring down the barrels of three pistols. "What the fu—"

"Must I remind ye that ye are in the company of ladies, and I would thank ye to watch yerself," Bridgette said.

The men looked past the women, toward the barkeeper. Elaina knew without turning that he also had a rifle trained on the men. She smiled at the tall one and waved him toward the back of the building with her pistol.

"I don't think you have the guts," he said.

"I wouldna try her, if I were ye," Bridgette said. "Even Cumberland himself can attest to what a crack shot she is. She could remove yer left bollock at a hundred yards. Think what she could do at five feet."

Elaina lowered the tip of her gun toward the man's crotch. "Through the back. Now."

The three men traipsed through the door, and Bridgette cast the barkeeper a wink as they passed by. He returned his rifle to its resting place under his bar and picked up his rag as if nothing had happened. The women guided the men through the rear of the inn and out into the close that ran behind it.

"Now, you may continue on to your previous destination, and we shall accompany you. We wouldn't want you to get lonely nor lost." Elaina poked the point of her pistol in the tall soldier's back. "Walk."

The soldiers led the women through the winding closes that the women had traversed four separate times the day before so as to familiarize themselves with the path.

When the one they called Barkley attempted to lead them astray down a different pathway, Rory shoved her gun into his back. "I believe ye are mistaken, sir. I do believe our destination lies in the other direction."

With a frustrated grunt, the man returned to his previous route.

When they reached the back of the gray stone building that they believed held the prisoners they sought, Bridgette nudged the scar-faced soldier. "Unlock the door and step inside."

"You will regret this. I promise you." Barkley growled at Rory through clenched teeth.

"I dinna think I will," she said, refusing to be cowed down.

They ushered the men through the door and into a larger room with two more soldiers.

Barkley's hand darted out, snatching Elaina by the hair. He yanked her toward him, and she shivered at the thin line of cold steel he held against her throat. "Now then," he said to Rory and Bridgette, "drop your weapons, ladies."

Rory didn't hesitate, but instead shot the man in the foot, sending him howling to the ground. The four remaining soldiers stared at their comrade writhing in pain.

"Shoot them!" he screamed, attempting to hold his bleeding foot.

They turned to look at the women, who now held two pistols apiece.

"If'n ye'd like to keep all yer parts, I suggest we make our way to the prisoners," Bridgette said with a brilliant smile.

With a glance at each other, the men all turned toward the hallway.

"Just you." Bridgette told one of them. "The others can remain here. Wouldn't want ye tryin' to overpower us in the hallway and such."

Bridgette and the officer disappeared through a doorway.

Barkley's screams had diminished to a whimper.

Rory clucked her tongue at him. "I tried to warn ye. Arrogant, ignorant bastard."

"About bloody time," Aron said as he emerged from the hallway two steps behind his father.

"Oh? Do you think we took our time about it?" Elaina said. "We can bloody well lock you back in there."

"Gentlemen, that way, if you will." Bridgette waved her gun toward the hallway. "Someone help your brother-in-arms off of the floor, if ye would. He'll be walkin' with a tilt from now on, won't he?"

Two of the soldiers grabbed Barkley by his arms and pulled him up.

Elaina handed one of her pistols to Aron, who readily ushered the soldiers down the hallway and locked them in the room he and his father had just vacated.

"Now, can we bloody well get out of here before the whole of the British army realizes what we are about?" Laird Beinnmaree said. "Thank ye, ladies, truly. Though I think I shall never live it down that a gaggle of women rescued me." His demeanor was lighthearted and jovial for a man who had just spent the last week in the captivity of the English.

The group turned to the door and stopped at the sight of Isobel standing in the open doorway. Elaina had never seen the woman look as fierce as she did in that moment, her fiery curls somewhat tamed into a braid down her back.

"Daughter," the laird said.

"Father. It seems ye have found yer stay here quite enjoyable. It doesna seem to have bothered ye o'er much." Isobel's gaze burned black with anger.

"Nay. Truly, it was none so bad, was it Aron?" The laird elbowed his son in the side.

Aron paid him no mind, his gaze transfixed on his sister.

The laird's nonchalant attitude seemed to get the better of Isobel, and she stepped forward, slapping her father across the face with a blow that threw his head to the side.

Before he had righted himself, his large hand darted out, taking Isobel by the throat. "I am yer laird," he growled into his daughter's face. If he thought it would intimidate her, he was dead wrong.

She glared at him with all the fires of hell burning in her eyes. "You are my father," Isobel squeezed out. "And Rhona's husband. Do ye even care if she lived or died, Da?"

"Of course I do." Laird Beinnmaree shoved his daughter away from him as if she were nothing.

Isobel would not be put off that easily. "Then where have ye been?"

"I have been fighting for my prince and for my country. My king comes before all. Ye should ken that by now, girl." The laird turned his back on his daughter and started to walk away.

"Well, then," she said, "ye should ken that she is dead."

The laird stopped and slowly turned to face his daughter. "You lie."

Elaina wanted to believe that she had only said that to hurt him. To make him understand what they had all gone through these last few months. But the set of her jaw and her blazing glare said otherwise, and Elaina's hand flew to her mouth.

Aron stared at his sister in disbelief, shaking his head as if his negative response would negate the horrid truth that his mother was gone.

"Yer grandson held her hand as she left this world," Isobel said in a choked whisper. "It should have been you."

The laird hung his head, his shoulders drooping. The room stood silent. When he slowly raised his head to look at his daughter, his eyes were dark with pain. "Aye," he said. "I should have been there to hold her hand."

"Nay, Da. Ye misunderstand," Isobel said to her father. "It should have been ye that died." Isobel shoved him aside and marched out of the stunned room, leaving everyone to come to terms with the fact that the Lady Beinnmaree no longer walked this earth.

Chapter Twenty-Eight

Elaina, Rory, and Eads, the butler of Duart Manor, stood a fair distance away from the small group of mourners gathered in silence around the sinking dirt of the Lady Beinnmaree's grave. They had missed saying their goodbyes by a week. Eads had taken everything to hand in his usual proficient manner and had Rhona laid to rest in the family plot beside Elaina's mother and father.

"You should be with them," Eads said, sympathy lacing his tone.

"I will in a moment. Trying to ready myself," Elaina whispered.

"That I understand, child."

Elaina sighed. "What happened? Did the procedure not take well?" The group had had no opportunity to question what had taken place to bring them to this point. The moment they had arrived at Duart Manor—well behind a furious Isobel, who had traveled by carriage and left the others to walk in stunned silence—Eads had two carriages readied for their group, and they had gone straight from the drive of the manor to the solemn cemetery that now held another person Elaina didn't know how she would live without.

"'Twas a difficult procedure, to be sure. But she seemed to have fared well. Her color had been brighter, and eventually she had wakened enough to know that her daughter and her grandson were present. She seemed to be rallying, albeit slowly. Then word came that the English had taken her husband prisoner, and it was but two days and she was gone from this world. I think the news was just too much to bear."

"No wonder Isobel is so angry at her father."

"Mistress Isobel is not the only one angry. You thought the lad a handful before. He is uncontainable now. He is wounded greatly and does not know what to do with his grief." Eads nodded to Jamie, who sat sullenly by a dead oak tree with his chin nearly touching his chest, his blond curls hiding his face while he banged one rock upon another.

Elaina's heart broke once again into a million pieces. She didn't know how many times a heart could be knitted back together, but hers must be reaching its limit. She glanced at the group huddled at the graveside.

Calum too watched his nephew. His gazed turned to her and the corners of his mouth turned faintly upward, and he motioned her to his side.

"Go," Eads whispered. "They need you, my lady."

Elaina crossed the distance between where she, Rory, and Eads had been keeping vigil and where the rest of the group stood. The sound of her boots crunching on the frozen sleet announced her approach, and Caitir glanced over her shoulder, eyes swollen and red from days of crying.

"Oh, Caitir." Elaina wrapped her friend in a crushing embrace while reaching for her husband's hand, who stood beside them. She comforted her friend, who had done the same for her too many times to think of.

Calum wrapped both of them in his strong embrace, drawing them close. The two friends rested their heads against the wide expanse of his chest and let their tears fall unimpeded.

"May I join the nest?" Isobel startled Elaina.

Without words, Elaina and Caitir drew her into their sanctuary.

"I'm nay certain ye've got enough arms for the lot o' them," Aron's voice rumbled from somewhere behind them. In the next moment, he too had wrapped his arms around the group, and the women stood huddled in a cocoon of warmth and strength.

Jamie's high-pitched scream separated them like a knife, and they all turned in his direction to see the laird attempting to speak to his grandchild.

"Come, now." He held out his hand to the young lad. "Let us go."

Jamie scrambled to his feet and backed away from his grandfather, a rock clenched in his small fist.

"Come, son. Dinna be difficult. We must go." The laird took a step forward.

The rock left Jamie's hand as if expelled from a gun, catching the laird on his left cheek. The lad turned and ran from the kirkyard before anyone could stop him. They all broke into a run after him, but when they exited the iron gates, the lad was nowhere to be seen.

"We must find him." Elaina's gaze darted frantically around at the trees surrounding the kirkyard, her heart squeezing in panic.

Isobel, however, remained calm to the point of it being odd. "Dinna fash the boy, sister," she said, taking Elaina's hand. "'Tis no' the first time he has disappeared in this fashion. He kens the way to the house and will return home when cold and hungry."

Elaina didn't know how the woman could remain so calm. "But…"

Caitir squeezed Elaina's other hand. "He has disappeared every day since Rhona passed. He escapes to the burn where he throws stones until he is cold and hungry. We watch him but dinna let him ken it for fear he might find a new place to hide."

The others could remain calm, but Elaina's heart was as if clenched in a vise. The day she and William had buried their parents here in this very kirk, what seemed like a lifetime ago, it had been pouring rain. Today, the sleet threatened to fall yet again. The boy would freeze to death. She turned a pleading look to Ainsley, who gave the slightest nod of the head and turned in the direction of the burn. Elaina watched Calum and Aron lead the group down the road toward the main house. They had all decided it better to travel afoot today rather than be seen in one of the Earl of Strafford's coaches. There was no sense taking a chance that someone would become suspicious of the earl's carriages being used in his absence.

When they reached the manor, Mrs. Davies met them at the back gate and took Elaina in her arms. "I cannae believe they took you. And right from under our noses. I swear if yer brother wasn't an earl…"

"No need to fret, Mrs. Davies. All is well, though I must say I may be frozen straight to the bone." Elaina entered the kitchen and sighed into the warmth that enveloped her.

Missie placed a steaming cup of tea with a splash of brandy into each of the women's hands. It was then that Elaina noticed the men remained outside. Calum and Aron needed a moment alone with their father, she was sure. The news of Rhona's demise had come as a blow to them all. The women all gathered around the table and recounted somewhat tearfully the weeks that had passed since Elaina's absence. She shocked them all with the tale of how the lieutenant had changed the path he had first chosen upon learning that it was she who had sat with his dying brother, nor could they believe how the Duke of Newcastle had acted toward the daughter of his long-time family friend.

Mrs. Davies fanned herself with a towel when Elaina told them how Jeanette and Harry Everson had shoved her beneath the seat of their carriage and helped her escape. "Jesus, Mary, and Joseph, child. Ye'll turn all my hair silver at one sittin'. Come, Missie, before we burn the hens."

The door opened, and Calum and Aron entered without the laird.

"Well, where is he?" Isobel asked the pair.

"Gone." Aron plopped himself down on the stone floor by the fire. "Says he cannae stay at a British soldier's house no matter his relations. He is gone to catch up with the prince and his group."

"Coward," Isobel said with a sniff, as if she didn't believe that was the true reason for the laird's disappearance.

Elaina silently agreed. The man was a coward. She had always thought him somewhat ruthless, but never anticipated that he would behave as such. Men processed grief in such different ways, and young men in yet others. She gave a worried glance to the kitchen door leading to the outside, willing Ainsley and Jamie to come walking through.

Calum slid onto the bench beside her. "Ainsley will find him," he whispered.

Elaina squeezed his hand. "It's just so cold, and it's getting dark." She glanced at Isobel, hoping that she was not worrying her sister-in-law, but she was in the middle of her own conversation with her other brother, who sat on the floor beside the hearth with his long legs stretched out, his arms and his ankles crossed. It was the first time Elaina had seen any resemblance between the brothers. He sat much like Calum always stood. Two brothers so different yet so alike in more ways than she cared to admit.

Her thoughts were interrupted by a whoosh of icy wind that sent the candles flickering and her heart jumping. Ainsley closed the door behind him with his foot, his arms full of a big Highland boy.

Elaina scrambled to his feet. "Is he—"

"Sleeping," Ainsley whispered.

Mrs. Davies scrambled to her feet and waved for Ainsley to follow her. She led him to a room where he deposited his burden. Isobel disappeared into the room, and Ainsley returned to the kitchen, shaking out his arms.

"Oi. That kid weighs as much as a small calf. I may never be able to lift a broadsword again. Have ye anythin' to eat, Mrs. Davies?" Ainsley fell into the chair beside Elaina and massaged his arms. "I cannae feel my fingers." He wiggled them in front of himself. "I followed him down to the little burn where

Isobel said he would go. He didnae run from me, but he kept askin' for Captain Spencer?"

Elaina cast a questioning look at Mrs. Davies, who stood carving a hen.

"Aye. Lord Spencer has been here. He was here when the missus passed. The lad had run off that time too. Lord Spencer went after him, and I believe he found him in the same place. He comforted the lad until he fell asleep and then carried him home as well. Jamie followed Lord Spencer around like a lost kitten after that. Always on his boot heels. I tried to keep the lad out from underfoot and away from the upstairs, but there was no keepin' the two apart. If he wasna upstairs, Lord Spencer came looking for him."

Elaina sat speechless.

"Lady Caroline as well." Mrs. Davies sliced a good portion of meat, put it on a plate, and slid it in front of Ainsley.

Elaina cocked her head and raised an eyebrow at Mrs. Davies. "Lady Caroline?" she asked slowly.

"Aye." Mrs. Davies glanced at Isobel as she came back to the kitchen.

"Jamie is furious with us all for lettin' his *seanmhair* leave this world. The only people he will speak to is yer brother and his lady friend…and Eads. The rest of us may as well be ghosts for all the lad cares." Isobel wiped a tear from her cheek. "I've lost my mother and my son." She lay her head on the table and wept.

Aron grunted as he rose from his resting spot on the floor. He came to stand beside her and patted her head. "There, there. He will come 'round. He is hurt, is all. 'Twill nay be long, and he will be underfoot so that ye will be wishin' he were following Lord Spencer around."

"Is William about now?" Elaina asked.

"Nay," Mrs. Davies said, dashing her hopes. "He has been called away. Cumberland is gathering all of his troops throughout the two countries. 'Tis no' bodin' well for the uprisin'."

Elaina chanced a glance at Calum and Aron. The look the two brothers shared with each other told her to prepare to leave Edinburgh and her former family home once again.

Chapter Twenty-Nine

JAMIE ATTACHED HIMSELF TO HIS new savior, Ainsley, and seemed infatuated with Rory and her "orange" hair. "Ye look like a carrot," he said the next evening around a bite of rabbit.

"Jamie," Isobel scolded.

"It's nay worries," Rory said to Isobel with a dip of her head much like a beaten pup, as if she were half afraid to speak to the woman.

Elaina understood the sentiment. Her feelings had been much the same upon her first meeting with Isobel. She was every bit as intimidating as her mother had been.

The lad acted as if his mother had never spoken. Not even a glance in her direction. He had grown very good at ignoring people.

Elaina felt a storm brewing, and the lad would not fare so well in the end. Either Calum or Aron or both would have stepped in already if Isobel had not held them back. "Give him time," she whispered. "He needs time."

"He needs a skelpin'," Aron growled but only narrowed his eyes at the boy.

"I happen to like carrots just fine," Ainsley said, causing Rory's face to flush the color of a beet.

Calum turned to the fire to hide his grin.

"Oh, me too, me too," Jamie said, nearly bouncing on the bench where he sat between his two new favorite people.

"'Tis a good thing I am not a carrot then," Rory said, narrowing her eyes at the lad, "or ye might have cooked me and eaten me up already. You, meanwhile, wee Jamie, look like a potato." She scrubbed her fingers through his blond curls. "And ye are just the right size to be thrown on the fire and roasted to a crisp." Rory grabbed him up like she would do just that.

Jamie squealed and struggled to get away.

Isobel turned away from the scene. "At least he is laughing."

Elaina's heart went out to her. She knew well the jealousies the woman harbored about her child. She had been on the receiving end of them more than a year ago. Perhaps it was the thought that the group would travel on in a few days that kept Isobel from voicing her unhappiness about the situation to Rory. They would be gone soon, and she would have all the time in the world to reunite with her son. For now, it seemed that Isobel barely had the stamina to stay standing, let alone volley for her son's attention. Elaina wrapped a shawl around her sister-in-law's shoulders, and Isobel lay her head on Elaina's shoulders with a heavy sigh.

"I am tired, *mo phiuthar.* So very tired," she whispered.

"Then rest," Elaina said, wrapping her arms around her. "Lay your weariness upon my shoulders and let me be your strength, if just for a little while. It is about time you let me return the favor." She thought back to the days after she had lost her child and how Isobel and Jamie had taken such good care of her, making sure she ate something every day whether she wanted to or not.

Many times, Elaina had put her head on Isobel's shoulders and wept. It was Isobel's turn to release her grief, and Elaina planned to give her as much time and strength as she could. That turned out to be a very little indeed, as the next afternoon a messenger arrived with the news that the prince had taken ill and what was left of the rebel troops were up in arms, so to speak, over the thought that their leader might perish.

"We must go," Aron announced after the messenger's departure. "We will leave on the morrow. Elaina and Rory can stay here, and the three of us will join the ranks." He nodded to Calum and Aron.

Elaina stood with her arms crossed. "I am not leaving Calum's side."

"As generous and welcoming as everyone has been here, I must remain with Elaina," Rory said.

Aron turned a steely glare on the girl. If he thought he was as intimidating as his sister, he thought wrong.

Rory lifted her chin a notch and stared him down in a rare show of stubbornness.

Good for you, Elaina thought.

"Stare daggers into me all ye want, Mr. MacKinnon, but I will stay with her. You cannae keep me from it."

"Aye, if I tie ye up and throw ye into the priest hole, I can."

"Ye leave her alone." Jamie kicked his uncle in the shin, then darted away from his snatching hand.

Rory didn't bother to hide her smirk as Aron cursed under his breath and rubbed his shin.

"I think the lad speaks for us all," Calum said with a chuckle. "Rory should remain with Elaina, and if Elaina willnae stay behind, then I guess that means she will travel with us as well."

"Me too," Jamie said, latching onto Ainsley's leg.

"Oh, no." Ainsley looked down at the boy. "War is no place for a boy."

"I'm no *boy*," Jamie protested. "I'm a Highland warrior, just like ye."

"Ye are a boy," Aron said. "And ye are stayin' wi' yer mam, and I'll hear no more out of ye, or I *will* tie *ye* up and throw ye into the priest hole."

"I hate you!" Jamie screamed at his uncle and bolted out of the door.

"Let him cool off a bit, and I will go after him," Ainsley said with a shake of his head. "I swear the lad's temper might be worse than yer own, Elaina."

"I'll show you my temper, Ainsley MacEwan, if you don't watch yourself." Elaina snatched up an empty tin cup and chunked it at him.

He caught it deftly out of the air and set it back on the table. "Point proved yet again," he said with a laugh, then sauntered out of the door and into the early winter evening.

<hr>

The following morning, Elaina, Rory, Ainsley, Calum, and Aron left in search of Prince Charles and his crew. Tears had been shed as the girls said their goodbyes to each other, and Jamie had grown furious once again and kicked and screamed as his mother held him tightly while the five rode off into the dim light of dawn.

The traveling was miserable, with sleet stinging their faces and the biting wind ripping through their layers of clothing. Elaina didn't see much of their surroundings as she kept her head down and her fur hood pulled over as far as possible to protect her watering eyes from the brutal wind. She focused on the ground in front of her horse as if she could control where he placed his feet and what lay beneath the layers of sleet in this driving, stinging misery. She had never been so ready for spring in all of her life. Perhaps she had made a poor decision by leaving the warm comforts of her brother's kitchen.

So lost in dreaming of sitting by the hearth with a hot cup of cider was she that she nearly toppled from her horse when it stopped abruptly.

"Where is yer mind that ye nearly fall from a horse?" Aron asked as he came to a stop beside her. "It's too dangerous out here for ye to be daydreamin' so. Get yer head out of the clouds and pay attention to yer surroundin's."

Even for Aron, his tone was unusually grumpy. Elaina wished she had a cup she could throw at him.

"We must stop here," her brother-in-law announced, his expression grim. "It is becoming too dangerous for the horses. We cannae afford for any of them to slip and break a leg. Besides, I think this is the only protected place we will come across this day, if memory serves me correctly."

Elaina looked around at the small cluster of naked, scraggly trees. If Aron thought this was protection from the elements, then she had better gird her loins for the coming days. It would be longer and harder than she had thought it would be.

Elaina slid from the back of her horse and stood surveying their surroundings with her hands on her hips. Surely the sleet could not last forever, even though it seemed to have stuck around for a fair amount of the winter. The men took up their axes and whacked at the trees, cutting limbs and branches to use for erecting a little shelter of sorts. Elaina and Rory set about gathering kindling and scraps for a fire. It reminded her eerily of the lieutenant and their hideous camping escapades while he had held her captive. She wondered where he was now. Not that it mattered. He would be in the company of the redcoats, of course. She prayed God would spare not only her family but the lieutenant as well. He was not as horrible as she had first perceived. The man did have a heart after all and a sense of duty to rival William's.

They built a small fire, and Elaina all but collapsed from the fatigue of their rough travels and the weight of the grief of burying her husband's mother and saying her goodbyes yet again to Caitir, Isobel, and the household staff at Duart Manor. Wee Jamie had grown furious and disappeared upon their leaving and refusal to take him with them. He'd made it clear, in no uncertain terms, the loathing he felt for everyone but Eads and the unfairness of the fact that he would once again be left behind.

The group huddled, wrapped in their woolen tartans and arisaids. Though they sat together, each had their head covered with heavy woolen cloth, making the world around them muffled, and Elaina was overcome with the sensation of being cut off from the world. All over this country, people she loved sat about in the same horrible weather. Elaina hoped that they at least had a roof over their head, but she doubted it. Auld Ruadh and Laird Beinnmaree were with the prince and his company, and William was possibly with Cumberland. Their worlds would collide unless something could be done to stop one side or the other. Something desperate. Something dangerous. Something Elaina had not thought of yet, but she sat listening to the sleet and pondering ways to keep the two sides from destroying each other and those she loved.

A hand on Elaina's caused her to emit a high-pitched squeak. Aron had opened one of the sacks Mrs. Davies had packed them for the trip and was distributing the cold bannocks and dried venison amongst the silent group.

"Ye ken when a person squeals like that, it means they are up to no good?" Aron said, closing the sack.

"I always thought when a person squealed like that it was because an over-grown oaf scared them."

Rory snorted.

Aron cast the usually silent girl a sideways glance.

She studied the bannock in her hand as if the noise hadn't come from her.

"I said yer name twice. Ye were not here with this group. I hope ye were no' plottin' any misguided heroic attempts at anything. God kens ye've been in enough trouble already."

Elaina had no snappy response to that remark. It, unfortunately, was true enough. "If you must know the truth, I *am* plotting." She raised an eyebrow at him.

"Not my demise, I hope." Aron leaned back against one of the rooted trees they had erected their makeshift shelter through and around.

"Don't give me ideas," Elaina said with a grin. "No." She turned serious. "I am trying to figure out a way to make this war go away."

"That would be quite the feat," Ainsley said with a snort. "Even for you."

"The only way that will happen is if ole Georgie abdicates the throne now, and obviously from the word we have received, that is as probable as this godfor-saken sleet lettin' up before summer." Aron glared up at the sky as if the sleet had control over whether or not it fell.

Much like the rebels. They had no control any longer. They had retreated back into Scotland, their victories over the redcoats fading into stories the survivors would tell their children and grandchildren. If there were survivors.

Elaina chanced a glance at Calum. Light and shadow from the dwindling flames of the small fire they had built fell across his face in a macabre dance. He turned to look at her, and for a brief moment, she saw the worry in his eyes before he drew down the curtain and hid it from her.

He gave her an impish grin. "All I ken is that if there is a person alive who can end this war, it is my innovative and scheming wife."

It was Aron's turn to snort.

"But I also ken this," Calum continued. "That same person can always fall into a fair amount of trouble by trying to do what is right and trying to protect what she holds dear." His gaze turned serious. "I fear that nothin' but trouble lies ahead, no matter if we do wrong or if we do right."

The group fell into silence again. This one crawled across Elaina's skin like snakes wrapping themselves around her chest until she felt as if she couldn't breathe. She attempted to eat, but the bannock felt as if it lodged in her throat and no amount of whisky could make that lump go away. The whisky, however, warmed her, and the effects of the spirits and exhaustion soon overtook her. In a haze, she remembered Calum taking the bannock from her fingers and gently laying her down and covering her with a fur.

Sometime after the fire had burned low and the wind had stopped howling about her ears, another sound snapped her awake. A much more subtle sound. She stifled a squeal as Calum's hand clamped over her mouth. He had heard it as well. A rustle. A snap of a twig. Then nothing. Calum slid his dirk from its sheath and sat up, stretching.

"Where are you going?" Elaina whispered.

"To relieve myself. Go back to sleep, hen," he answered loud enough for any would be assailant to hear.

Elaina lay her head back down but drew her *sgian dubh* from its hiding spot. She felt the change in the surrounding group, everyone in the camp now on alert.

Calum disappeared into the dark. There was a sudden movement followed by a dull *thunk* and Calum's strangled oath. A high-pitched screech split the night. That could only mean one thing. Jamie had followed them.

"Ye little shite," Calum growled in a rare show of frustration. "I've a mind to turn ye over my knee and skelp ye a fair one." Swiping at the blood running down his forehead, Calum emerged from the brush with a livid Jamie kicking and fighting. "He's a wicked shot with the bloody rocks." He plunked Jamie down in front of the dying fire and held him there by putting his boot on the lad's legs, pinning them to the ground.

"Lemme go!" Jamie yelled.

"Haud yer wheesht, lad."

Jamie must have heard that tone from his Uncle Calum before because he immediately stopped squirming and buried his chin in a pout.

"How in the hell did ye keep up wi' us?" Aron asked.

Jamie glared at him and opened his mouth to reply but glanced at Calum and thought better of it.

"He stole a horse."

All knife points twirled in the direction of Isobel's voice as she and Caitir stepped out of the shadows.

The blood drained from Jamie's face, causing his scattering of freckles to stand out against the stark white of his skin. Even the pink from the cold seemed to disappear.

"Is this true?" Calum glared down at his nephew. "Do ye ken what they do to horse thieves, James Michael? How would ye like to hang from the end of a noose? Or better yet, be shot and just left there in a pool of yer own blood for yer mam to find? Would ye like that?"

"Lord Spencer would never." Jamie stuck his lip out in defiance. "He gave me that pony. Told me it was mine as long as I remained."

"As long as ye remained, eh?" Calum raised his brow at the boy. "And where are ye now? No' on Lord Spencer's land. So, remain ye didnae. Ye stole the man's pony. A lord and a redcoat captain. A man who put his faith in ye to care for the steed, no' make off wi' it. I suppose we must turn back on the morrow and return this rapscallion and his hijacked steed to the manor."

"No." Isobel surprised everyone.

"Yes," Aron said, earning him a glare.

"There is nothing there for me, Aron. We will continue on with you until preparations can be made for us to return home. I want to go home." Isobel's voice broke.

Caitir squeezed her hand.

Aron remained silent but kept his look of annoyance on display.

"Very well," Calum said. "But what about the horse?"

"I will send Lord Spencer recompense for the pony," Isobel said.

Calum stood quiet for a moment before looking down at Jamie. "Ye better be glad ye have such a kind mam, or I would turn ye over to Lord Spencer myself. How in the hell did ye get the damned thing saddled and get yerself on it, anyway?"

"The fence," Jamie said, the tone of his voice telling Calum just what he thought of his uncle's ignorance.

Calum must have increased his pressure on Jamie's leg, for the lad grunted with a grimace. Jamie sat sullenly, looking between Calum and his mother before dropping his chin to his chest and ignoring everyone.

"Can I return to sleep now?" Aron asked. "Tie that boy to his mam and let's get some rest. We've a hard journey on the morrow."

No one took Aron's advice of tying Jamie to his mother, but they lay down again. Isobel wrapped Jamie up in her blanket next to her, and much to Elaina's amazement, the boy eventually cuddled against his mother's chest and fell fast asleep. All of his exploits must have exhausted him as well. They were all bone weary, and she felt things would only get worse from there. Perhaps they, too, could return home.

Unfortunately, home seemed to be an evasive destination, an always shifting mirage. The closer she seemed to think they were getting to being able to return home, the farther it seemed out of reach. She wished once again that she could awaken from this nightmare and be back home… But where was home now? Duart Manor? Gleann Eader? Right where she lay? Wrapped up in Calum's arms, is what she decided. Anywhere her husband was, that was her home. It didn't matter the house, the castle, the hovel—as long as her husband was by her side, she was home.

Did he feel the same about her? Would Gleann Eader feel like home without Rhona to grace its halls? Was Isobel chasing a ghost in search of happiness?

Chapter Thirty

IT TOOK NEAR A WEEK to reach the rebel encampment at Inverness. Between keeping up with a rambunctious four-year-old, Aron's horse going lame, and the tumble Isobel had taken coming down a slick embankment, the fact that every one of them arrived at all seemed a miracle.

The sight that greeted them made them wish they had stayed in Edinburgh in Mrs. Davies's cozy, inviting kitchen.

"Ye've quite the entourage."

The voice sounded like Auld Ruadh, but the man standing before Elaina did not resemble her memories of the man, though he had not been very long gone from her presence. He was thin, and his clothes hung loosely on his sturdy frame. His hair had lost its vibrancy and taken on a fair amount of gray in the short time since she'd seen him last. He greeted his family with hugs for everyone. No matter how he looked, his grip was still as strong as ever, and Elaina fought for breath when he squeezed her.

"Ah, and there is the lass who saved my bloody life." Auld Ruadh wrapped Rory up in a hug, just as tight as Elaina's.

Rory touched him on his arm, surprising Elaina. "How are ye healin'?" she asked.

"Well enough, I suppose," Auld Ruadh said, patting her hand.

"Oh. She'll talk to him." Ainsley waved a hand at Auld Ruadh. "All I get are snorts and other odd noises."

Auld Ruadh barked out a laugh. "I have the touch, lad. Ye should pay attention. Ye could learn the ways of women."

Now it was Ainsley's turn to snort.

Rory just looked from man to man and shook her head. "Maybe if I'd seen ye on the brink of death and yet ye managed to pull through, I might be just as friendly to ye," she said.

Everyone gaped at Rory with their brows raised before breaking into laughter.

"What's so funny?" Jamie demanded from his mother's side.

That seemed to be the first moment that Auld Ruadh saw him, and he sobered immediately. "What in the name of Hades is *he* doin' here? Have ye lost yer mind, Isobel?"

Isobel glared at her uncle. "No, I havenae lost my mind. I've lost my mother, and my son ran off to join the rebel Cause. Stole a bloody horse in the process. I'm nay any more happy about it than ye are. I just want to bloody well go home."

Auld Ruadh removed his bonnet from his head and bowed it, muttering an unintelligible prayer while crossing himself. He raised his gaze to Isobel. "Ye needn't remind me of my sister's death. I relive it every day in my mind. I should have been by her side, but at least she had her daughter and her grandson. As far as going home to Gleann Eader, I'm nay certain how we accomplish that feat. Glengarry MacDonalds are deserting several a day. They are no' taking the death of Angus Og, their chief's son, well. 'Twas an accidental shootin', and they received recompense of an eye for an eye, but that has nay helped their enthusiasm at all. Then the damned MacDonalds of Clanranald are nay happy about havin' to watch an execution of one of their own for the death of Angus Og, so they are droppin' out too. Damned bastards, all of them. Pardon me, my ladies." Auld Ruadh bobbed his head in apology to the women in his presence.

"I've heard Mistress Elaina say worse." Ainsley earned himself a glare from Mistress Elaina.

"What of the prince?" Aron asked.

"He is recovering well enough. Though not well enough to come to his senses. After our retreat from Derby, the Irish Quartermaster General has his ear, and he heeds no' what his Lieutenant General Lord George Murray says on nearly every matter. He no longer has as much faith in the man, but what in the hell do the Irish ken of this land? They are out of their heids and acting like power hungry fools! Every one of them! I've half a mind to…" His voice having raised an octave during his little rant, Auld Ruadh now stopped and cleared his throat. In a calmer tone he added, "Yes, well, morale is low. The men are starvin', and exhaustion has overtaken the ranks. Driven the soul right out of some."

"Includin' ye, Uncle?" Aron asked, his forehead wrinkled as he studied his uncle's haggard face.

"It doesnae matter whether I am tired or not. I made a vow to our prince, and I'll no' break it. A man is only as good as his word, and upon my death there will be nay doubt whether I was a man of integrity or no'. Come. Yer da will be wantin' to speak wi' ye…and we will have to decide what to do wi' that one." Auld Ruadh cast a pointed look at his great nephew.

Jamie simply glared right back. Damn, but the boy had nerve.

They made their way across the muck of a camp to a canvas cover erected beside a large dwelling where Laird Beinnmaree was holding court just under the edge of it, out of the endless sleet and rain.

No more scared of his grandfather than his uncle, Wee Jamie stood in his presence, returning his stony glare. Elaina thought she might burst out in laughter and pinched herself to keep from doing just that. Laird Beinnmaree made her knees quake most of the time, whether or not she showed it. Jamie did not seem to suffer the same malady. The lad certainly had spunk.

"Ye've nothin' to say then of yer actions?" the laird bellowed at his grandson.

Jamie didn't reply. He didn't blink nor flinch. He glared in defiance at his grandfather.

"Get the little shite out of here," the laird growled when nothing he said nor yelled seemed to intimidate the lad. "Ainsley. Take the womenfolk and the runt to the tent across the way. They will give them shelter, and they can help with camp needs. God knows there are enough needs to go around. The rest of ye stay. There is much to discuss."

Elaina glanced at Calum, who gave her a somber nod.

She returned what she hoped was an encouraging smile before turning and joining the already moving group. Ainsley led the parade of Elaina, Caitir, Isobel, and a sullen Jamie across the sodden ground where numerous horses and men had trampled what was left of the dormant grass until nothing but mud remained. Mud and horse excrements, from the smell of it. Could be other excrements as well, but Elaina didn't want to dwell on that unpleasant thought. She lifted her skirts and stepped over a particularly large mud hole and ran into someone, nearly sending them both tumbling down into the questionable brown ooze around them.

A pair of firm hands grabbed her as she was going over and caught her moments before she hit the ground. "Woah there, lassie. Ye dinnae want to take a tumble into that quagmire. Ye willnae get clean until *Bealtaine*."

Elaina looked up to thank the man, but then slapped him on the arm instead.

"That's some show of gratitude," Ruske teased. "I ought to roll ye through the muck, now." He made a move to drop her to the ground.

Elaina squealed, wrenching herself away and diving behind Ainsley. "You scared the life out of me. For a moment I thought you a ghost."

"Oh, I came close to it. Caught a fever from all the wounds, but the *diabhal* isna ready for me yet."

"Well, I'm sure the devil doesn't want the competition," Elaina said.

"Ah, look at that. Learnin' ye a little *Gàidhlig,* are ye?" Ruske said.

"Elaina!" A feminine voice called to her before she could reply. She turned to see Bridgette with her skirts fisted in her hands and her raven black hair drawn into a tight braid that hung over her shoulder and bounced with every step as she jumped gingerly from somewhat dry spot to somewhat dry spot.

Elaina wrapped her up in her arms when she reached them.

"Ah, I see the welcome ye get compared to the one Elaina offered me. I feel verra unappreciated," Ruske said.

"Dinna be jealous, love. Ye scared the daylights out of her for the first few months that ye kent her. I cannae blame her for holding a grudge." Bridgette's words were muffled in Elaina's coat. When they broke free from their embrace, her eyes glittered with tears. She wiped them on the back of her woolen mittens. "Thank ye again for bringing him back to me. Hopefully, we can return home soon and get on with our lives."

"From your mouth to God's ears," Isobel said.

"To be certain," Caitir chimed in.

Elaina introduced Isobel to Bridgette and Ruske.

"Ye are the one they call the Calhoun?" Isobel said.

"I see my reputation precedes me." Ruske gave Isobel a bow.

"I'm nay certain that is a good thing," Bridgette said with a laugh.

"Let's walk." Elaina slid her arm through Bridgette's and the other through Ruske's. It was an odd feeling, for Ruske was so tall and Bridgette no taller than Elaina. Quite the difference in height. They walked a short way before Elaina turned to look behind her. "Well, all of you, too." She laughed at the group she had left behind standing in the cold, looking like the lost and weary travelers they were. Elaina wanted to see the camp. There were questions that needed to be asked and answered. She wanted to know why Auld Ruadh looked so beat down and had seemed to age years in a matter of months.

She didn't have to twist Ruske's arm to get him to divulge all he knew about the lack of funds, not to mention the lack of support promised from France and the other countries. There was no money to pay the men and no food to feed them. Supposedly funds were coming and just hadn't reached the prince's hand yet.

"Also, Cumberland has moved his troops from Aberdeen across the Spey. He is close. Verra close, indeed."

"That is of no matter." Aron had come up beside Ruske. "We will make them wish they had never stepped foot in Scotland. We'll send him and his pompous, bilious father back to Germany, where they belong. The throne belongs to the Stuarts."

"That is the fightin' spirit we need," Ruske said.

"Well, that is the fightin' spirit ye shall have."

Aron turned to Bridgette. "Take the ladies and the child to the women's tent. I've need of the Calhoun. Ainsley, come along as well. Ruske, have ye caught sight of John Roy within the last hour?"

"Stewart?" Elaina asked. "John Roy Stewart, the poet?"

"Aye, that's the redheaded bastard. But he is no' just a poet. He is a fighter and loyal to the Stuart crown."

"I've no doubt," Elaina said, glancing about warily.

"Now, that is no way to be, lassie. He helped to save yer husband's life. No' to mention yers truly as well." Ruske thumped himself on the chest.

"I do owe the man a debt," Elaina conceded.

With a curt nod to Elaina and a swift glance at Rory, a look that was almost unnoticeable...almost, Ainsley fell into step with Ruske the Calhoun and Aron.

"Oh, no, you don't," Isobel ran after Jamie, who had caught up with the men, and grabbed him by the scruff of his coat.

He struggled and howled with rage. "Let me go! I'm no' a girl!"

"Ye may no' be a lassie, son, but ye are certainly acting like one at the moment." Aron snatched Jamie out of his mother's grasp, pinning his arms to his sides and forcing the boy to look at him.

"Stop yer bloody haverin' and go wi' yer mam. I dinnae wish to have to skelp ye in front of God and everyone, but I swear ye're pushing me to it. Now, go without argument." Aron set the boy on his feet beside his mother.

Jamie shrugged himself from his uncle's grasp, then folded his arms and glared at Aron, his face showing red either from the cold or his recent struggle with his uncle. Elaina took it to be the latter. The lad was hurting. He had watched his grandmother die, holding her hand as she'd passed from this earth. He had been torn from his home and thrown into this uncertain mess. He had lost William and Caroline, the only people he felt he could confide in, and now here he stood in a camp full of injured, exhausted men who still fought on, and he, the poor lad, had to tag along with the women. Elaina wanted to wrap him up in her arms and comfort him the way he had given her comfort after the loss of her baby, but she sensed he was not ready yet. He followed the group of women as Bridgette led them across the muck to a small house with a thatch roof that was filled with other women in various stages of mending torn and bloody articles of clothing, treating the wounded, or sitting beside a wall with their heads buried in their hands.

Jamie found himself an empty corner to curl up in, rolled himself into a ball facing the wall, and pulled his knitted hat down over his face.

Isobel shook her head as she watched the performance. "I hate to beat the lad, but he is pushin' me to the edge. The sooner we can get back to Gleann Eader, the better."

Elaina felt much the same, but there was a niggling in her gut that made her think they might never see Gleann Eader again. *Nonsense,* she thought, as she took up a torn and bloody tunic, fingering the fabric. An almost overwhelming sense of pity washed over her as she took in the state of the clothing. She felt so sorry for whose ever it was, not only because it looked as if they had sustained a terrible injury but also because she was a horrid seamstress.

Chapter Thirty-One

MUD PULLED AT HER BOOTS as Elaina squeezed her cloak tighter around her tiny frame. Her dress hung loosely, and her stomach rumbled. They were starving. There had been very little to eat on the weeks' ride to Inverness and all but nothing since they had arrived weeks ago. A biscuit in the morning, if they were lucky. Now, the Jacobite army had made its way from Inverness to Culloden house, rousting Lord Culloden, who was the Lord President of the Court of Session, only the most senior legal officer in Scotland and an ardent supporter of King George, but the prince had run him out of his own lavish house.

Elaina's gaze traveled over the men huddled around the fires across the field. Earlier in the day, she had overhead Lord George Murray and Cameron of Lo-cheil speaking with Auld Ruadh. None were happy about the location in the least. Drumossie Moor was boggy and flat. The Highlanders had better luck when they could descend on their enemies in a horrific roust from above. What could they do here? It was too level, too wet, and a vast open space. They did their best to convince Prince Charles that the chosen moor was unfit for his intentions, but alas, O'Sullivan's flattery held more sway than Murray's experience. The only chance they stood was if they could lure the English between the two dikes.

An arm snaked around her waist, and Elaina emitted a tiny shriek as it pulled her to a stop.

Calum whispered in her ear, "What are ye fashin' about so, *mo chridhe*? I called yer name."

"Not *fashing*, just thinking, and kindly stop sneaking up on me." Elaina looked up at him over her shoulder.

His hazel eyes twinkled in the light of a nearby fire. He leaned closer, his lips grazing her ear, sending her into a fit of shivers. "Come wi' me. We shall escape all of this if just for a bit. I've somethin' to show ye."

"What is it?" She didn't know whether to be wary or excited.

"Never ye mind just now. Ye'll see." Calum took her by the hand and led her through a maze of campfires and rumbling voices.

She stumbled along, the ground uneven and black as pitch. The third time her toe caught a rock in the dark and she stumbled, Calum caught her, scooping her up in his arms and continuing his journey through the men amongst whistles intermingled with Gaelic shouts and laughter.

"I can walk, you know." She felt the flush creep up into her face as Calum hollered back at one particularly boisterous man. She squirmed in his arms, trying to break free from his grip.

"Ye can? Then why were ye stumblin' 'round like a wean? I'm only savin' yer dignity."

She could just make out his dimple in the glow cast by the fires. "Saving my dignity? Then what's all the Gaelic noise about?" She tugged at his queue hanging down his back.

"No' fit for a lady's ears."

"That's what I thought. Put me down."

"I will soon enough. Ye just be still and enjoy the ride."

The ride ended in a copse of trees well beyond the other men. A small fire burned, and Calum deposited Elaina on her feet before adding wood to it, pushing the flames higher into the night. She huddled up beside it, holding her frozen hands over it. She smelled the heated wool of her gloves before she felt it.

Calum took her hands in his, rubbing them vigorously. "Ye are goin' to catch them on fire."

"Well, maybe that would warm them. I don't think I have felt them for near a week now."

"Mine too." Calum chuckled and pulled her down beside him onto a blanket of fur, then wrapped her up in his arms, his legs encircling hers, and pulled another fur around their shoulders. "I do believe this may be the coldest winter I've ever lived through."

"Maybe it's because you are starving like the rest of us." Elaina squeezed his thigh. Though still rigid with muscle, it was decidedly smaller than it had been.

"Aye, that could be it as well. I will be glad when all of this is over and done, and we can return to Gleann Eader and a decent meal, a decent bed, and work on a house for the two of us. It must be large, though."

"We do not need a large home for the two of us."

"We must, so we can fill it with all the babes we are to have."

"With all the babes?"

"Aye. A woman spoke to me this verra mornin'. She had the sight. Told me our home would be filled with weans."

"She did, did she? And just where did you run into this seer?"

"In Culloden when I got us this." Calum pulled a wad of fabric from inside his coat. He began to unwrap it but moved with the speed of an elderly man, one corner at a time.

Elaina arched a brow at him.

He continued his torture while he stared into her eyes, studying her as if he wanted to devour her.

Heat flooded through her, and she leaned in for a kiss when he unfolded the final bit of fabric. "Cheese." The word escaped her mouth on a foggy sigh and all thoughts of kissing fled her brain.

"Yes, cheese." Calum tore the small wedge in half, handing Elaina one of them.

Holding it close to her nose, she inhaled the heady, sharp aroma of it. She wanted to devour it all at once and cherish the sight and the scent of it longer. She took a small nibble and groaned with ecstasy.

"I like that sound, *mo chridhe*. I would like to make ye do it again." Calum leaned closer.

"I'm busy," she said, taking another nibble of the cheese, letting the salty morsel sit on her tongue. She closed her eyes, savoring. "Tell me more about the seer."

Calum chuckled and pulled her in tighter. "She stopped me on the street, told me she had a vision for me."

"Well, I could tout to being a seer too and traipse around asking for coin to tell people they were going to have lots of children."

"I didnae give her coin, and there is more." Calum's voice grew somber, and Elaina could feel the change in his body. He lay his chin on top of her head. "She told me that our child rested in the arms of those who loved him, no' to worry about where his little soul abides."

Elaina's breath caught in her throat. Babes died so often it would be nothing to assume that a person had lost a child. But she'd said, "his soul."

"She also told me that blood would flow through the streets of Edinburgh and fires would burn the countryside. I want ye all to return to Gleann Eader. I will send Ainsley wi' ye."

"I will not." She looked up at him, appalled at his words.

"Ye must, *mo chridhe*. It would kill me if anything happened to you."

"I feel the same for you, and that is why I cannot go."

"I dinna wish to argue this night. Put that thought aside. We will discuss it more in the mornin'."

After a drawn out moment of silence, Elaina asked, "Did she say whose blood?"

"Nay. She couldna or wadna tell me the outcome of the risin'. But she told me my home would be filled with weans."

Elaina tried not to put stock in the seer's words, but if they held true, that meant Calum would survive whatever was to come. But what about herself? What if she couldn't carry children? She had already lost one. What if Calum's house was filled with another woman's babes? The thought suffocated her soul, and she fought to hold her tears at bay.

"What is it, love?"

"Nothing, I just…I just… I don't want to think about any of this anymore. I want to go home to Gleann Eader and raise a family with you. I don't want to be here, and I don't want you here, either."

"I promise to leave as soon as possible. Surely to God, Prince Charles will come to his senses."

"We can try to take leave on the morrow. So many have left already. What are two more?"

"I cannae abandon my clan. If my laird leaves, I will leave. Until then…"

Elaina knew the ending of the sentence full well and felt a small bit of shame for having suggested leaving at all.

"Now," Calum said with an air of finality, "let's see if we can forget our unhappy bellies for a few moments." He turned her toward him and lay his forehead upon hers.

She stared into his ever-changing eyes. Dark as pitch at times, then the flames of the fire would glint off of them, sending them into ripples of gold and brown. "I do love you so, Calum MacKinnon," she whispered.

"And I you, Elaina MacKinnon. To the end of my days."

As he lay her back on their bed of furs and his warm hands contrasted with the chill of the soft snowflakes drifting onto her cheeks and clinging to her lashes, Elaina prayed with everything she had that the end of their days was a very long time away.

Chapter Thirty-Two

THE CHANTERS AWOKE THE CAMP at dawn, the pipes screaming their orders for the clans to come forth and assemble. Elaina, Bridgette, Isobel, and Rory stood on a knoll beside a tree and stared out at the sea of men before them and the expanse of the moor after that. Isobel kept one hand firmly on Jamie's shoulder, holding the lad in place lest he attempt to dart out into the oncoming fray. But the fray never came. The clansmen stood for hours searching the horizon for the first signs of the king's army, only to be disappointed or relieved, depending upon who one asked. At around eleven that morning, the prince gave the order to break. Weary, with bellies rumbling, the men returned to camp with orders from the prince for them to be fed.

"With what?" Aron grumbled. "There is nothin'. The bloody rations are still in Inverness. That idiot, Hay, cannae find his own arse with both hands, let alone organize damned carts full of oats, and God forbid there be any kind of meat involved."

"It will be got, dammit," a waif of a man with strings of gray hair shooting every which way from his red scalp yelled at Aron. Likely, he was the man Aron called Hay, and he truly must have been none too bright to raise his voice to Aron MacKinnon.

Aron took a step toward the man, his fists curled at his sides. "Get on wi' ye, then. Why are ye standin' about as if ye've nothin' better to do?"

The man swallowed hard before turning and scurrying away like a rat.

Laird Beinnmaree, Caitir's father Donald Murray, and Locheil joined the group that had gathered under Laird Beinnmaree's tent cover. Auld Ruadh and Ainsley soon joined the group as well.

"As much as I would like for it to be over and done wi'," Locheil said, "it is just as well nothin' came of the mornin'. The Frasers and MacPhersons, from what I gather, are no' even to Inverness at the moment. The bloody MacGregors are north in Cromarty. No offense, Mistress MacKinnon." Lochiel bobbed his head at Elaina over his foul language at her clan of birth.

Elaina nodded back, not a small amount relieved that at least her Uncle Graham and her cousins might be spared a certain death for the moment.

"Aye, some of the men have gone home to defend their homesteads from the Campbells that have been let loose upon the Highlands," Auld Ruadh said.

Laird Beinnmaree lifted his head to look at something over Elaina's shoulder. She turned to see a rather annoyed Lord George scouring the grounds. He caught Laird Beinnmaree's eye and jerked his head toward the grand Culloden House. "Come," the laird said to the men. "There is much to discuss."

Calum placed a kiss on Elaina's forehead before following his brother, father, and the others toward the house.

A silence crushed the group of women who stood watching the retreating men. They all exchanged glances and joined hands without a word. Apparently, Elaina was not the only one to have the cold hand of dread squeezing her heart.

⸻ ❦ ⸻

"We are to bring an attack this night," Ruske said without the excitement that his voice usually held at the thought of a good fight.

"In Nairn? Now?" Isobel asked, unable to hide the disbelief in her voice.

Elaina couldn't believe it either. The men of their group had spent the day either in meetings within Culloden House or pacing the frozen muck outside of it. The women had stayed on the other side of camp and out of the matter completely. Now, there was no staying away.

"Aye. My understandin' is that it's the day of the good ol' duke's birth, and the powers that be expect them all to be merry with drink and therefore easier to catch unawares." Sarcasm laced Ruske's statement.

"Let me guess. It is the blasted Irish responsible for this nonsense. These men have had no more than a biscuit to eat in days and some no' even that! I cannae even remember the last time any one of us ate meat," Bridgette growled in frustration, expressing what everyone else was feeling.

"Nay. No' the Irish this time, but Lord George. The prince refuses to entertain the idea of retreating farther and luring the English onto more stable ground on which to fight. Lord George thought if he could no' convince the prince otherwise, then we should attack tonight in Nairn, to stand a better chance at victory," Ruske said.

Lord George Murray stormed from Culloden House, his face twisted with a dark unhappiness as he gathered the troops together. Though it was his plan, he still seemed none too happy at the prospect.

Elaina met Calum's eye, and the regret that swam there made her want to weep.

"Ye must wait here, *mo chridhe.*" Calum took Elaina's face in his hands. "Please," he said as she opened her mouth to argue. "For me. I cannae defend myself if I feel I have to defend ye as well. Stay with the women, and I will ken that ye are safe."

Elaina placed her gloved hands on his, wishing it were skin on skin instead of wool. She closed her eyes, willing the tears to stay. Tears would help nothing. "Come back to me, Calum MacKinnon," she whispered.

"Always," he whispered against her lips.

Though his nose was cold, his lips were warm. She drew a measure of comfort from the ferocity with which he kissed her. But then he was gone, blending in with the straggling regiments on a desperate mission into the black night.

Sleep evaded the women all through the night. Elaina paced through the encampments surrounding Culloden House, passing Rory and Bridgette as they sat by a dwindling fire. Both of them were unaware of the happenings around them as they stared into the dancing flames. If any of the women spoke to another, it was with the hushed tones of standing in a graveyard.

A hand grabbed Elaina's arm.

She looked back at Isobel's ashen white face. "Bloody hell, Isobel. You nearly scared me to death." Elaina clutched a hand to her chest, her heart racing beneath it.

"I cannae find Jamie," Isobel hissed, her eyes wide with fear.

"You don't think..."

"I dinna ken. Damn that boy! I should have known. I should have tied him to me. How many times has he run off?" Isobel's hands were clenched and shaking around the folds of her skirt, the trembling climbing her arms and her eyes growing wider with each word she uttered.

"Yes. How many times have we had to hunt for him, but we have found him every time, mostly unharmed?" Elaina had a flashback to the lad's pale face and blue lips as he lay on the banks of the loch back home at Gleann Eader. The boy was like a cat with nine lives, but his odds of remaining unscathed were growing slim. "Come." She took Isobel by the hand and dragged her through the camp to where Bridgette and Rory sat.

Elaina hadn't time to utter a word before Rory had scrambled to her feet. "What is it?"

"Jamie," Isobel said.

"Again? I'll skelp the boy!" Rory looked like she meant it.

"I'll gather torches," Bridgette said, fisting her skirts in her hands as she spun out of the glow of the firelight.

"We cannot call out to him in case there are redcoats about, but should we head in the direction the men took?" Elaina asked. Traversing the moor at night was not a pleasant thought.

"I'm fair certain that is where he would go," Isobel said with a sigh. "What am I doin' wrong, Elaina? Why can I no' control my own child? He's just a lad, for heaven's sake." She swiped an angry hand across her face.

"You are doing nothing wrong." Elaina wrapped her arms around her sister-in-law. "Look at your brothers. Did they not act the same as wee Jamie when they were but lads?" She knew for certain that Aron had. She had heard stories.

"Aye, but that doesnae make it easier." Isobel sniffled into Elaina's hair.

"I know. But it's the only thing I could think of to say."

That got a chuckle out of Isobel.

"Here," Bridgette had returned with torches. "I brought two in case we need to split up. But I thought too many and we might alert the English that something is amiss."

Elaina's stomach churned with the thought of the possibility of betraying their men and their mission, and she decided when they found Jamie this time, she would skelp him herself.

It wasn't long into their search before a sour taste formed in Elaina's mouth and grew increasingly worse with every step they took. They had somewhat fanned out, her and Isobel together and Bridgette with Rory, but the ground they traversed was little more than a quagmire, and the thought of the men having to do battle where they could lose their footing at any time was unsettling. Their mission must be successful this night.

Isobel let out a squeal as the ground swallowed her near to her knees. "Bloody hell," she hissed through her teeth.

Elaina gave her a hand and tugged her out of the quagmire, only to lose her footing minutes later. What came out of her mouth was not near about as nice as what Isobel had said. She pushed herself to her feet. The moor sucked at them, trying to swallow them. She could only imagine what it would do to a young lad.

They struggled on for what felt like forever, the two sets of women growing farther apart. They had taken to hissing Jamie's name into the black night. For all they knew, the damned moor could have swallowed him up.

Isobel stopped to catch her breath and stood with her hands on her hips, panting. "No wonder Lord Murray is none so happy about doing battle here. 'Tis impossible. Surely the prince and his other commanders can see that? I mean, here I am a lowly woman, and I can tell that this is no' a place where ye would like to face down the enemy. Ye cannae run. Well, if ye had redcoats blazing down on ye possibly, but for the love of all that is holy, I pray their mission is successful this night."

"From your mouth to Go—"

A faint wail silenced Elaina's thoughts.

"That way," Isobel pointed, and the two of them began to make their way toward the sound.

Elaina felt as if she could lose a boot at any moment. Thank heavens she had cinched them up tighter before they left. The sound grew louder and more distinct the farther they waded and struggled, and Elaina's heart began to sink. She could see the slump in Isobel's shoulders that meant she had determined it too. Instead of a five-year-old boy, they were tracking down a lost sheep. They kept their trajectory and soon stumbled upon the helpless creature bogged down in the muck. Elaina attempted to scoop the sheep up and help it gain its footing on slightly more stable ground, but then she toppled over as the blasted sheep scrambled to safety and out of her arms. She heard a muffled snort behind her.

"A hand?" she said, holding an arm straight up in the air.

After a moment, she began to think that Isobel was just going to stand there laughing silently instead of helping her to her feet when finally, a hand gripped hers. It was larger than Isobel's and had no problem yanking her to her feet. She smacked directly into a firm chest. A chest covered in a uniform. A captain's coat, no less. Of his majesty's army. She looked up into the face of her brother and her knees gave out from the relief of the moment, his tightening grip the only thing keeping her from sinking to her knees.

"William. Thank God." She dropped her forehead against his chest.

"What in the hell are the two of you doing trapesing around the moor in the dead of night? Do you know just how dangerous it is?" He gave Isobel the same glare that he gave Elaina.

She closed her eyes as she heard Isobel suck in a breath behind her. *Well, now he's gone and done it,* Elaina thought to herself.

"With all due respect, Captain Spencer, or do I call you *my Lord* Spencer?" Isobel asked, her voice dripping with disdain.

Elaina wondered how the two of them had survived being in the same house together during the time she had been gone.

William stood in silence, but his grip tightened on Elaina's arms as if she were the one speaking to him in such a manner.

"Does it look like we are having a bloody good time? Do ye truly think that we thought, 'Oh, let us go for a jolly jaunt through the muck and the mire in the freezing sleet. Let us get buried to the waist in ice cold sludge. What fun that will be?' "

Silence.

Afraid to look up at him, Elaina kept her eyes closed instead. She could imagine the daggers he was shooting through Isobel. She had been on the receiving end of many an intimidating, baleful glare from the Spencer men. Though frightening, Elaina assumed Isobel would react the same as she did, with more tirade and a stubborn will.

"Have ye happened to come across a wee lad rompin' 'round out here? Oh, he is about so high with a head full of blond curls and is a wicked shot with a stone?"

"Jamie? Is out here?" William dropped Elaina's arms with that stunned statement.

"I dinna ken where the hell he is, but he is no' at camp. We thought he might…" Isobel had come close to disclosing the whereabouts of the rebel army.

"You truly think he would wander out on the moor…in the pitch black of night?" William sounded incredulous.

"Have ye met the lad?" Isobel asked.

Elaina could sense in her sister-in-law's tone that she was about thirty seconds from throttling William.

"Yes…well…you do have a point," William conceded.

"What are *you* doing out here?" Elaina asked, suspicion dawning on her.

"I was making a patrol and saw the light." He turned his burning gaze to her.

Elaina raised an eyebrow at him. "Why are you making patrols and not your men?"

"Because they are having a raucous good time and someone had to keep an eye out for souls lurking about in the dark, looking to do harm. Are you just using Jamie as an alibi for being on the moor, headed straight for enemy camp?"

With a growl, Isobel slapped William, nearly knocking him off his feet. He grabbed her hand as she started coming back for more.

There was a tense moment of silence, during which Elaina was afraid to breathe.

"Obviously, I was mistaken, and I apologize." William held both of Isobel's wrists while also holding her gaze until the heaving of her chest slowed and her shoulders slumped.

"I'm sorry, Captain Spencer." Isobel's voice hitched.

"I deserved it, and I *am* sorry. Come and let me help you look for him." William took the torch from Elaina, turned into the black night, and yelled, "Jamie!"

Elaina thought her knees would buckle beneath her. If the rebels were any-where close and heard them, they might be in trouble. William, most definitely. Elaina and Isobel exchanged a look behind William's back. What were they to do?

They were coming up on dawn. Elaina had no idea how far they had trav-eled in their search, but she had heard no sounds of battle and certainly the rebels should have attacked already. If William were here, she could be assured of his safety, if only for a short time. But Calum? And Ainsley? What of the other part of her heart? They stumbled on through the ever-changing light until two figures emerged from the haze of sleet.

"Anythin'?" Isobel asked as Rory and Bridgette stopped short at the sight of William.

Both stood frozen like statues, except for the slight shake of their heads, their gaze never leaving Elaina's military companion.

"This is my brother," Elaina said. "Captain Spencer, this is Bridgette and Rory. They've been helping us."

The two women, as if pulled by the same marionette, bobbed their heads in unison.

"Ladies," William only cast them a cursory glance before his gaze returned to their surroundings. "How certain are you that the lad came this way?" he finally said.

"I dinnae ken in which direction he went," Isobel said. "We just took up torches and set out."

"From the rebel camp?" William asked.

Elaina felt Bridgette stiffen beside her.

William took notice as well. "We know where your camp is, just as your men know where ours is. This is war…Bridgette, is it? But I am not on this moor at the moment as a soldier but as a brother and a friend looking for a lost little boy who probably needs warmth, and food, and… What did Mama always say?" His gaze turned to Elaina.

Their mother had said a lot of things. Elaina didn't know to which he referred.

"Ah, a skelping. Is that the correct term?" William asked Isobel.

"Aye, 'tis. And he needs a good one."

They had taken no more than five more steps when a faint thumping sound echoed across the open expanse. Everyone came to a stop. It was not the rant of the pipes that the women had been expecting all night but a rhythmical tapping.

William looked toward the sound and back at the women. His countenance had turned grim in that brief span of time. "I must go, and so must you," he said. "I do not think that Jamie is on this moor." He took Isobel's hands and squeezed them. "I will continue to watch for him, and I will do everything in my power to protect him if I find him, but this is no place for a lad, nor a woman."

They had traveled much farther than Elaina had thought. Just how close were they to the enemy camp and where were the attacking rebels? Had they missed their window of opportunity, for that is what it seemed?

William turned his gaze to his sister. "This is where we part ways yet again, Elaina."

Elaina nodded, then William wrapped her up in a tight embrace. She buried her face in his coat, trying to inhale the scent of him in case she never saw him again. Two siblings on the opposite side of a war. There were several like her in the camp. She had heard that even father and son might face each other on the battlefield soon. But she didn't want it to be this way. She didn't want him to leave. She wanted to gather all of those she loved and cart them away, back to the colonies and far away from this entire blasted mess.

William kissed the top of her head before he let her go. "Stay safe, sister," he whispered, clasping both of her hands.

A hoarse whisper was all that Elaina could muster. "And you, brother."

William nodded to those standing around them. "Ladies. Good luck, Isobel," he said. "I promise I will keep looking."

"I do thank you, truly," Isobel said with a rare hint of a tear in her eye.

"Well…" William said.

They all stood around awkwardly, not quite knowing what else to say or do.

"I believe there is a road that direction." William pointed off to the right. "Now, I must go." And he did, as fast as the boggy moor would let him.

When he was out of earshot, Bridgette blew out a sigh. "The night's mission was a loss, then? We havena found Jamie, and our men havena attacked."

"That is how it would seem," Elaina said.

"Let us go for the road," Isobel said, marching off in that direction. "Mayhap that is the direction he went, for we have no sign of him here."

Rory, as usual, remained silent, and she walked beside Elaina as they struggled to make their way to the road.

It was the shuffle of feet that drew her attention first. Many of them. Then, the closer they got, they could make out line after line of ghostly shapes in the dark. The women quickened their pace until they came to the road and stood to the side, watching the defeated passing of many a Jacobite traveling in the wrong direction. The prince rode up and down the ranks, attempting to get them to turn back, attempting to rally their spirits to no avail.

One gentleman just sat down. "I havena eaten meat in days. No' even a biscuit last eve, and he thinks we could do battle starved and exhausted from marching all night? I shall sleep here, and when I awaken, I shall find some meat." True to his word, the man curled up beside a brush of dormant heather and covered his head with his plaid.

"What is happening?" Bridgette rushed to one of the men, a Cameron.

"We didnae make it in time. Too much arguing and posturing between the heads and not a damned one of them with any sense." The man's voice dripped with disdain for both of the leaders. "So now we return to camp and hopefully sleep and, prayers to God, find food."

Isobel made inquiries about Jamie, but head after head shook their answer. Elaina didn't know if the men saw much at all. Many of them, their eyes glazed, merely stared at Isobel in confusion before shaking their heads.

"Well, ye look like a fine mess," John Roy Stuart said as his regiment dragged past Elaina.

Elaina raised an eyebrow at him. "Yes, well, we all can't appear as dandy as you all the time."

"No. I suppose not. What are ye doin' nearly in the enemy camp?"

"We are looking for my nephew, Jamie. I don't suppose you have seen him or my husband and his clan?" Elaina fell into step with the poet turned soldier.

"If he is the rotten blond-headed scoundrel I think he is, then nay, I havena seen him. But I would like to get my hands on him." John Roy rubbed the back of his head as if he had been the recipient of one of Jamie's stones. "But in any matter, nay. I havena seen him, but as ye can well see, this is a most unorganized march. We are losing men by the minute. If they hadna stopped to argue so many times on the way, we might have won the damn war already. Beggin' yer pardon."

"No need to apologize, Mr. Stuart. But would you please keep an eye out for any short, blond-headed heathens?"

"Aye, I will if ye promise to look for some food as well as yer boy. These men cannae go on much longer."

"That I promise," Elaina said, and then she disappeared into the straggling men, searching for anyone who was a relation.

Dawn broke, if one could call it a dawn with just the palest of sunlight peeking through wave after wave of sleet and rain with no young boy in sight. Nor Elaina's husband. The women had become separated as well, as they weaved in and out of the exhausted rebels. When she finally found Auld Ruadh, he said he thought Calum had accompanied the prince into Inverness in search of food for the troops. Prince Charles had been incensed at learning that his men had not eaten a proper meal in weeks.

Elaina explained Jamie's disappearance to Auld Ruadh, who shook his head in anger. "I ken the boy has seen much and lost much, but for God's sake, can no one contain him? He is like a ghost constantly slipping away. I will spread word with the men to be watching for him."

"Thank you, Uncle." Elaina wrapped him up in a massive hug before kissing him on the cheek and returning to her search for Jamie.

Worn to the bone, Elaina shuffled in and out amongst the throng of men, some who fell and slept where they lay, whether it be in a ditch, under a tree, or in the road. She found shelter under an eave of Culloden House, where she sank down against the wall and pulled her knees into her chest. She needed to find Jamie, but she also needed to rest her legs and her eyes for just a moment. When someone plopped to the ground beside her, she glanced up from her knees to find Rory studying her with concern.

"Are ye bonnie, then?" Rory asked, drawing her knees up as well.

"Aye," Elaina answered.

Caitir dropped to the ground on the other side and followed the other two women's lead of drawing her knees in. "I cannae move another step," she said, her hands kneading the muscles in her calves.

"Bridgette?" Elaina asked.

"She is with Ruske," Caitir said around a yawn so big Elaina could see the back of her throat.

"I need but a few minutes to rest and then I can go on." Elaina attempted to stifle a yawn and failed.

"Just a short nap," Rory said, scooting closer to Elaina.

Caitir did the same.

The three women huddled together under the dripping eave of the grand house like a brood of hens and drew warmth and comfort from each other as they drifted off to sleep.

Chapter Thirty-Three

THE RANT OF THE PIPES pierced through Elaina's dreams. She buried her head farther into her knees. She wasn't ready. Just a few more minutes.

The blasted noise only grew louder.

Elaina raised her head and looked around with bleary eyes that she had to blink several times to get to focus. Most of the men were already gone. A small brigade of them rooted and rummaged through everything around the camp.

She clambered to her feet and grabbed a passing Cameron by the arm. "What is it? What is happening?"

"The English, madam," he said, intensity pouring from his body.

She could feel the knot of muscle under her hand that shook slightly from the grip the man held on his broadsword.

"Clans MacKintosh and Lochiel came back to announce that bloody Cumberland was on the move. We've been standing in wait for hours, but nothin' has happened, and we are starved. Do ye have anything edible? I dinna care if it is covered in mold or worms. I haven't the strength to wield my own sword."

Elaina shook her head, and the man shrugged his arm free and returned to his shuffling trek to the far edge of Drumossie Moor. She turned to find Caitir and Rory on their feet as well. The immense crush of dread that coursed through her could be read easily enough on her friends' faces. As the wailing of the pipes died off, the echoing rhythmic beating of the English army's drums could be heard staccatoing the air and the sleet with their interminable rhythm that was enough to put a chill in one's heart. The men about them froze, then with a dissolute air, snatched up their weapons and returned to their ranks.

There were so many. The drumming was so loud Elaina imagined the English already upon them. She turned toward the moor and the tap, tap, tap that never wavered from its rhythm. Snatching her skirts out of her way, she ran in the direction the men were headed. She had to see for herself.

There. The prince! That meant Calum had returned as well. She became distracted by that thought, and her search turned from attempting to gauge the range of the enemy to attempting to find her husband. Prince Charles looked pale and drawn from his night's adventure and the morning's continuation. As Elaina approached him to inquire of Calum's whereabouts, a group of men, MacDonalds possibly, were bending the prince's ear about the right side being their side by tradition, the MacDonalds, Clanranald, Keppochs, and Glencoes. It had been thus since the battle of Bannockburn when Robert the Bruce had battled King Edward the Second all the way back in 1314, but now Lord George Murray's Atholl men had been granted the position and not a one of the Mac-Donalds were happy about it in the least. The prince seemed none too happy to have a history lesson, either.

Elaina didn't have time to wait for the bickering to end. Her gaze searched the surrounding men, looking for his curls. The blasted drums made it impossible to think. She ran, not waiting to be certain that Rory and Caitir followed, through the ranks of men, searching for the MacKinnons…Ruske…Laird Beinnmaree…John Roy, anyone who could tell her where her husband was.

When she came to a stuttering stop, Rory and Caitir, who in fact had been with her all the while, crashed into her, nearly taking them all to their knees.

"This is nay place for a woman," a Fraser beside her growled. "Get ye back out the way."

Elaina ignored him, her gaze upon the far side of the moor. His mouth stilled at her expression, and he turned in the direction she was looking.

"Shite," the man said as crimson topped the curve of the moor, the British standards glowing against the gray skies. "It seems today is the day, and this is the hour."

Elaina squinted against the sleet and the rain and watched as the group of English soldiers came to a stop in a line at the top of the hill. The bloody drums continued, pounding through her as the sleet stung her face in an oddly matching rhythm. Mayhap that was just the thumping of her heart. To her horror, the blood red line continued to grow on either side. Soldiers marched into view, the horizon filling with their numbers, stretching until they filled the whole of the horizon. Then the surrounding men began to huzzah and bravado even as the crimson line grew to a terrifying length. The rebels pounded their swords against their targes and shouted insults at the English, but they returned not one shout. The English stood stoic and unmovable on the far hill.

A hand shoved Elaina, and she nearly fell to the ground. "Get out of here before ye get yerself killed!"

This time, Elaina's feet moved. She grabbed Rory and Caitir and they ran, zigzagging through the ranks and up the knoll to where the prince paced his gray gelding back and forth. She continued to scan the thousands of heads before her, looking for Calum, the prince occasionally blocking her view. Cries of "Close up!" rattled over the pipers that continued to squeeze out each clan's rant until they all blended together in a screech that took Elaina back to the hill at Balquidder.

She felt the concussion before she heard the rebel cannons firing. It had begun. The smoke from the cannon fire blew back into the rebels' faces, joining the sleet and rain in blinding Prince Charles's army. Elaina stood on a rise along with the prince, who was surrounded by his footman, a guard of men on horses, and his young aide. The cannon shot seemed to fly over the entirety of the British army. The Jacobite men were unskilled in cannonry, and the better of them had abandoned their duties. The rebels continued scatterings of unsuccessful cannon fire.

A blast rippled its way across the moor, the shock of it hitting Elaina in the chest, but the actual cannonballs themselves bounced over the heads of the front lines of Jacobites and caught the second line with their force, removing limbs and sending them flying about like scatterings of birds. There was no time to take a breath nor to scream before another round of blasts rocked the air. Smoke and sleet hid part of the horrors, but even the cannon blasts could not drown out the screams of the wounded.

Without warning, a cannonball smashed into the earth beside the prince's horse, splattering him and those around him with mud, but worse, killing his footman and wounding his steed.

Elaina lay on the ground, stunned by the impact of a shot so close. She felt about her person, but she seemed to be intact. She turned to look for Caitir and Rory and found them on their hands and knees with their heads covered. They seemed to be smarter than anyone else standing on that bloody hill. Elaina crawled across the frozen ground to her family as cannon after cannon fired from across the moor.

Calum. A tear slid down her cheek.

Somewhere in the carnage was her husband. Her entire family, fighting for their country and their prince, who traded one horse for another. The pipers continued playing, but the rebel cannons had stopped. The yelling of orders was near drowned out by the screams of the wounded and the pounding of Cumberland's cannons. There was not much to be seen, however, for the smoke of the Royal army's cannons blew directly into the faces of the rebels along with the deadly balls. Darts of crimson cut the smoke from across the way, and Elaina wondered why nothing more was happening. No one had moved from their starting positions except for those blown away. Someone had come yelling at the prince.

Elaina turned toward the sound and watched an angry and anxious officer all but demanding that the prince give the order to charge. The rebels could not move until he gave the order, and there stood his men in an onslaught they could not withstand much longer.

Finally, the prince conceded and waved his aide, young Lachlan MacLachlan, into motion.

Young MacLachlan sprinted toward the front lines, yelling "Claymore!" the signal to charge. Before the young lad even reached the clansmen at the back of the formations, before anyone could hear him yelling to charge the enemy, a cannonball ripped through the air, removing his head.

Elaina felt herself falling, her vision going black.

Chapter Thirty-Four

S MOKE SWIRLED IN A MACABRE dance with the shards of ice stinging Elaina's face. She stared at nothing, blinking the sleet off of her lashes. An occasional shot split the air, but mostly moans and screams mixed with the *ssht* of the sleet falling all around her. She didn't want to move. She didn't want to look. The image of the cannonball taking the young aide's head played over and over in her mind, along with the urgent yells of the front line begging their prince to let them advance as their comrades fell hundreds at a time around them. She closed her eyes to the thoughts and felt the tears freezing on her cheeks. She wanted to lie there for eternity, still with her eyes closed, so that then none of this would have happened. No blood would have been spilled on this miserable day. But unable to stand the surrounding sounds anymore, she pushed herself up, her frozen clothing crackling as the sleet broke away from her person as if she were a body rising from the dead.

She stumbled to her feet, looking around her. She was no longer on the hill. Someone had taken the time to move her under a bramble of bushes. Neither Rory nor Caitir were in sight. In fact, not much was in sight besides smoke and carnage. She walked toward the sound of moans and screams. Wailing. She stared in horror at the piles of bodies, some alive. Most dead. In the moments that the wind blew the smoke and sleet clear, she could see those who had not perished in the fight being helped along their way by the blade of a bayonet. There was not one Highlander standing. None. If any had lived, they had retreated under the onslaught offered so handily by the English.

Elaina took a stumbling step toward the bodies. MacDonalds here, Frasers there. The names of the clans continued as she stumbled around and over the maze of bodies. MacGillvaries.

The sleet continued to fall, covering the dead men and making them look not quite real. The entire scene was a living nightmare. She raised her gaze toward where the English had stood, destroying her family. The family she had found not two years earlier.

English soldiers moved through the crowd of bodies laughing and joking with each other as they pierced the dead and near dead with their bayonets. They gave no quarter. The soldiers spit on the Highland dead and rammed their bayonets with such glee that they looked like schoolboys hunting for frogs. They took what they wanted from the dead, searched the bodies for whatever baubles they might find.

"The spoils of war," Elaina whispered.

"You, there!"

Elaina turned to the sound of the voice to see two English soldiers running at her as fast as men could move on the boggy moor and over the dead. "Spoils of war," she said again.

Calum. Where is Calum? He would save her. He needed to save her. "Calum?" Elaina took a hesitant step into the abyss of bodies. "Calum." Her voice came hoarse from her throat as if she had screamed for a very long time. "Calum!" she yelled. Her steps quickened as her body began to awake from the numbing slumber it had been in. "Ainsley!" She could feel the sob rising in her throat. "Aron!"

She stumbled on some of the dead. There was nowhere to step except on them.

"Auld Ruadh," she whispered as she looked down at his body. His bonnet had fallen away, his hair loose from its queue pooled out around him in a halo of auburns and grays. One leg was no longer attached to his body. If it was nearby, another body covered it. Blood stained the front of his plaid in several spots as if hit by grapeshot. She thought he twitched ever so slightly. She knelt beside him. "Auld Ruadh. Can you hear me?" She tried to smooth a strand of hair from his face, but it had frozen to his skin.

He moved then, ever so slightly turning his face toward hers. "My child," he whispered, his tongue coated with a wet sheen of blood.

Her tears flowed freely now. "Yes, *m 'uncail,*" she whispered, taking his frigid hand.

No warmth remained in it. He was not long for this world. She sat down hard, upon what she did not want to know, and pulled his head onto her lap.

She wanted to wrap what was left of him in her arms, but his head was the only strength she could muster. "I love you, you know." The words were nothing but breathed sounds as she choked on a sob. She brushed her fingers across his forehead and smoothed his mottled hair as she would a child.

"Aye, *mo nighean,* my lass. I pray ye ken what ye mean to me." He closed his eyes with a grimace.

"Yes. You have made that clear, Uncle." Elaina pulled him close and wept into his hair.

"Dinna cry for me, child. Just pray wi' me."

Elaina took a hiccuping breath, not certain that she could say the words. "Eternal rest, grant unto him…" The rest of the prayer came out so choked one could hardly understand the words.

"Thank you, child," Auld Ruadh whispered, a tear rolling down his cheek. He looked up into her eyes, his own clouded with his coming death. "Now," he whispered again, "kill me."

Elaina stared at him in horror, then shook her head. "No. I cannot!"

His hand moved, and he patted his dirk that had fallen by his side.

Someone jerked Elaina to her feet, causing Auld Ruadh's head to land on the ground with a thud.

"What've we got, 'ere? A Scottish whore?" A soldier sneered in her face.

"It doesnae matter whether she is or whether she isn't. She'll do all the same." The other gave a chuckle at his own cleverness.

Auld Ruadh made a noise, and the soldier looked down at him.

"Friend of yours?" he asked Elaina, giving her a terrible grin with his head cocked to the side. He leaned toward her, his sneering face mere inches away. "Not anymore," he whispered, his breath foul and his eyes glazed with hate. He stared Elaina in the eye as he drove his bayonet into some part of her uncle. The soldier thought he was performing a horrific act meant to wound her greatly, but he'd unknowingly granted Auld Ruadh his final wish.

Elaina refused to look. She refused to scream. He had done the man a favor, after all. He no longer had to lie in pain and freeze to death. But the tears fell anyway, with or without the scream. She closed her eyes and all but collapsed. It was as if Auld Ruadh—her friend…her mentor…her family—caressed her cheek as his soul passed from this life to another. The two soldiers took her by the arms and dragged her from the field, stumbling as they went.

"Calum!" she called out as they dragged her over body after body. "Aron!

Ainsley! Ruske!" She screamed the names of the men she knew if not for them to hear her and save her, then in remembrance.

"Shut your bloody mouth," one of the soldiers said through clenched teeth.

"Donald Murray! Locheil! John Roy—"

The soldier's fist collided with the side of Elaina's head, making her ears ring and black dots dance in her eyes. "There is no one left to save you."

A scream broke through the din in Elaina's head, and the soldier whose punch had caused the ringing tumbled to the ground, taking her with him but releasing her arm as he went. It was the demons of hell, for surely that was where she was. This…this thing, these bodies on which she now lay. She had never seen such horrors. This could not be the world she lived in. Man could not be that evil. The screaming continued. Elaina rolled onto her back to witness these demons, only to see Rory's orange hair standing stark against the gray of the day. She was beating the soldier who had laid hands upon Elaina.

The second soldier wrapped his arms around Rory, who fought with the wrath of a demonic being.

"Stop it," the soldier said, pinning Rory's arms to her sides, but he couldn't contain her legs, and her foot connected with the fallen soldier's mouth and nose before the man holding her took two steps backward. "Rory. Hush. Be still."

Rory and Elaina looked at the soldier's face at the same time. Lieutenant—No, Captain Perry held her captive. Rory collapsed in his arms.

"That bitch should die," the soldier on the ground said with his hand covering his mouth.

Elaina assumed the man had lost some teeth with Rory's kick because the words came out something more like "that bith."

Rory raised her chin in triumph.

"From what I could see, she was protecting her friend from deplorable treatment from a member of the king's army. You punched a woman in her head. A defenseless woman."

"Well, Cap'n," the man mumbled, "she was too thupid to keep her mouth thut. Ain't nothin' but a Scottith whore. They thaid take what we want."

"A woman is not the same as a knife or a fur. We will take the prisoners from here. You clean yourself up and get on with your duties." To the other soldiers accompanying him, Captain Perry said, "Help the lady to her feet."

As the soldier followed his captain's command, Elaina whispered, "You will let me go? Let me find my family?"

"I cannot do that, my lady. I may be able to save your virtue at the moment, but I cannot guarantee that I can save your life, and I am damned certain that I cannot procure your freedom. You are under arrest for high treason and crimes against the house of Hanover."

Elaina's legs collapsed under her, but the soldier holding her didn't let her fall.

Captain Perry emitted a sigh that intoned deep regret. "Come, ladies." He led the treacherous journey to a wagon waiting at the edge of the field of bodies. The very road that all of these dead men had traversed just this morning. "You may take them." He passed Rory on to another set of hands, and someone pushed both women into a wagon loaded with the shivering bodies of captives, their heads hanging, buried in their chests.

Two benches were built into the back of the wagon. Bloodied prisoners filled one and most of the other. Elaina and Rory huddled together on one of them, wrapping their arms around each other. Elaina lay her cheek upon Rory's head as if she were comforting her child, which was absurd because moments ago it had been Rory scrapping and fighting to free Elaina. Rory now sat with her face buried in Elaina's blood-soaked cloak and wept.

Elaina watched Captain Perry mount a horse before he gave a curt nod to the driver of the wagon. It jerked into motion, causing its load to sway as one, all but toppling them over onto each other. She watched the battlefield with its swarm of red demons collecting the remaining souls as the wagon bumped along.

Captain Perry followed the wagon, and as long as he did, they had protection. They might be headed to prison and a probable execution, but they would not be raped or tortured under his watch.

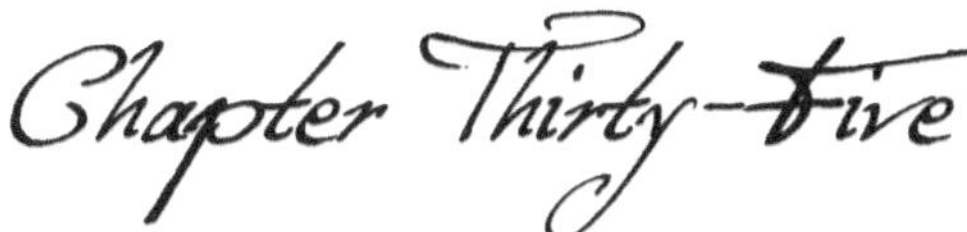

ELAINA TUMBLED OFF THE SEAT, landing hard on her hands and knees, when the cart came to a stop. Rory helped her back up onto the seat as three other people were shoved in amongst them.

"Ye dozed," Rory said in explanation of how Elaina ended up on the floor.

There was no more room to sit except the floor, and the new woman scooted back until her back leaned against the front wall of the cart. She kept her head down, but Elaina knew from the color of her hair that it was Isobel.

"*Mo phiuthar*," Elaina whispered.

Isobel did not move.

"Sister," Elaina repeated louder in the king's English, and someone kicked Isobel's leg, which was not the right thing to do.

Isobel lunged up at them, grabbing them by their throat.

The other woman's eyes bulged with fear and the inability to breathe. "Yer sister." The words were nothing more than a hiss, and the bulging eyes darted in Elaina's direction.

Isobel's head whipped around, and the fury that warped her face into someone Elaina almost didn't recognize faded away; the grief that replaced it shattered Elaina's heart into a million pieces.

"Elaina," Isobel whispered, releasing her victim. She crawled on her knees to lay her head in Elaina's lap, where she wept and clutched at Elaina's skirts.

Elaina didn't want to ask, but she needed to know. "Jamie?"

Isobel shook her head, and Elaina wanted to retch.

"I dinna ken," Isobel whispered into Elaina's skirts. "I dinna ken if my son lives. I never found him."

"Then there is hope," Rory said.

"Hope?" Isobel looked up into the girl's face, anger overtaking the grief. "Hope?" she all but yelled. "Look where we sit," she said. "There is no hope. We will hang, and I will never know what has become of my boy. Perhaps it is better that way. For when I die, I can imagine him healthy and happy back home in Gleann Eader, growing into a f-fine young m-man." She collapsed back onto Elaina's lap.

"I apologize," Rory herself was crying as she fell to her knees and wrapped Isobel in her arms. "I meant no offense."

"Oh, child, it is I who should apologize. Ye meant nay harm." Isobel wrapped her arms around Rory, and the two women wept together.

For either of the two women kneeling on the floor to show such emotion, and to each other no less, was nothing short of a miracle…or a tragedy. Perhaps they would never know the fate of the rest of their family, and maybe it was all the better.

The smell of smoke filled the air and grew stronger the farther they traveled, until the wagon pulled to a stop in front of a building that raged with fire.

"What of it?" the driver of the cart asked a soldier who stood leaning on his gun, watching the building burn with the glee of a small child having received a piece of candy.

The soldier snorted. "Told 'em we were takin' 'em to treat their wounds. Gullible bastards." He threw his head back, laughing.

One of his companions added, "Lit 'em on fire, we did, the rebel scum. Burned 'em alive!" He, too, looked hysterically gleeful.

Caught up in the excitement of the kill, they relished it, the death of others. A horrific death at that. A sentiment Elaina could not understand. She looked toward the back of the wagon where Captain Perry sat on his horse and stared at the building in disgust before turning an angry glare on the jovial soldiers.

"Get back to camp," Captain Perry ordered the men, sobering them immediately.

"But our orders were to kill any rebels we found," one of them argued.

"And that you have done in a most inhumane and crazed manner. Get back before I have the lot of you shot."

The soldier looked like he wanted to argue more, but Captain Perry pointed his pistol at the man, daring him to say another word. He did not. As their small group turned, grumbling, back toward Drumossie Moor, Captain Perry waved the wagon back into motion, his face twisted with rage.

Elaina watched the building continue to burn as it grew smaller and smaller with the sway of the wagon. Any of their clan could have been in there. Her gut twisted, and sweat broke out on her neck. The dark spots danced in her eyes again, and she put her head down and closed her eyes. She couldn't even offer a prayer for the dead or the dying. Not for herself or even for wee Jamie. She hung her head and wept. She was not the only one. She could hear the hiccuped breathing of those around her. The grief-stricken made their own music with the sniffles and the occasional wail. If Elaina had had it in her, she would have wailed just like the others. But she couldn't. She could do nothing but sit and cry and wonder how they'd ever gotten to this place. How someone could be so indifferent to a human life as to burn someone alive? There was no honor in the way the soldiers were behaving. No humanity. They were crazed animals.

They traveled for hours, or days. Elaina had no comprehension of time. Rory insisted Isobel take her seat on the bench. Rory sat with her head in Elaina's lap and her arms wrapped about her legs. Elaina kept a hand on her head as she herself leaned her head against the bumping wagon and slept fitfully, dreaming of red dragons who lit everyone in their path on fire before crushing them under their massive paws.

It was dark when they stopped. Guards stood on either side of the wagon, watching the captives. Elaina no longer saw Captain Perry. Perhaps he had already retired for the evening. She imagined him sitting down to a warm meal. Snuggled up in a warm bed. They had offered neither to the prisoners, to no one's surprise. It also stood that no matter how much the prisoners begged, they were given no water and not allowed to leave the wagon for indelicate reasons.

"Take care of it where ye sit," one guard said, standing at the opening of the cart with his bayonet pointed at them, daring them to move.

A prisoner stood and aimed his privates out of the wagon, pissing on a guard. They dragged him from the bed of the cart and beat him so severely that the women covered their ears in an attempt to drown out the sound of whatever weaponry the English used this time. The guards threw the man back in the wagon where he lay on the floor, making small hissing sounds as he attempted to breathe. Several of the prisoners fell to their knees around him, trying to help, but what could they do? Nothing but comfort. Elaina felt certain that he would die during the night.

Elaina thanked the gods that she couldn't remember the last time she'd had a drink of anything, for her urge to relieve herself was not as great as others.

It might have been by morning, however. Women defiantly lifted their skirts and squatted, eliminating their water, including Rory, whom Elaina then pulled onto her lap so she would not have to sit in a river of urine. The three women held each other and slept fitfully until the breaking of dawn when one of the redcoat soldiers yelled into the cart and threw in a loaf of bread. The starving prisoners clamored like rats to get to the bread, some trampling the now dead prisoner. Men and women fought and scratched like wild animals.

Rory leaped from Elaina's lap and dove at the foray.

Elaina tried grabbing her skirts to drag her back.

Rory tugged her skirts free and then grabbed a woman by her hair with one hand and a man by his ear with her other. "Stop it!" she yelled down at the remaining scrappers. She pushed one of them over with her foot. "Stop acting like savages! Ye are acting exactly how the English and lowlanders think we act. Stop lowerin' yourself to their expectations. Get up from there and hand me the bread." She released the man and the woman, patting them on their heads like children. A triumphant prisoner retrieved the loaf of bread and opened his mouth to take a monstrous bite, but Rory snatched it out of his hand.

"It's mine," the man growled and lunged at Rory, but Isobel's foot shot out, tripping the man, and he landed with a hard thud on his face.

Rory held him there with her foot. Several feet joined Rory's in keeping the man down. "It is *ours*," she said, breaking off a piece and handing the man under her foot the first piece.

He stared up at her, his jaw slack and a measure of disbelief on his face.

"Can ye act civilized, sir?" Rory asked the man. Her voice that had boomed through the wagon like a man's was now soft with compassion.

The man stared at her a moment before nodding, and Rory lifted her foot, as did the others.

The man pushed himself from the floor and took his seat once again on the bench on his side of the wagon.

Rory tore the bread into pieces and distributed them evenly to the captives. When she started back to Elaina's lap, one woman stood up from their side of the wagon and took the dead man's spot on the other side. She nodded to Rory and nibbled on her bread. Strangers scooted down, making room for Rory to take a seat beside Isobel.

"Well done, lass," Isobel said as she patted Rory on the leg.

"All we have is each other." Rory's voice cracked. "We cannae kill each other over bread." She took a nibble of her piece, then snorted a laugh as she wiped away her tears. "Horrid bread at that."

That brought a modicum of smiles to the surrounding faces. It was true. All they had was each other. Everyone else who they loved was gone. Alive or dead, no one knew. They were just gone. Life as they knew it was gone.

A short time later, a handful of soldiers came and dragged the dead man out of the cart. The wagon started up again, but this time there was no Captain Perry behind it to protect Elaina. He, too, was gone.

━━◆◇◆━━

Elaina didn't know how many days they traveled, each one like the next. One loaf of bread. One small bucket of water passed around. It was all Elaina could do not to just turn up the bucket and drain its contents. She sensed that the entirety of the wagon felt the same as they stared longingly at the bucket making the rounds. They were allowed one stop a day to relieve themselves, but they did it beside the wagon with no privacy and a bayonet at their chests. They had yet to stop today, and Elaina was growing anxious. When she thought for certain that she could hold her water no longer, the wagon pulled to a stop yet again, but what she saw darkened her heart with fear.

The wagon sat before the Tolbooth Prison in Edinburgh. The prisoners were unloaded, and before they could send them marching through the doors of their new home, Elaina squatted beside the wheel of the wagon. Before she had finished, however, she was slammed in the head by what felt like a boot heel and sent sprawling into the stream of what she had been trying to avoid.

"Ye bastard!" Isobel's voice came through the ringing in Elaina's ears.

"Shut your bloody mouth unless ye want some of the same," a man's voice growled as a pair of hands eased Elaina to her feet.

Isobel wrapped an arm around Elaina as they were herded like sheep to slaughter inside the worst prison in Scotland.

Chapter Thirty-Six

T HE RUMORS SHE'D HEARD ABOUT the prison held no light to the true horrors that dwelled within its cold stone walls. Weeks had passed with almost no food, women injured and crying or howling in pain, or dying, only to be shoved in a corner and left to rot. The stench was unlike anything Elaina had ever encountered, and she found it impossible to keep anything of substance in her wame no matter how much her companions tried to force down her. They all shared their bread, though Elaina argued that they should not waste it. She would only expel it once it hit her stomach. Rory and Isobel took turns holding her while she wretched each day with nary a complaint. Most of the time it was only bile, for they went days sometimes without food. When they received any, it was usually molded bread.

There was a rattling of the door to which Elaina paid no mind. They were finally coming to remove the two women who had died days ago. They were never in a hurry to remove the dead. They were never in a hurry about anything.

"What are ye doin'?" Isobel said.

Boots appeared in the dimness in front of Elaina. "We've orders." Soldiers dragged her to her feet and carried her from the cell as her two caretakers protested all the way to the door. With a grunt of frustration, one man turned. "If you don't shut that pie hole of yours, I'll fill it with something you'll no like o'er much."

There was a scuffle that had Elaina hitting her head on the bars of the cell door, and she thought she heard someone hit the ground. She hadn't the strength to fight. She let the men drag her down the stone corridors, winding their way out of the rancid smell of the prison cells and into an area that merely smelled of damp air and wet stone. Elaina's wame settled with the fresher air, somewhat. They stopped before a door and one of the guards knocked.

"Enter," said a voice from within.

They did just that, shoving Elaina through the open doorway where she landed with a teeth-jarring thud on her knees. She hadn't the strength to lift her head. She sat with her hair hanging in strings around her face, trying to stop the trembling that now encompassed all of her body from their little jaunt from the cells to wherever this place was. The door slammed shut behind her. The silence rang in Elaina's ears, and she thought herself to be alone until a voice called out from across the room.

"Pull her to her feet." His tone swam with a mix of annoyance laced with disinterest. "Look at me, child," he ordered after his men had dragged her near-lifeless body from the floor, though her feet would not hold her.

Elaina raised her head, and through the veil of her filthy hair, she saw the Duke of Cumberland seated behind a heavy oak desk with his legs crossed. The sight of his portly frame would have made her knees buckle had she been using them, but they were useless. She hadn't the strength to stand.

Cumberland rose from his chair and crossed the room in three easy strides. He stood before her, the buttons on his vest straining against the substantial girth of his waist. The duke was eating very well indeed. Much better than the Highlanders had all those weeks past. With a gentle hand, he pushed the hair away from her face. "Not nearly as lovely and elegant as the last time we met." His eyes roamed over her filthy and torn dress that now hung loosely from her frame.

"I'm sure that is so, Your Grace. I am sorry for my shabby appearance in your presence. Had I known where I was going, I would have tried harder." Elaina performed as much of a curtsy as she could muster while being held in the air by her arms.

The duke merely grunted at her attempt at levity, then turned his back to her and paced to the hearth, his hands clasped behind his back. He stared into the flames. The only sound in the room was the crackling of the peat bricks in the fireplace. Just when Elaina thought she could take no more, someone else entered the room. Not just one someone else but two, and when Elaina turned her head to see who her new companions were, she thought her heart would shatter into a million pieces.

William stood before her with his wrists shackled in front of him and his uniform in tatters, the evidence of a fight written in blood upon his clothing and his face.

"William," she whispered, wondering if his own people had dealt out punishment for a sister turned rogue.

He stood stoicly, his chin held high, but he could not disguise the concern in his eyes when he took in her appearance.

"Now that everyone is present, let the party commence," Cumberland said from across the room. "Leave us," he ordered Elaina and William's accompanying soldiers.

Elaina crumpled to the floor as her support abandoned her. Following their commander's orders, they turned on their heels and the click of the door closing behind them sent chills down Elaina's spine. She harbored no doubt that everything had taken a dire turn. Sitting in the frigid cell with hundreds of other women and rats scurrying over you in the dark and biting at your legs was bad enough. Not to mention the eye-watering stench of human excrement and bodily fluids. Then there were the dead that lay bloating in the cell until what few guards they had decided it was time to remove them. None of that compared to the nausea roiling in her belly at being shut in a room with Butcher Cumberland and her innocent brother shackled as a common prisoner. She had heard the stories. Every time a new person joined the other prisoners, they would share their stories of the horrors taking place on the outside. The murders…the rapes…the burning of houses and barns…the confiscation of everything people owned. Cumberland's bootheels sounded hollow against the floor as he came to stand in front of her and William.

"The two of you are quite the pair." Cumberland stood before them.

If he wanted a response, Elaina had none. Her mouth had gone dry, and the trembling had returned.

"I am disappointed with you, Captain Spencer. I would think you could better control your traitorous sister. Your father would roll over in his grave. You have shamed his name and this country."

"I have done nothing, Your Grace," William said.

Cumberland landed a blow to his nose that almost took him to the ground.

He caught himself and straightened, his chin high and blood pouring from his nose, across his lips, and dripping from his chin.

"He is not my keeper," Elaina said.

"Is he not?" Cumberland turned on her with fire in his eyes.

Elaina struggled to find her tongue again. "N-no. I am wed. I left his care not long after we first met, Your Grace."

Cumberland narrowed his eyes at her. "It does not matter that you are married, my dear."

"Does it not? He has not been in my life for over a year now. I turned my back on him when it became apparent just how loyal he was to his king. Meaning no disrespect, Your Grace."

"Elain—"

The Duke of Cumberland squatted in front of her, snatching Elaina's chin and cutting off her brother's protestations.

"Do not speak ill of my father," Cumberland growled into her face.

"I am not." How she got the words past her lips, she was not sure. "William is loyal to England and to your father. You must believe me. He tried to stop me many times, but my blood lies with Scotland, Your Grace."

His hand squeezed harder at her words, and she thought he would snap her jaw in two. "How in God's name does the daughter of one of my most revered captains turn her back on her home country and support a fool? Was the MacKinnon's cock that good, my dear, to turn you against king and country?"

If his words were meant to shock her, they had done their duty. He knew of her association with Calum. Was he alive? Had the duke already served his punishment and did her husband lie in a grave, or had he burned alive with some of the other prisoners? Had he died on the moor at Culloden? An unwanted tear slipped down her cheek.

"M-my husband did nothing to turn my heart, Your Grace. You see, I am not the daughter of your most revered captain. I am the daughter of Mairi and Thamas MacGregor of Balquhidder. I am Scottish by birth, by blood, and now by choice. William is innocent in all matters. He has only ever done his duty for his country. He is your most loyal and humble soldier, sir. His name is as clean as was my father's...*his* father's."

"Elaina, please," William begged as Cumberland dropped her face and paced the room.

"But you are not innocent, are you, Elaina MacKinnon? You aided your father-in-law and your fool of a prince in their treachery against the king."

Elaina remained silent. She would not protest her innocence in the matter, though she had done nothing to promote the rebellious Cause. She had still stood beside her Scottish family, even by the prince himself. Innocent, she was not. Guilt surged through her like a burning fire. Guilt for her father's name, the man who had raised her as his own. Guilt for her brother standing beside her like a common prisoner, a man who had committed no wrong except loving her even when she had turned her back on England. God help her, she had heard the screams of the tortured. *God, please show mercy, though I do not deserve it.*

"Captain Spencer. There will be a full investigation into all aspects of your life and your career before I make my final decision about your guilt or your innocence."

"I understand, Your Grace."

"You will find nothing detrimental to his name. I assure you," Elaina said.

Cumberland turned on her. "Shut your mouth."

Her mouth snapped shut, fear shooting through her like lightning.

The hatred in his eyes burned like fire. "Elaina Spencer *MacGregor MacKinnon.* I sentence you to death for treason against your just and rightful king. I shall hang you from the gallows in the square for all the country to see what happens to traitors, women or otherwise."

If Elaina were not already kneeling on the floor, her legs would have given way. As it was, it was her arms that gave, and she rested her forehead on the cold stone floor.

"Your Grace," William pleaded. "Show mercy. I beg of you."

"Why? Are you not as innocent as she claims? Why would you beg for the life of a traitor to your country if you are as loyal as she has made you seem?"

"She is my sister. Blood or no blood, Your Grace. I offer to take her place. Please spare her life."

"No, William," Elaina said into her hair, sounding calmer than she felt. "I will take my punishment."

"I surrender my life for hers."

"William, please. You have committed no wrong." Elaina raised her head to look at her brother.

William stood straight and defiant, ignoring his sister's plea.

"You would give your life for this wretch who would not go free, I assure you. She would live out her days in prison, what little of them she has left, by the looks of her."

"I would."

Cumberland sneered at William, "How very gallant of you, Captain Spencer."

"I remind you, Your Grace, that I was taken from the field of battle where I fought for my king and my country, where I carried out your orders. I am giving you a life for a life."

"You cannot make demands of me, son. I am like God, judge and execu—"

"Forgiving," Elaina said. "God is forgiving."

The duke snorted with laughter. "Forgiving? That is what you think I am, lass? I assure you I am anything but. To your feet." Cumberland grabbed her elbow, hauling her up. "Very well, Captain Spencer. I will spare your sister's life."

"No!" Elaina took a stumbling step toward the duke, who drew a pistol and held it against her forehead.

A knock on the door interrupted the fiery exchange.

"What!" Cumberland bellowed.

Elaina cringed.

The door opened, and the Duke of Newcastle lumbered into the room. "My apologies for interrupting, Your Grace, but I would request an audience with you before you lay down your punishment. 'Tis quite urgent, I assure you." His gaze flitted from the pistol at Elaina's head to Cumberland's face before briefly lighting on each sibling.

Cumberland lowered his weapon. "I will give you five minutes and not a second more."

"It will be brief and well worth your time, I assure you."

Elaina sat hard on the stone floor as the door closed behind the two men.

"Eat this quickly." William knelt by her side with a wedge of cheese extended in his hand.

"How? What?"

"It doesn't matter. I knew you would be starved, but I never dreamed you would be like this."

"I-I don't know if I can eat it and keep it down."

"You must try." William held the back of her head and fed her the cheese like a babe.

Elaina fought to keep the rich morsel on her irate stomach. She had eaten nothing but a few bites of moldy bread in days and her wame worked hard to reject William's offering.

"That's it. Swallow." He rubbed her back like her mother used to do when she had woken from a night terror.

She wished she could awaken from this terrible situation, but there would be no escape. Then she grabbed her brother's hand and pleaded, "Calum? Have you any word?"

"No. I've none. Ainsley was captured, but he lives. That much I know."

Elaina didn't know whether to be grateful or to weep.

"On your feet," Cumberland bellowed, throwing the door open and barreling through the doorway. "Lord Spencer, in exchange for your sister's life, you will receive 50 lashes in the center of the town square while Madam MacKinnon watches, and in return, she will carry out her days in servitude in the Royal colonies. She will be transported aboard ship and sold as an indentured servant for the rest of her days. Of course, that is should she survive the voyage, which at present looks as if she may not. To which I may add that I do not give one damn either way. You may thank the Duke of Newcastle Upon Tyne and Captain Reginald Perry for sparing your life, Madam MacKinnon. Now, I've better things to do than stand here with the likes of you." Cumberland left as fast as he came.

Two soldiers entered after him, taking Elaina and William by the arms.

The Duke of Newcastle and Captain Perry stopped them in the hallway.

"How?" Elaina asked.

"That is of no consequence," Captain Perry said. "You are fortunate, Elaina. His Grace is not a forgiving man."

"That I have learned."

The Duke of Newcastle said nothing as he studied William, not deigning Elaina with even a glance. He had done this for William. Did he know William was to be flogged in the town center? Would he have that prim, smug look still pasted to his face as he watched? "I am sorry I could not free you as well. It is a miracle in itself that he has spared your life," Captain Perry added.

"You have done enough, Captain. Thank y—"

The soldier jerked her into motion down the darkened hallway.

Elaina watched the duke, Captain Perry, and William stare after her until she disappeared around a corner.

Indentured servant. It could be worse.

He could have had her drawn and quartered.

Chapter Thirty-Seven

ELAINA KNELT ON THE FROZEN stones that made up the center of High Street in Edinburgh. The ominous Tolbooth rose like the gaping mouth of a monster waiting to devour man and beast alike. She wanted to look anywhere but at the flogging post and the gallows erected in the center of the town square. She supposed she should be grateful that William was tied to the first and not the latter, although she would prefer neither. Her brother stood bare from the waist up, the chains on his wrists looped over the iron hook above his head. He stood stoic and proud, his muscles taut and shivering with the sleet that pelted him and the seemingly oblivious onlookers.

One thing Elaina had found to hold true in this terrible world was that humans were drawn to the gruesome and terrifying treatment of others like flies to a corpse. They feasted on the disadvantages of those around them. Even their murmurings now sounded like the hum of swarms of flies devouring the flesh of the dead.

The first lash made the bile rise in her throat. She had done this to her brother. It should be *her* punishment, not his. He had committed no wrong. He was perfect as ever. If she wanted to be honest, Micheil MacKinnon, the Laird Beinnmaree, had put her brother in this position. If he had stayed by his wife's side after her injury and looked after her as he should have and not followed the Bonnie Prince all over the godforsaken country, then Elaina and Calum would be home at Gleann Eader in front of a warm fire with Jamie running amok throughout the household, traumatizing the household staff. Caitir and Isobel would not be in the filthy prison cell awaiting their fate, being starved and used as rat bait. Her husband's fate and the fate of the rest of her family would not be a mystery to her. Auld Ruadh would not be lying dead, buried in a mass grave as if he had never blessed this earth and her life with his presence.

By the thirty-first lash, blood flowed from William's back and rushed through Elaina's ears. Darkness clawed at the corners of her eyes, threatening to overcome her, when a soul piercing scream snapped her back to life. Her gaze drifted along with the crowd's to the source of the sound. Lady Caroline stood with one hand over her mouth, the other cupping a curly blond head to her skirts.

Jamie! Jamie lived. Blessed holy mother, the boy lived and was safe in the arms of Lady Caroline. The color had drained from Lady Caroline's face, terror twisting her features. And there stood Mrs. Davies, drawing the woman to her in a comforting embrace as Eads stood stoically by their side.

Elaina followed Caroline's horrified gaze, not to William's beating and the blood oozing from his back, but to a site beyond him and higher.

She struggled to search the gray skies, the sleet burning her eyes. Then she found it. The two severed heads of Micheil MacKinnon, the Laird Beinnmaree of Gleann Eader, and Lady Caroline's father, Lord Taylor. Butcher Cumberland's souvenirs displayed on two pikes erected in front of the prison.

Elaina turned back to her friend, a sob lodged in her throat. Caroline lay prone on the ground with the household help kneeling around her. Tears froze to Elaina's cheeks and darkness crept into her vision like the fog drifted in the early mornings. She railed against the darkness. Her time of fainting was over. She drew herself up, clenching her chattering teeth as two soldiers unhooked William from the post and eased her brother down the steps, his back flayed open.

"Uncle William!" Jamie launched toward William, almost reaching him by the time William's feet touched the ground.

Two guards caught Jamie by the arms, and he kicked and fought, biting one of them on the hand. The soldier howled before backhanding Jamie and knocking him onto his back. If he thought that would deter the boy, he was mistaken, because Jamie came up swinging and landed a solid punch to the soldier's bits, which took him to his knees.

"Jamie!" Lady Caroline was on her feet, her face red with tears and with the cold. "Get away from him! He is only a boy. How dare you?" She snatched Jamie up off the ground, and he buried his face in her neck. "That is his uncle. Have you no decency, not to allow the boy to see to his own kin? His *only* kin." She glanced at Elaina.

She had written Elaina off then, probably blaming her father's death on her and the whole of the Cause. 'Twas no matter. *All the better,* Elaina thought. It would keep her and William safe. Enough people had suffered.

Jamie's head raised at that moment, and his eyes lighted on Elaina, still on her knees on the frigid stones. He squirmed out of Lady Caroline's arms and ran to Elaina, nearly toppling her over. The strength of his hug amazed her. His arms squeezed her until she couldn't breathe, but she wouldn't protest. She wrapped him in her embrace and never wanted to let him go. Her tears fell like rain.

"Dinna cry, Annie Lanie," Jamie whispered into her neck.

Caroline appeared in front of them. She stood in silence, not making a move to separate Elaina and Jamie, for which Elaina would always be grateful.

After a moment, Elaina pulled Jamie's arms from around her neck. "I want you to go with Lady Caroline."

Jamie merely stared at her, his own eyes wet with tears.

"She will keep you safe. Do you understand?"

After a moment, Jamie offered her a small nod.

Elaina struggled to get to her feet, her frozen knees not wanting to change their shape.

Lady Caroline grabbed her under the arm and helped her to her feet.

"Thank you," Elaina said. "For everything. You will take him and care for him?" she whispered, glancing down at Jamie.

"I will."

"God bless you. I am so sorry for everything."

"There is nothing to be sorry for," Caroline said.

"But your father…you said William was Jamie's only kin. I understand that you blame our family—"

"My father's actions are his own. He knew the dangers." Caroline held Elaina's gaze for a long moment. "How he hid it all from the family is beyond me. You are not to blame, Elaina. You needn't carry the weight of the world on your shoulders. As for the boy's only kin. If they thought him the son of a rebel, do you think they would let him go with me? 'Tis only to keep him safe. The child's mother?" Caroline asked as Mrs. Davies approached and took Jamie by the hand, leading him a few feet away. "Do you know what has come of her?"

"She is alive. She is with me in the prison. I do not know what her fate will be, however, whether she will live or she will die. But I will relay to her that her son is well and with good people. It will bring a peace to her heart no matter her future. How did he come to be with you? We searched all night for him before the…the battle." Elaina's voice choked on the last words.

"William found him and brought him to me."

"William," Elaina whispered. A part of her had hoped that it was Calum who'd found him and Calum who had delivered him to safety, then she could imagine Calum safe and alive.

Lady Caroline wrapped her arms around Elaina.

Elaina tried to push her away. "You shouldn't touch me. I'm filthy. There is no telling what disease I am covered with."

Caroline's grip tightened instead of loosening, as it should. "I do not care. We will see each other again, Elaina. I promise it. We will not abandon nor forsake you."

"We?" Elaina asked.

"William and I have married."

Elaina jerked away and stared at Caroline, studying her face, then looked wildly around for William. He hadn't told her. Why did he not tell her when they had been alone in Cumberland's study?

"I am sorry," Caroline whispered.

"Sorry? For what?"

"We did not tell you." Caroline's lip trembled. "He…he married me to save me from a fate similar to my father's."

Elaina cupped the woman's face. "You are so very mistaken, dear Caroline. William married you because he loves you. He always does the honorable thing, and he would not have married you if he didn't love you. He would have found another way to save your life."

"Let's go." A guard grabbed Elaina's arm and shoved her into motion.

"Keep him safe," Elaina called over her shoulder as the guard pulled her stumbling along. "Keep them both safe."

Chapter Thirty-Eight

"GE' UP." THE SOLDIER SHOVED Elaina with his boot. Isobel and Rory all but carried Elaina as the guards prodded the women out of their cell, down the dank hall of the prison, and out into the fresh Scotland air. They loaded the women into wagons, so many bodies that they near sat upon each other.

Though the breeze was frigid, the sunlight shining down on them brought Elaina to a more alert state, and she squinted against the brightness of the day.

"Where are they taking us?" She watched the nightmarish prison grow smaller behind them.

"To the ship," a woman answered. "To the colonies."

"Thank the lord," Elaina whispered, laying her head against Isobel's chest.

The wagon bounced and jostled toward the shipyard.

It took several minutes for Elaina to realize that Isobel was crying, the warmth of her sister's tears dripping onto her cheek being the evidence. "What is it?" She raised her head.

Isobel's gaze remained on the retreating city of Edinburgh. Her silent tears streamed down her cheeks.

"Jamie." The dawning of the reality hit Elaina like a tidal wave.

"I will never see my son again. Nor my country," Isobel whispered.

It was Elaina's turn to comfort, and she pulled Isobel close, the two of them weeping together. Rory encircled them with her arms, and they huddled together, their tears mixing in with the sounds of other women weeping for their families, or their country, or both.

The wagon lumbered to a stop, spilling the women upon each other. They had no time to right themselves before soldiers began dragging them from the back of the wagon. Elaina and the other three stood on the dock shivering from the wind coming off of the North Sea as they stared at the ship that would be their home for the coming weeks, if not months.

"Mam!"

They all turned in time to see the curly blond head darting in and out of the crowd with Caroline and William fast on his heels.

"Oh, my son." Isobel fell to her knees, wrapping her chained arms around Jamie. "*Am fear fiadhaich agam*," she whispered into his hair. "My wild one. My son." She wept as she rocked him back and forth.

He clung to her, his hands twisting in her filthy hair that hung loosely down her back.

"What's this?" A soldier ripped Jamie from Isobel's grasp by the scruff of his coat and held him squirming and kicking in the air. "What d'ya think, Parker? Shall we feed 'im to the fishies?"

His companion laughed and pushed a furious Jamie with the butt of his gun, which was decidedly the wrong thing to do as it gave Jamie the momentum to swing up and catch him under the chin with the toe of his boot, sending blood pouring from the man's mouth along with a string of obscenities and two teeth.

The redcoat holding him reared back his fist to hit Jamie, but William caught the man's arm before he could land the blow.

"Is this the best use of your time, soldier?" William barked at the man. "I believe you have other duties that need tending. I do not think that touting your prowess over a tot of a boy is one of them. Move on." He scooped Jamie into his arms and away from a furious soldier.

"Aye, ge' on wi' ye, ye bollock licker," Jamie yelled after the retreating men.

"James Michael," Caroline scolded, but only half-heartedly.

"What are you doing here?" Elaina asked William as soldiers began filing women up the plank and to the awaiting ship.

"I couldn't let them take all of you without letting Isobel say goodbye." William's voice cracked, and he focused on something past Elaina's shoulder. "I will guard him with my life. I swear it to you." His gaze turned to Isobel.

"I can never repay ye, Lord Spencer. Never."

Caroline laid a comforting hand on Isobel's shoulder. "All will be well, Mistress MacKinnon. You concentrate on staying alive so that you may be reunited someday," she said.

"Cap'n?" the soldier addressed William as he took Elaina by the arm.

"Mistress MacKinnon. May God go with you," William whispered, then he laid a kiss on his sister's forehead.

Elaina could only nod. No words would pass her throat.

Jamie's howls drowned out Isobel's goodbyes and continued as the women were dragged toward the ship.

The sound of the blood rushing through Elaina's ears and the sobs tearing from her throat echoed through her as she tried to tune out the screams of her nephew for his mother.

Captain Perry stepped in front of Elaina, causing her to smack into his chest as he blocked their progress to the boat. "One moment, soldier." If he had not caught her, she would have surely slid to the ground, but he pulled her back to her feet.

"You look terrible, Elaina," he said, looking her up and down.

"You look well rested, Captain," Elaina replied.

"And you are full of horse shite, my dear. I looked in the mirror this morning while shaving."

Elaina quirked him a smile. "What can I do for you, sir? You are delaying my journey into a life of servitude."

"At least it is not a journey to the gallows." He arched a brow at her.

"Touché."

"I have a small bit of news that I wanted to share with you before you leave on your journey."

"How very generous of you?" Elaina said, her brow furrowed.

The captain leaned toward her. "Your husband lives," he whispered into her ears.

Elaina collapsed in his arms.

Captain Perry caught her just before she hit the ground.

"You…you are certain?"

"Aye."

"Where is he?" Elaina asked, looking around.

"Not here, I'm afraid," Captain Perry said, regret lacing his tone and his eyes turning sorrowful with sympathy. "He will travel by ship to a destination I have not been able to learn. But I thought you would want to know. Perhaps it would help you retain hope."

"And why do you care?" Elaina asked. "No offense, but you captured me and put me in prison."

"I also talked Cumberland into sparing your life. I lied, I covered up, and I put my name, my rank, and my life on the line."

"Why?" Elaina asked again.

"You saved my life. You did not abandon me in my time of need. You released me from the captivity of your people. It is the least I could do. Not to mention that I discovered you have a very large heart, madam. A quite prickly personality, but a large heart. Now godspeed."

Before Elaina could respond, a soldier took her by the arms and ushered her toward the ship.

The sound of her name being called penetrated the din of the sobs she hadn't even known she still cried, and her head darted up, her gaze searching the crowd for the source. Searching for his face.

"Elaina! I will come for you!" Ainsley's shaggy head lurched forward as a guard shoved him up the plank of a neighboring ship. "I will find ye!" He was near unrecognizable, with a full beard and hair that had grown down his back. He, too, had been starved, by the looks of him. But he was alive.

"I love you, my son. I have faith," she yelled, even though she held little hope of being reunited unless by some slim chance they would arrive at the same port.

Her declaration brought the lad up short. He stood staring at her, blocking the flow of prisoners onto the ship. His mouth formed the words, *My son*. He gave her a formal bow even as the soldiers shoved him into motion. Their gazes remained locked as Ainsley was shoved aboard the ship and disappeared from view.

The women were crammed into the hull of the ship where it was dark, reeked of urine and waste already, and where things scurried in the dark. The lid slammed shut, and the prisoners sat in darkened silence. The four women clung to each other in the dark.

After a few moments of silence, a voice hissed into the inky darkness, "Who is here? State your clan. They may take our freedom, but they cannae take our voices. Let us tell each other of our families and may we get answers from one another."

There was a moment of silence before a woman at the far end of the hull said, "Clan Chattan. All of my men are dead." Her voice was emotionless, as if her life had been taken from her as well.

"Clan MacDonald. I have had no word of my son, Anndrais."

"Anndrais MacDonald? I am sorry. I believe he perished on the moor," another woman said from across the ship.

Sobs erupted into the darkness, and sounds of comforting followed.

"Clan MacKinnon. I—"

"Caitir?" Isobel hissed into the darkness.

"Isobel? Isobel!" There were scrambling and scuffing sounds as Caitir made her way across the ship.

"Watch it, will ye?" a woman growled.

"Speak again, Isobel," Caitir said, ignoring the grumbling woman she had possibly stepped all over.

"Over here," Isobel said.

A moment later, Caitir was upon them, and Isobel and Elaina both wrapped their arms around her. "Who else is here?" Caitir asked, touching Elaina's arms.

"It is I," Elaina said, and Caitir broke into a sob and squeezed her tight.

The names of clans continued to be called, and the women shared what information they knew about each other's loved ones.

"What of Calum?" Caitir whispered as if she were afraid to ask.

"He lives. Captain Perry told me as we were being brought aboard," Elaina said.

"Can you trust him?" Caitir asked.

"Yes, I believe I can. He would have no reason to lie. We will never cross paths again. He did not have to make the effort to find me…to speak to me."

"That is true," Isobel said. "Ainsley lives as well. We saw him being boarded on another ship."

"Praise God," Caitir whispered.

"Aron?" Elaina asked.

"I dinna ken," Caitir said. "I dinna ken about the Calhoun either, but Bridgette…Bridgette is no longer of this earth. She died in the prison."

A wave of nausea overcame Elaina at Caitir's words and as the ship began to sway with the rhythm of the sea. *Dear Bridgette.* So many had perished. Elaina felt certain there would be many more, as the Duke of Cumberland had all but told his men to take no quarter. It seemed there would be no end to the repercussions of war. She felt bile rise in her throat yet again. "I need to—"

"Pot. Is there a pot in this place?" Isobel called out, not needing Elaina to finish her sentence to know what she meant.

"Over here," someone said.

Elaina fought the nausea down as Isobel scrambled with her across the ship, stepping on numerous women. Caitir held onto Elaina's dress and followed with them. "Ye'll no leave me behind again," she said as they reached their destination and Elaina vomited the molded bread she had eaten at first light that morning.

"What is wrong wi' her?" asked a woman, her voice laced with suspicion. "What's she got?"

"A baby," Isobel said.

"No, I don—"

"Dinna say ye are no' wi' child. Ye have been vomiting for weeks now, and ye've yet to have yer menses. We've been in that terrible place for over a month. Ye are carryin' a babe, and by God, if I have anything to do wi' it, this one will live, dammit! It has to." Isobel choked on her words.

A baby. A baby, alone and in a life of servitude, without a father.

Elaina buried her head in Caitir's shoulder as the ship swayed even more. They were leaving the dock. They were leaving everything they knew and loved behind. An uncertain future lay ahead for all of them, not just her and the child she carried. She had had suspicions, but the thought of it terrified her, so she had tamped it down. Now it had been spoken, which made the truth of it all too real.

"Dinna be afraid, Elaina. We are here, and God willin', we will remain together. We must. We have lost too much already. Be strong, *mo chridhe*," Caitir whispered, using the term that Calum always used for her, my heart. "If Calum is truly alive, he will come for you."

Elaina lay a hand on her swirling stomach, fear squeezing her heart, but there was something else there as well. A touch of hope. It was but a small flicker, but a bit was better than none. She closed her eyes to the dark and leaned her head against the rocking hull of the ship and whispered into the dark, "Calum."

TO BE CONTINUED

Thank you for taking the time out of your busy life to be a part of mine. I ask that you please leave an honest review on your favorite retail site. Reviews are invaluable tools to help authors rise above the flood of books on the market and possibly be seen by more readers.

Note to the Reader

Dearest readers. So many things to talk about, I don't even know where to begin. "Begin at the beginning," you say? Where is the beginning?

First, I would like to express my gratitude for you showing up and partaking of Elaina's little world. These novels have been so fun to write (when I'm not sitting in the corner, rocking back and forth and crying). Every novel goes through its highs and lows. Moments when you can't type fast enough to keep up with the visions in your head and times when you have to pull every word kicking and screaming from your feeble mind. But that is no different from the ways in which we live our lives. It can't be all fun and games. It takes the bad times to help you truly appreciate the good ones.

That being said, let me explain a few things. I took great liberties in this book. Possibly more than usual, but that is my style, mostly fiction with a little history sprinkled on for flavor.

Let's talk about the chapter at Falkirk, for instance. The one where Elaina and the crew help out at the makeshift hospital and meet Ollie and Lieutenant Perry for the first time. Slaton House is roughly based on a home owned by one Colonel James Gardiner, a Scottish man who faithfully fought for the British and King George. But Colonel Gardiner was not at the Battle of Falkirk because he had been killed many months earlier at the Battle of Prestonpans, where this scene originally took place. The Battle of Prestonpans, near Edinburgh, took place in September of 1745. The Battle of Culloden took place in April of 1746. What in the heck were my characters going to do for seven months? I didn't know either, so I changed the battle to the Battle of Falkirk but kept Colonel Gardiner's home, changed the name from Bankton House to Slaton House and voila! Magic. Poor Colonel Gardiner was mortally wounded at the Battle of

Prestonpans within sight of his home and died later that day less than a mile from home. After the battle, his home was taken over and served as the main field hospital for both sides. See, a little bit of history and a whole lot of liberties. I just thought it a compelling story and felt it needed to remain as part of the book.

Now, on to Donald Cameron of Lochiel. He did exist. Often referred to as Gentle Lochiel, the chief of Clan Cameron at first was not eager to serve Prince Charles Edward Stuart on his mission to overthrow the king of England and return the Bonnie Prince's father to the throne. He tried to convince the prince many times to return from whence he came, but not to be deterred, the prince soon pressured Lochiel into joining the Cause. Lochiel had short notice to try to gather his clansmen together. After threats of seizing their land and assets, many of the Cameron men obeyed their chief and took up arms. Some of the more stubborn ones were later convinced by Cameron of Lochiel's brother, Dr. Archibald Cameron, who came through Cameron lands weeks later, killing cattle and threatening to burn the homes of the resistors. A clan chief's declaration of war was binding on all of the clan. The men who disobeyed were considered dishonorable. Such was the world, whether it be in the Highlands of Scotland or within the British army. Both sides pressed men to fight who did not wish to, and many of them never returned home. But nothing else that happened in this book concerning Donald Cameron of Lochiel actually took place…fiction.

Let's talk about the Battle of Culloden. It was real. It was horrendous. One of those bits of history that makes you want to sit and weep. It did take place on boggy land where horses screamed as their legs sank into the muck. I'm not sure what the powers that be were thinking, unless it was only of their pride and stubbornness. Poor Lachlan MacLachlan *did* exist and *did* have his head removed by a cannonball on his way to give the order to charge. It didn't matter though. There was no winning. The rebels were starved and exhausted. The land was harsh and unforgiving. They were out of their element. The land was perfect for the British army, who advanced as one with bayonets. It was horrible for a group of Highland rebels who relished the surprise attack, the screaming ferociousness of catching the enemy unawares and streaming out of mountains and hills like hordes of demons wielding swords and scythes banded to poles for lack of weaponry.

But the fate of the Highlanders during and after the epic battle was mostly determined by a piece of tampered information "intercepted" from the Jacobite forces stating that "No quarter is to be given," therefore, the Royal forces believed that the Jacobites were ordered to show no mercy. Not true. But the false information served its purpose of riling the British army into a frenzy. After the horrific battle that lasted less than an hour, leaving thousands of Highlanders dead on the field and only a little over a hundred British, the losers were given "no quarter." It is not completely clear whether that order came directly from the Duke of Cumberland himself or if he merely turned a blind eye to the whole matter. He set out on a campaign to decimate any semblance of life in the Highlands of Scotland, resulting in what some consider a genocide, where the Royal army burned homes, and raped, imprisoned, and murdered their way through the Highlands.

His horrid tactics were better received in the lowlands of Scotland where he was offered a Chancellorship of Aberdeen and St. Andrew's University. In England, the famous composer, Handel, produced a special anthem in honor of his victory. But Prince William, Duke of Cumberland, younger son to King George II, could not outrun his murderous reputation and has been referred to throughout history as Butcher Cumberland.

If you love Elaina and her independent, stubborn streak as much as I do, you can learn more about her and the infamous Richard who left her at the altar in *The Gift of a Broken Promise* when you sign up for my email newsletter at www.reneegallant.com. It is just a little thank you from me to you.

My newsletter will provide you with occasional updates about my works in progress, recommendations for books I love, and the odd whacky story about my crazy life. I will never spam you and I am also fairly inconsistent with writing newsletters, so there will not be an avalanche of emails to your inbox.

But, if the thought of more emails (though few) turns your blood cold, no worries. You can follow me on any of your favorite online retail platforms and find me as @thewriterenee on Facebook, Instagram, and Pinterest.

About the Author

Renée Gallant spent the biggest part of her childhood growing up in north Texas, hiding behind bushes or sitting in trees immersed in stories of mystery and adventure and scratching out her own Trixie Belden fan fiction.

It was only after reaching middle age, having an empty nest, and being bitten by a creepy little eight-legged foe that she thought to pick up pen and paper once more and lose herself in a fictional world where anything was possible. Unfortunately, no, she did not turn into Spiderman nor even The Tick but instead became an advocate for auto-immune sufferers, a grandmother, and finally, a published author.

After a twenty-year hiatus where she was all things to all people, Renée Gallant switched her focus back to herself and her first love, words.

You can find Renée, her books, and all her info at

https://www.reneegallant.com

https://www.facebook.com/thewriterenee

https://www.instagram.com/thewriterenee

https://www.twitter.com/thewriterenee

https://www.pinterest.com/thewriterenee

Don't be shy. Her fans make the world go 'round, and she would love to hear from you.